SALMAN RUSHDIE
NEW CRITICAL INSIGHTS

Volume - II

Edited by
Rajeshwar Mittapalli
Joel Kuortti

ATLANTIC
PUBLISHERS & DISTRIBUTORS (P) LTD

Published by

ATLANTIC

PUBLISHERS & DISTRIBUTORS (P) LTD

7/22, Ansari Road, Darya Ganj,
New Delhi-110002
Phones : +91-11-40775252, 23273880, 23275880, 23280451
Fax : +91-11-23285873
Web : www.atlanticbooks.com
E-mail : orders@atlanticbooks.com

Branch Office
5, Nallathambi Street, Wallajah Road,
Chennai-600002
Phones : +91-44-64611085, 32413319
E-mail : chennai@atlanticbooks.com

Printed in India at Nice Printing Press, A-33/3A, Site-IV, Industrial Area, Sahibabad, Ghaziabad, U.P.

Preface

For well over a quarter century Salman Rushdie has been an impressive presence on the world literary scene. Starting with *Grimus* (1975) he has published eight novels, the latest being *Fury* (2001). Despite their relatively small number, the impact Rushdie's novels have had on common readers and critics alike is profound by any reckoning. His *Midnight's Children* (1981) gave a new direction and orientation to fiction all over the world. The intellectual, intercultural and intertextual richness of this novel, and indeed of every other novel of Rushdie's, teases the readers and challenges them to comprehend and come to grips with them. His books create tension, induce anticipation, and evoke conflicting emotions between (and within) the readers. With each new novel Rushdie initiates fresh discussion and debate. All this attests to a creative genius which compels us to re-evaluate every so often.

Rushdie has been a much discussed author, and a great number of critical studies have already appeared, the earliest being the essays in 1982 by Maria Couto in *Encounter,* Uma Parameswaran in *Toronto South Asian Review,* and Tariq Ali in *New Left Review.* But what happened in 1988-89 was something unprecedented in the history of literature. With the publication of *The Satanic Verses* in 1988 the discussion of Rushdie went beyond the realms of literary criticism. This book inaugurated what has come to be known as the "Rushdie Affair," and highly polemical views began to be expressed, sometimes to the complete exclusion of any mention of his novels. The intercultural conflict which ensued, with its deep interest, is now a part of history, but it is not a point of discussion in these two volumes. Still, they acknowledge the implications of this 'affair' for the image of Rushdie the novelist. An important consequence of the 'affair' which merits special mention is that to read

Rushdie without reference to his (auto)biography has been rendered difficult, even in the current postmodern, post-structuralist literary context.

However, Rushdie has since emerged from the political and religious quagmire and re-embraced the literary world. It is therefore important to continue the 'literary-critical' study of his works, a task which these volumes set out to accomplish by bringing together some of the very best critical essays written in the post-'*Verses* controversy' period. We believe that these seventeen articles (including the eight in volume I) present fresh insights into Rushdie's works, not necessarily overshadowed by the controversy that surrounded him at one time. They represent varied critical and theoretical approaches and attempt an honest assessment of Rushdie's novels by creatively engaging with the issues each of them raises.

The articles have been organized in the order of appearance of Rushdie's novels so that discussion proceeds from *Grimus*, through *Midnight's Children*, *Shame*, *East, West*, *The Moor's Last Sigh*, and *The Ground Beneath Her Feet*. Towards the end of this volume there are three articles that discuss Rushdie's novels from general and comparative perspectives. A useful bibliography of Rushdie's works and another of recent Rushdie criticism have been appended to Volume I and Volume II respectively.

We would like to thank the contributors for their cooperation and for permitting us to include previously published (although often revised) material.

—Rajeshwar Mittapalli
—Joel Kuortti

CONTENTS

1

Schema Disruption in the Re-writing of History: Salman Rushdie's *East, West*

CELIA M. WALLHEAD

0. Introduction

Salman Rushdie has consecrated his life, at great risk to it, to the post-colonial re-writing of world history. While he explores those "most contentious fault-lines of cultural debate-metropolis/periphery, atavism/modernity, fundamentalism/multiculturalism" (Bhabha 29) he works in the interstices of another pair of opposites: the momentous/the insignificant. Indeed, his reviewer, the writer Homi Bhabha, says he has "a fine sense of the little things of life" (Bhabha 29). Another Rushdie hallmark is a tremendous sense of humour, manifested through verbal wit in the tradition of Laurence Sterne. It is small wonder that in one of his latest collections of short stories, *East, West* (1994), there is a pastiche Shandean re-writing of *Hamlet,* called "Yorick."

This collection questions the strict dichotomy of East/West (it uses a comma rather than a stroke to separate them), and brings the two together, especially in its final section. It has three sections, each with three stories. Section One ("East") has three modern but Oriental tales, Section Two ("West"), starts with the "Yorick" story and ends with one about Spain and the discovery of America: "Christopher Columbus and Queen Isabella of Spain Consummate Their Relationship (*Sante Fé,* AD 1492)." The final section, ("East, West"), has three stories which explore East-West relations in literature, the occult, the cinema, and such modern ailments as terrorism. So, for example, in the second story, "Chekov and Zulu," we have diplomats involved in the assassination of Indira Gandhi playing out *Star Treck* fantasies.

On the front cover there is a remark about Rushdie by Nadine Gordimer: "The most original imagination writing today." Like all Rushdie's fiction, *East, West* is a feat of the imagination. For imaginative writing to be successful, the writer must have some control over the imaginations of his or her readers, in order to be able to carry the reader along. Homi Bhabha describes Rushdie's unorthodox method of creating narrative suspense:

> In *Midnight's Children,* it is the tic and twitch of Padma's thigh muscles, as they respond to every twist and turn in the story of Cyrus the Great, that provide Saleem Sinai with his first lesson in storytelling: "[...] what happened is less important than what the author can persuade his audience to believe." [...] The silences in these stories occur when the narrator pauses to make sure, like the young Saleem Sinai, that he is carrying his audience with him; that their muscles are twitching in time with the tale. (Bhabha 29)

The path of the imagination is run in leaps and bounds by Rushdie, with significant silences interpolated. In this essay, we contend that Rushdie is able to make these leaps and bounds and carry the reader along because he works with schemata which are recognisable to the reader. He may jump from one field to another, there may even be apparent incompatibility of schemata, but because they are inherently structured, the writer knows that some element in the structuring of one schema will tie in somehow with one or more elements in the other schema or schemata evoked in the reader's mind.

To illustrate this thesis, we are going to focus upon the tale about Christopher Columbus. The model for analysis which we are going to use is that invented by Guy Cook to detect, analyse and describe the functions of schemata in texts. It sets up frameworks in the form of scenarios in which the events are re-enacted. Rushdie recreates momentous events of history-here the discovery of America-and asks us to review them in a new light, which invariably involves the "little things," the quotidian. In the Columbus story, he explores the interface of power and sex. But the seriousness of the momentous occasion is subverted by his disrupting the tone and register of the formal discourse with a contemporary informal discourse. Firstly, we will map out the schemata that dominate the tale, and then briefly describe Cook's schema theory model. Finally, following Cook's approach, we establish the structures in the different schemata and trace the relationships between them that account for the coherence and also the verbal wit in the tale.

1. The Principal Schemata Invoked in "Christopher Columbus and Queen Isabella of Spain Consummate their Relationship" (Santa Fé, AD 1492)

The opening of "Christopher Columbus [...]" evokes, quite naturally, the schema of KINGSHIP, but curiously, it evokes at the same time a WOMAN schema, as the anonymous narrator refers to *Queen Isabella*: "Columbus, a foreigner, follows Queen Isabella for an eternity without entirely giving up hope" (107). But the next schema evoked is that of LOVE, for an anonymous commentator then speaks: "*In what characteristic postures?*[...] But, on his first arrival at court, when the Queen herself asked him what he desired, he [...] murmured a single, dangerous word. 'Consummation'" (107).

The next schemata introduced are those of a MAN schema, and of a DOOR-TO-DOOR SALESMAN, with a "confidence-man's charm." This "confidence-man" has already been described as a foreigner, so the schema of NATIONAL/ FOREIGN is introduced. A more striking schema is that of the KNIGHT in shining armour, where Columbus wants to "tie the Queen's favour to his helmet, like a knight in a romance" (107). This is subverted by the addition "(He owns no helmet)," and the next statement of the narrator's which is from an informal register: "He has hopes of cash," thus breaking the formal tone of the narration. The final scenario evoked in the opening passage is that of children reciting poetry or playing with words at school: "in fourteen hundred and ninety-two, sailing across the ocean blue" (107).

2. Guy Cook's Model for Analysing Schemata in Texts

While the main work in which Guy Cook describes his findings is his 1994 *Discourse and Literature*, he offered a preview of his ideas on schema theory in a plenary lecture at the *Primeras Jornadas Internacionales de Lingüística Aplicada* held at the University of Granada on 11-15 January 1993:

> The general proposal of schema theory concerning discourse processing is well-known: a schema is a mental representation of a typical instance, and various types of schema have been proposed. The relationship of schemata to discourse would be as follows: enough detail is given in a discourse to trigger the selection of a schema in the receiver's mind. This schema is then used in top-down processing. Other than that, details are given only where there is a divergence from the schema. Unmentioned details-default elements as they are called-can if necessary be retrieved from the share of knowledge, from the share of schema. (Cook, "Top-down" 146)

In his "Introduction" to *Discourse and Literature*, Cook states his intention to clarify certain processes in writer-reader relations that underlie and account for the power of some texts. He says the following: "there is a type of discourse which has a particular effect on the mind, refreshing and changing our mental representations of the world. [...] It derives, I believe, from an interaction of textual form with a reader's pre-existing mental representations" (Cook, *Discourse* 4). Cook traces the history of schema theory from its origins in the Gestalt psychology of the 1920s and 1930s. In reviewing the general principles of schema theory, he acknowledges that pragmatic analysis of discourse assumes both shared knowledge and processing rules, and that he personally belongs to the school which stresses the importance of the former. His definition of the function of schemata is as follows:

> A theory of knowledge in interaction with text is provided by the notion of 'schemata.' These are mental representations of typical instances, and the suggestion

> is that they are used in discourse processing to predict and make sense of the particular instance which the discourse describes. The idea is that the mind, stimulated either by key linguistic items in the text (often referred to as 'triggers' [...]), or by the context, activates a schema, and uses it to make sense of the discourse. In this sense schemata are 'norms' and individual facts are 'deviations.' (Cook, *Discourse* 11)

The mental ability in the reader to add to the norm, to supply details by reading them in in their absence, is of particular relevance to literary narrative. The reader is prompted by a point of reference and left to use his knowledge or imagination to fill in the possible gaps. This filling in is not totally arbitrary, but governed by the limits of the schema.

The postulation of the functioning of schemata at both a conscious and a subconscious level can help to account for the mechanisms of ommission and retrieval and the background conditions for the activation of these processes. Charles Fillmore, in his article "Frames and the Semantics of Understanding" had shown how certain word groups are held together by "the fact of their being motivated by, founded on, and co-structured with, specific united frameworks of knowledge, or coherent schematizations of experience" (Fillmore 223). He uses the general word "frame," drawing upon Minsky, Winograd and Charniak, while pointing out that his own earlier "scene," Bartlett's "schema" of 1932, taken up by Rumelhart (1980) and favoured by Guy Cook, Schank and Abelson's "script" (1977), de Beaugrande "global pattern" (1987), and Lakoff and Johnson's "experiential gestalt" (1980) are all essentially describing the same phenomenon. Meanings are not "contained" within the text, but are constructed in the interaction between the text and the interpreter's background knowledge. The goal of Fillmore's model of "U-semantics" is to uncover the nature of the relationship between linguistic texts and the interpreter's full understanding of the texts in their contexts (Fillmore 231). He shows how a frame is invoked when the interpreter, in trying to make sense of a text segment, is able to assign it an interpretation by situating its content in a pattern that is known independently of the text (Fillmore 232). But Fillmore, with his semantic theory, is not the only one to take up frame or schema theory, it has been pressed into service in other areas like second and foreign language learning (e.g. Carrel et al.).

Cook picks upon the seminal model of schema theory put forward by Schank and Abelson in their 1977 book *Scripts, Plans, Goals and Understanding.* Despite ongoing modification by the authors, Cook maintains the superiority of this model for his purposes. The main advantage of schema theory, as set out in their model, to explain effects in literature, is that while schemata enable us to omit a sequence of well-known causal links, thus saving time and making for compression of thought, they enable us to provide them if needed. Hence a writer can assume that a reader is following him or her, since once a schema has been activated, the links in the chain underlie the overt representation made by the selected items, and the reader may be either consciously or subconsciously aware of them. If a writer wishes to explicitly mention all the links, he or she has that option available for whatever purpose.

Cook claims that the Schank and Abelson version is one of the most "detailed, rigorous, well-known, and influential" versions (Cook, *Discourse* 80) of schema theory, but before we can apply it in *East, West,* we must obviously show how Cook explains and applies it himself. We refer particularly to Chapter Three of *Discourse and Literature.* Here, Cooks shows that the basic claim of schema theory is that human understanding, and here, text understanding, can be represented as a hierarchy of levels of schemata in which failure to understand on one level can be corrected by referring to the level above. A theory of coherence may be extrapolated from this, whereby failure of correction at a lower level may be referred to a higher one. What exactly are these levels that we are talking about? Schank and Abelson define them in the following paradigmatic terms:

THEMES
GOALS
SUB-GOALS

PLANS
SCRIPTS

Cook explains these, working through the categories from bottom to top.

Scripts

Scripts are structures "that describe appropriate sequences of events in a particular context [...] a predetermined, stereotyped sequence of actions that defines a well-known situation" (Schank and Abelson 41). They fall into three main categories: situational, personal and instrumental. A script may have a number of "tracks," which are different but related instances of the same general category. Each script is represented from the point of view of one of the participants and his or her role in it. Each script also has an "essential precondition" and a "main consequence." In addition, each script has a number of "slots" (similar to default elements) whose realization can be assumed unless there is information to the contrary. The slots in a script are: a number of props, the roles of participants, the entry conditions, results and scenes and their sequence.

The distinguishing feature of scripts, as a type of schema, is that these slots are instantiated by quite specific entities and events. Cook (*Discourse* 81) gives us the example of a "trial" script from the point of view of a judge. The props would be a wig or a gavel, and the roles would be defendant, lawyers, witnesses, etc. The entry condition would be "being appointed to hear the case"; the result would be the verdict and punishment or exoneration, and the scenes would be indictment, plea, defence case, etc. A script, it is claimed, is activated by any one of a number of "headers" concerning the preconditions. It can be activated by specific mention of one of the participants, the occupant of a slot, or a location habitually associated with the script. In text understanding, script activation enables details to be bypassed, or provided by the default elements of the script, as required. Almost no script would function in a straightforward way within a text, however, or it would have little to recommend for itself. Most are complicated with obstacles, deviations, and errors, usually to foreground one aspect or other. Cook lists the following to look for: the incidental mention of potential "headers" for other scripts, the concurrent activation of rival scripts which will then compete to be the one used in understanding, the concurrent running of more than one script, or of one script as part of another, "headers" which may create "scriptal ambiguity" as to which of a number of scripts that share them is the one to activate, obstacles to the course of events which may necessitate either a loop back to an earlier point, or script abandonment, unexpected events which may lead to scripts being abandoned or held in abeyance until the event has run its course, movement from one script to another. (Cook, *Discourse* 82)

Plans

Schank and Abelson define plans and distinguish them from scripts by saying that there are experiences which are so novel and unpredictable as to demand interpretation with reference to a structure which is not so specific in its elements. A "plan" is therefore a schema in the sense that it consists of ordered slots, but it is far less explicitly connected to specified places, individuals, or locations. Plans are ordered in that they realize goals, which may themselves be subordinate to higher goals. The recognition of the goal, or sub-goal, and the stages of the plan to realize it, establishes coherence. Suspension of goal revelation by the writer is accompanied by growing demand for knowledge of the goal on the part of the reader, which must be satisfied at some later point.

Goals and Sub-Goals

Schank and Abelson identify five main goals as objectives of possible plans or scripts of agents in a discourse. They are: satisfaction, enjoyment, achievement, preservation and crisis handling. The dividing line between goals and plans is fuzzy, but there are certain "basic" goals most people can agree upon. Literary writing very often concerns itself with departure from expected goals.

Themes

Just as plans and scripts demand goals, so goals need

explanation too. In text comprehension, if a goal is not recognized, or is unfamiliar, recourse may be made to some higher level. Schank and Abelson propose the category of themes, divided into three, as follows: role themes, interpersonal themes and life themes (Cook, *Discourse* 80).

Cook refers to G. Edelman's *Bright Air, Brilliant Fire,* in his conclusion about themes and our understanding of them in texts. He refers to a possible genetic role in the interface of "intelligence" and neurophysiological activity:

> This process of explanation at higher and higher levels is potentially endless, but the explanation of themes, as *SPGU* point out, is beyond the scope of the investigation of text understanding. Further speculation would need to consider such issues as the interaction of the nature of intelligence with the neurophysiology of the brain, and the degree to which an intelligence is 'programmed' genetically or environmentally. Indeed, the notion of themes correlates well with the neural Darwinist notion of an innate, individually variable, value system dictating the development of cognitive structures (Edelman 1992). (Cook, *Discourse* 90)

Cook summarises his theory of schemata before making his analyses in Chapter Four, and offers the following symbols:

$ = script
P= plan
I = goal (sub-I = sub-goal)
O = theme.

Cook discusses his analysis, noting that the naming, classifying and assigning of schemata in this way is "highly speculative and highly problematic." Yet it is worth the attempt as the results emerging make our intuitions about schemata and coherence more explicit (Cook, *Discourse* 109). Coherence is created, or may be, depending on the reader, when the reader perceives connections between schemata. The connections may be causal, or inclusive, in that one schema may be contained in another.

Excluding processes may signal deviance. "Deviance" as part of a mutually defining binary pair along with "normality," can only have significance in relation to this norm. Since schemata represent the norm, for they encapsulate the reader's expectations once they have been triggered, the essence of schema theory is that "discourse proceeds, and achieves coherence, by successfully locating the unexpected within a framework of expectation" (Cook, *Discourse* 130).

Cook postulates a theory based upon a combination of discourse analysis, schema theory and literary theory: "A theory of discourse deviation: schema refreshment and cognitive change" (Cook, *Discourse* 181-211), in which he shows how defamiliarization, to use the Russian formalist notion, can make a crucial contribution to a theory of the relation between literary text and reader's mind at work on the text. A writer may introduce a schema only to disrupt and radically alter it. In its static nature, an altered or subverted schema suffers the foregrounding of certain of its components or aspects. This deviation may have a meaningful or aesthetic effect which contributes to the power of the text. The levels at which the defamiliarization may take place are at those of language schemata, text schemata and world schemata. Cook demonstrates three aspects to the introduction of changes in schemata: existing schemata may be destroyed; new ones may be constructed, and new connections may be established between existing schemata. Cook calls this "schema refreshment," for which disruption is a pre-requisite. The different procedures are reinforcing, preserving and adding, and the disruptive procedures are refreshing through destroying, constructing and connecting. Cook claims that it is the primary function of certain discourses-particularly literary and publicitary ones-to effect a change in the schemata of their readers.

3.0 Analysis of the Schemata of "Christopher Columbus and Queen Isabella of Spain Consummate Their Relationship (Santa Fé, AD 1492)"

We have seen that the opening paragraphs of the story activate schemata concerning kingship, salesmanship, love and medieval chivalry, as well as the man/woman and the national/foreign dichotomies, since Columbus is presented immediately as a foreigner. They also establish a formal narrative tone which is occasionally broken, either by a sudden descent to an informal tone, or by the introduction of humorous word-play. The text also modulates between third person narration by the anonymous narrator, and use of a theatrical approach including the actual dialogue of characters on the scene who appear to be two courtiers. The schemata in this tentative list fall into two categories: schemata about discourse types and schemata about the world.

3.1 Schemata About Discourse Types

3.1.1 Text Schemata

$S	(script-like schemata)	Π	(realising plans)
$S	NARRATION (WRITTEN)	Π	INFORM, ENTERTAIN
$S	DRAMA (ORAL)	Π	INFORM, DRAMATISE
$S	CHILDREN'S POETRY (ORAL)	Π	ENTERTAIN, INSTRUCT

3.1.2 Language Schemata

$S	(script-like schemata)	Π	(realising plans)
$S	FORMAL LANGUAGE (WRITTEN)	Π	INFORM, INSTRUCT
$S	INFORMAL LANGUAGE (ORAL)	Π	INFORM, ENTERTAIN

3.2 World Schemata

$S	(script-like schemata)	Π	(relevant plans)
$S	KINGSHIP	Π C	RULE KINGDOM
$S	SALESMANSHIP	Π C	SELL A PRODUCT
$S	MEN	Π C	PROTECT, EARN LIVING
$S	WOMEN	Π C	LOOK AFTER FAMILY, DO DOMESTIC TASKS
$S	NATIONAL	Π C	BE BETTER, FAMILIAR
$S	FOREIGN	Π C	BE DIFFERENT, SUSPECT

$S	LOVE:	
	MALE HETEROSEXUAL	Π C PURSUE WOMAN
	FEMALE HETEROSEXUAL	Π C BE PURSUED BY MAN
$S	KNIGHT	Π C REPRESENT KING OR WOMAN WIN IN COMBAT

3.3 Discussion

3.3.1 Text Schemata

As Cook points out, "knowledge of what types of evidence are reliable is of crucial importance to an individual. To call assumptions into question is to undermine the basis of all knowledge" (Cook, *Discourse* 232). In this story, traditional versions of the account of Columbus's persuading of Queen Isabella and King Ferdinand to be his patrons for the enterprise of sailing westwards to the Indies are called into question through the device of presenting, not one, nor two, but three, eye-witnesses. The narrator is the first eye-witness, as he or she presents the events as developing before his or her very eyes. This effect is achieved in several ways: firstly, through the use of the present tense, which is maintained throughout, right to the end of the tale: "'Yes,' he tells the heralds. *Yes. I'll come*" (119). The second way is in the narrator's recall of the actual words of the protagonists, as in this quotation. Another way is through the omniscience of the god-like narrator; he has all the answers: "Obvious answers first" (107). The second and third eyewitnesses are the unnamed characters who speak in the text, breaking up the narrator's discourse. The first is introduced by a single curved line and the second by a double one. This discourse is dramatic and like a play in that it is pure dialogue, with no stage-directions. The lack of stage-directions produces silences in between which force the reader to deduce information about the speakers. At the end of the story we deduce that these commentators are heralds, as we see them speaking directly to Columbus, persuading him to return: "The heralds dismount. They offer bribes, plead, cajole. [...] *She's waiting for you in Santa Fé. You must come at once*" (119).

As heralds or courtiers, they are able to give inside information about Queen Isabella's intimate reactions. This, in turn, contrasts with the traditional children's poem "in fourteen hundred and ninety-two, sailing across the ocean blue," thus providing an intimist re-writing of the event.

3.3.2 Language Schemata

The tale is begun by the narrator using a formal register, referring to "preferment" (107) and "Italianate blandishments" (108). The anonymous narrator's tone evokes a schema of history books instructing us in the orthodox version of important historical events. This tone is then subverted by the narrator introducing colloquial and unconventional speech from a lower register. This is done by the use of exaggerations and anachronisms: "man-sized diapers" (112), "a one-man debauch" (109). Anachronistic modern usage, bordering on the disrespectful and offensive, subverts with humour, such as when a herald comments on Columbus's behaviour: "'*The nerve!*'" (107), or Columbus mentally calls the Queen a bitch (117). Colloquial and metaphorical expressions such as "take a hint," "turn a deaf ear," "go too far," "look after herself," "cuts him dead," "eats like a horse," contribute to the intimist tone of the "inside story" version of the events. The two contrasting scenarios are brought together in exchanges like: "'Her face is a lush peninsula' [...] 'Her legs are not so great'" (113).

3.3.3 World Schemata

Our assumptions about kingship are that the model is usually patriarchal, and that if the monarch is female, then she is, in a way, usurping male power, or at least assuming it. The traditional view of Queen Isabella as being powerful, almost masculine, is maintained. Her husband, King Ferdinand, is called by the narrator "an absolute zero: a blank." There is also humorous word-play here, in that "absolute zero" contrasts with the reference to her as "an absolute monarch" (110). This is no feminist sub-plot, however, as her power lust, her efficiency and energy: "The more of the land she swallows, the more warriors she engulfs, the hungrier she gets" (112) are replaced by a more capricious motivation. Her enigmatic refusal to be satisfied with the known and knowable, is shown to be the hidden reason for her change of mind and decision to become Columbus's patron. Her initial unwillingness is not attributed to lack of faith in his enterprise, or to personal and institutional avarice, as it was in the current mythical views of the events. Her fascination for the new in terms of kingship and imperialism is tied in with a similar sexual curiosity. Rushdie here explores the interface of desire on the imperial level and on the personal level. When Columbus is cast as a foreigner and as a travelling salesman, he both attracts through difference, and has to attract with his product. In this schema, Queen Isabella is turned into a housewife, and as Columbus gets his foot in the door, she is seduced by his product: a paradoxical and risky, but apparently viable, plan to obtain great wealth through travelling to the East via the West. The riskiness for the Queen is emphasised by the fact that his foreign unreliability is exaggerated by his drunkenness and dirtiness, probable side effects of his peripatetic profession. But a step further on from the schema of Columbus as salesman, is that of the great discoverer as lover. This is made explicit in the text by paradigmatic comments by Columbus on his own story:

> 'The search for money and patronage,' Columbus says, 'is not so different from the quest for love.' (112)
>
> 'The loss of money and patronage,' Columbus says, 'is as bitter as unrequited love.' (115)

Medieval knights are also often unrequited lovers, and can be "errant" like travelling salesmen, so again, the next schema is easily assimilated. A model for the Queen Isabella - King Ferdinand-Christopher Columbus triangle, which brings together both the LOVE and CHIVALRY schemata, would be that of King Arthur, Queen Guinevere and Lancelot. In our story, the king is never mentioned by name, his nonentity is summed up in that the only reference to him is as an adjunct to her: "her husband." The fact that King Ferdinand served as a model of the modern prince for Machiavelli and had four children out of wedlock does not seem to back up this idea historically, which reminds us that Rushdie is re-writing history for fictional purposes.

Queen Isabella's susceptibility to the charms of Columbus

as salesman, lover and knight, therefore disrupts the schema which attributes a monopoly of power and decision to the monarch, not to mention the chaste connotations of the *Catholic* Monarch. In her caprice, based on desire and dream, there is implied negation of the rationalism that was beginning to be felt with the transition from the medieval world to that of the Renaissance. As we examine all the details in the text which belong to the most important world schemata in the story, it will become apparent that these details interrelate and create connections and implicit cohesion.

4. Summary of a Reader Interpreting World Schemata

We can postulate the following script-like schemata ($S) for the world knowledge in the story. Under each $S we name the words and phrases from the text referring to defaults, and the relationship they have to the main concept. These words are all "headers in the text." We see a dominance of qualities and attributes (IS or HAS) and actions (EVENTS). As Cook says: "it is often shared attributes and actions which create a metaphoric link from one schema to another" (Cook, *Discourse* 219).

1. $S KINGSHIP

INSTANCE:	QUEEN ISABELLA OF CASTILLE
PROPS:	HAS a court, a military victory, *a ring often kissed, appetites,* castles, armies, battle plans, conquests, citadels, flags, triumphs, *treasure chests*
IS:	an absolute monarch, a tyrant, all-conquering, omnipotent, (default element: IS *not* a man)
EVENTS:	foils conspiracies of assassins, negociates treaties, swallows land, wins battles

2. $S LOVE

INSTANCE:	QUEEN ISABELLA OF SPAIN
PROPS:	HAS an olive hand, hair to braid, breasts to fondle, *a ring often kissed,* sexual *appetites,* flirtatiousness, infidelities, *treasure chests* (= breasts)

IS: touched by tentacles of warmth, a turbulence

EVENTS: offers the ecstasy of her glance, reaches peak of ecstasy

INSTANCE: CHRISTOPHER COLUMBUS

PROPS: HAS sexual *appetites*, quest for love, *charm*

IS: (at end) [like] a requited lover, a groom on his wedding day

EVENTS: *offers the possibility of embracing his scheme with a lover's abandon*

3. $S SALESMANSHIP

INSTANCE: CHRISTOPHER COLUMBUS

PROPS: HAS *a scheme*, a confidence-man's *charm*, a certain saucy vulgarity, shoes a little thin

IS: knee bent, fawning, ingratiating

EVENTS: is running out of sales talk, *offers the possibility of embracing his scheme with a lover's abandon*

4. $S MEDIEVAL CHIVALRY

INSTANCE: CHRISTOPHER COLUMBUS

PROPS: HAS tuneless serenades, coarse epistles

IS: a medieval knight, a hero, a knight in a romance, a man of action, unrequited, (default element: is not the husband)

EVENTS: ties the Queen's favour to his [non-existent] helmet, carries her flag and her favour, wears man-sized diapers under [his] armour because the fear of death will open the bowels

5. $S FOREIGN

INSTANCE: CHRISTOPHER COLUMBUS

PROPS: HAS sea-dog raffishness, excessively colourful clothes, the dusty patchwork cloak of his invisibility

IS:	(default element: a traveller), invisible
EVENTS:	dreams of entering the invisible world, is [pushed] beyond the frontiers of [the] self, [...] beyond his mind's rim

5. Conclusions

In terms of plans and themes, the enterprises of Queen Isabella and Christopher Columbus associate through a common plan on two levels. Isabella's "treasure chests" are to be both filled and fondled by Columbus, and her ring is to be kissed as Queen and mistress, just as his scheme is embraced by both with a lover's abandon. Rushdie conveys the urgency of the desire and the inevitable coupling of the two names for all time:

[H]e must must must carry her flag and her favour beyond the end of the end of the earth, into exhaltation and immortality, linking her to him for ever with bonds far harder to dissolve than those of any mortal love, the harsh and deifying ties of history. (117)

Isabella's plans are to extend her sphere of power, and with the hindsight that the advantage of time affords us, we know that it was the beginning of a great empire. She used the foreigner Columbus to achieve her ends, thus engulfing the foreign. Rushdie comments ironically on the controversial centre/periphery dichotomy through one of the heralds: "there are quarters in which (hard as it is to accept) we ourselves would be considered foreign, too!" (108). Within the FOREIGN schema, we have another apparent paradox, which takes us from the visible and concrete to the invisible and abstract, and that is the idea of coloured /colourless. At first, Columbus's colourfulness is censored, but then, in the course of the story, it becomes positive. Columbus depends on Isabella's crucial decision, because it will, and did, make or break him. He is caught in the interstice between the old and the new worlds: "This old world is too old and the new world is an unfound land" (115). He is going mad in a no-man's land of nothingness. Her decision to be his patron saves him from oblivion, or invisibility to history, and makes his foreign colour or colourfulness visible to history and no longer culturally negative. We see from the level of the quotidian that it was a hit or miss affair.

In terms of schema connections, the contents evoked in the text yield a number of cross-references, which we have emphasised with the use of italics. The most obvious is the paradigmatic relationship between the structure of kingship, with the position of the king or queen at the top, and that of love or chivalry, with the lover or knight looking up to the lady. If the cross-reference of "treasure chests" is not understood at the level of the script, then meaning must be sought at higher levels, those of a king/queen or lover's plans and goals, and the general theme of kingship.

Finally, we appreciate the disruption of the KINGSHIP schema when we find the default element of a strong, rational, male monarch absent. In its place, we find contradictory elements in the interplay of strong and weak, rational and irrational, male and female. The accompanying discourse deviation is seen in the disruption of the written, history-book norm by the low-register oral interventions. Rushdie is reviewing history in fiction, where fact matters but is inconsequential, where the momentous is seen to depend upon the "little things of life," and where historical personages turn out to be (fictional) real people with personal problems that are often as interesting as the great feats they have accomplished. Thus the event or the person is not an isolated phenomenon, but part of a complex context, and the novelist has a much freer hand than the historian. The lingering suggestion Rushdie throws out to the reader who has followed his imaginative leaps and bounds, is that the original historian may have been as partisan in the creation of history through discourse, as a novelist like him.

Works Cited

Bartlett, F.C. *Remembering: A Study in Experimental and Social Psychology.* Cambridge: Cambridge UP, 1932.

de Beaugrande, R. "Schemas for Literary Communication." *Literary Discourse.* Ed. L. Halász. Berlin: de Gruyter, 1987. 49-99.

Bhabha, Homi K. "Exploring the Place of Silence." *Guardian Weekly* 16 Oct. 1994: 29.

Carrel, P.L., J. Devine and D. Eskey, eds. *Interactive Approaches to Second Language Reading.* Cambridge: Cambridge UP, 1988.

Cook, Guy. *Discourse and Literature: the Interplay of Form and Mind.* Oxford: Oxford UP, 1994.

____. "Top-down Misunderstanding." *Temas de Lingüística Aplicada.* Ed. J. Fernández-Barrientos and C. Wallhead. Granada: U Granada P, 1995. 139-55.

Edelman, G. *Bright Air, Brilliant Fire: On the Matter of the Mind.* Harmondsworth: Penguin, 1992.

Fillmore, C.J. "Frames and the Semantics of Understanding." *Quaderni di Semantica* 6.2 (1985): 222-54.

Lakoff, George and Mark Johnson. *Metaphors We Live By.* Chicago: Chicago UP, 1980.

Minsky, M. "A Framework for Representing Knowledge." *The Psychology of Computer Vision.* Ed. P.E. Winston. New York: McGraw-Hill, 1975. 221-77.

Rumelhart, D.E. "Schemata: The Building Blocks of Cognition." *Theoretical Issues in Reading Comprehension: Perspectives in Cognitive Psychology, Linguistics, Artificial Intelligence and Education.* Ed. R.J. Spiro, B. Bruce and W. Brewer. Hillsdale, NJ: Lawrence Erlbaum, 1980. 33-58.

Rushdie, Salman. "Christopher Columbus and Queen Isabella of Spain Consummate their Relationship (Santa Fé, AD 1492)." *East, West.* London: Jonathan Cape, 1994. 105-19.

____. *East, West.* London: Jonathan Cape, 1994.

Schank, R.C. and R. Abelson. *Scripts, Plans, Goals and Understanding.* Hillsdale, NJ: Lawrence Erlbaum, 1977.

2

ORIGIN, ORIGINS, ORIGINALITY: SALMAN RUSHDIE'S *EAST, WEST*, DAVID MALOUF'S *ANTIPODES* AND WILSON HARRIS' *THE WOMB OF SPACE*

ELSA LINGUANTI

A bridge between here and there, and now and then

In 1998 we gathered in Turin for a seminar whose title was: "From one Ocean to the Other: the Expressions of Originality." The group included academics studying Anglophone, Francophone and iberophone literary cultures. It was the twenty-fifth anniversary of our meetings.

The first thing that came to my mind when I saw the title/ subject of that meeting, was (a typical case of idiolectic association) the moment, almost twenty years ago, when I had opened what was then the latest novel by the West-Coast Canadian Jack Hodgins, entitled *The Resurrection of Joseph Bourne, or A Word or two about Those Port Annie Miracles,* published in 1979, and found, among the epigraphs, a quotation from *An Imaginary Life,* by the Australian David Malouf, which in the previous year, 1978, had been a real revelation for me.

> What else should our lives be but a continual series of beginnings, of painful settings out into the unknown, pushing off from the edges of consciousness into the mystery of what we have not yet become, except in dreams [...].[1]

At the time, it seemed to me that, across the oceans, from one hemisphere to the other, the voices of the two writers were rising in unison to remove limits, borders, thresholds, signs of division and separation ("the edges"), and to draw closer, starting again from scratch every time, to a potential idea of man: "what we have not yet become," or "what we might have been," to quote a more recent verse of Fay Zwicky, the Australian poetess.[2]

Twenty years after the publication of those books, among the various possibilities suggested by the title/subject of the seminar, I decided to follow a route which linked together two specific works: the first, a collection of stories, *East, West* by Salman Rushdie, published in 1994, which forms a link across the oceans because it visits India, and the West of Christopher Columbus and Hamlet, Prince of Denmark, narrating also of encounters between the two worlds; the second, David Malouf's collection of stories published in 1985, *Antipodes,* because the stories connect Australia with Italy, Belgium and Austria. Worth mentioning seemed also the volume *12 Edmonstone Street* in which Malouf describes, with his meditations and comments, the two most important addresses where he has lived for the longest periods: 12, Edmonstone Street, Brisbane, Australia and Campagnatico, in the province of Grosseto, Italy, and tells of a trip of his to India.[3]

The third book I refer to, a collection of essays by Wilson Harris, *The Womb of Space,* moves the subject ("From One Ocean to the Other") onto a totally metaphorical level.[4]

As regards "the expressions of originality," we know that the word "expression" indicates language, and in our case, literary language. What is not so easy to define is the meaning of "originality." It is true that the word is used in our professional, critical-academic jargon to mean an innovation (something is born *orior* and is therefore new), *in contrast to* an imitative respect for tradition, and thus the word has to do with a semantic field that Western histories of literature discuss freely, displaying a fair degree of certainty. However, then what kind of tradition(s)? All the writers using English in our times are fully acquainted with the tradition of Western culture, even if they were born in countries bordering on other oceans, but at the same time other traditions have either partially influenced them (the Aborigines in Australia, the Maoris in New Zealand, the Indians in Canada) or wholly permeated them (that of the Indian subcontinent in the specific case of Rushdie, of Africa with its different nations, of the West Indies, etc, in other cases) with their different stories, legends, myths and interpretations of the world, and their different techniques of narrating and of composing poetry. Thus originality is a term that invites reflection.

Etymologically speaking (*orior, origo*), the word is connected with birth and origins, as we consider them in a spatial synchronic sense (origination). In this sense, the writers that we study are natives of, and were born on, the shores of other oceans, and come to us from far away: Rushdie, for example, from India to London, as an expatriate, Malouf from Australia, but with Lebanese and British connections, to Campagnatico, but not on a stable basis.

But origins may also exist in a diachronic sense, as Wilson Harris does not fail to observe; he comes originally from Guyana (but what a mixture of ethnic, biological and cultural components in the person of Harris!). Reflecting upon origins, upon the Origin, is a cultural imperative for Harris. In order to find the "gateway" that makes it possible to go beyond limits, edges, borders, thresholds, and all kinds of signs of division and separation that keep man imprisoned in the monolith of the dominant culture, Harris searches for the resources of the imagination "that may alter perception through and away from fixed habit, greed and monoliths of terror" (*WS* XVI), trying to detect the possible alternatives to the 'mainstream' which has become the foundation of the life of man on our planet, and returning to the potential that has been removed, and discarded, but which can and must coexist.

When the origin—seen as a synchronic provenance from other oceans—and the memory of the Origin—seen as a diachronic, fossilized, largely forgotten but potentially coexisting alternative—are combined, the linguistic-literary expression that is created is likewise "original" in the above sense. Not just an originality of literary forms, to which modernism and post-modernism have accustomed us (to saturation point, I might add, arousing the suspicion of a conformity to anti-conformity), but an originality of metaphors which appear to me to be capable of gathering into new *topoi,* in contrast with worn-out fields of metaphor and exhausted, over-worked topics.

On the basis of these premises

1. The contrasting relationship between "the Old Country" and "the New World" is frequently presented in the collection *Antipodes*: on the one hand, philosophy and the music of Beethoven and Mahler, and on the other, "the desolate shore" (*A* 7) which is the Australian continent; on the one hand, Bruges, "our dear sad Bruges," "this old and impressively dead city" (*A* 88), and on the other, the antipodes, where one of the protagonists is "deep in his dream of sunlight and youth" (*A* 90).

But it is not the binary separations that interest Malouf. In the first story, "Southern Skies," an English teacher at Brisbane is the link, "a last link" (*A* 9), between the two worlds, but also the anonymous boy who forms a relationship with him in the story, always riding his bicycle, is "a kind of centaur" (*A* 12) and consequently a creature that belongs to two worlds, both human and non-human, both realist and mythic. The story moves towards a climax, when the boy is presented with a revelation: the beauty, grandeur, and mathematical order of the spectacle of the stars, revealed by the telescope that the English teacher always keeps trained on the "southern sky."

> The sky, which looks so still, is always in motion, full of drama if you understand how to read it. Like looking into a pond. Hundreds of events happening right under your eyes, except that most of what we see is already finished by the time we see it—ages ago—but important all the same. Such large events. Huge! Bigger even than we can imagine. And beautiful, since they unfold, you know, to numbers of infinite dimensions like the ones

> you deal with in equations at school, but more complex and entirely visible (*A* 18).

The clumsy boy, who is hampered by an excess of adolescent hormones, is overwhelmed by the vision of

> blossoming abstractions, equations luminously exploding out of their own depths, brilliantly solving themselves and playing the results in my head as a real and visible music (*A* 24),

which recalls the passage at the beginning of the third chapter of Joyce's *A Portrait of the Artist as a Young Man,* with the difference that Stephen Dedalus is obsessed with himself, whereas the anonymous boy of "Southern Skies," who is sexually manipulated by the English teacher—with all the ambiguities and the irony of the coincidence—when he perceives the relationship between the stars and mathematics and music, feels as if he is "bursting into the life of things" (*A* 25), and the experience thrusts him beyond his modest individual dimensions.

Roughly at the centre of the collection, in the story "The Only Speaker of his Tongue," a linguist-anthropologist reflects upon the ancient mystery of language:

> O holiest of all things! We touch here on beginnings, go deep under Now to the remotest dark, far back in each ordinary moment of our speaking, even in gossip and the rigmarole of love words and children's games, into the lives of our fathers, to *share* with them the single instant of all our seeing and making, all our long history of doing and being, [...] back before syntax (*A* 69, my italics).

In the language of the aborigine,

> a whole alternative universe, since the world as we know it is in the last resort the words through which we imagine and name it (*A* 69).

In that language, the aborigine

> holds [...] the whole circle of shabby-looking trees, the bushes with their hidden life, the infinitesimal coming and going among grass-roots or on ant-trails between stones, the minds of small native creatures that come

> creeping to the edge of the scene and look in at us from their other lives (*A* 71).

And in the same way, in the context of a story set in Italy, the non-human world is present in the sound of cicadas, that can be heard in the silence of the siesta,

> whose generations beyond counting might go back here to beginnings. They were dug in under stones, or they clung with shrill tenacity to the bark of pines. It was another language. Immemorial. Indecipherable (*A* 110).

In the last story, "A Medium," there is once again "a link" between two worlds—those of the living and of the dead—and once again an anonymous boy, "standing at an angle to the half-open door" (*A* 158), his attention divided between the music that is being played in one room, and a *séance* that is taking place in the other one. As he answers the music teacher's questions ("she played intervals and I named them, or struck chords and I named them. It wasn't difficult. It was simple mathematics" *A* 159), the boy feels that at a moment of excitement he has gained "a glimpse through a half-open door" (*A* 160) of a reality that is bigger than him, but of which his voice is a part.

Also in *12 Edmonstone Street,* there is on the one hand "the ghost of England" (ES 25), and on the other, Australia, like "another planet" (*ES* 35) where the "are "invisible," but here too, the adolescent boy's curiosity is aroused by "the magic that glows along a threshold" (*ES* 9), and by verandas, which are "no man's lands, border zones" (*ES* 20), ambiguous places in contact with the house, but also opening on to the street, the night, the world of mystery, and the area below the houses, where clocks and language have not yet been invented, and "the freedom and mystery of a time before houses" dominates (*ES* 47). "The world is full of odd, undisclosed connections" (*ES* 51), he observes, and some photos of creatures that are half-human and half-animal give him "a marvellous sense of possibilities, of how the world of animals and men might be connected" (*ES* 60).

What strikes Malouf on his travels in India is the plural density, the "invigorating, indestructible" inclusiveness (*ES*

110) of a life "closer to primitive beginnings" and perhaps, as a consequence, "further off from the distant, inconceivable end" (*ES* 111):

> India seems never to have heard of this absolute distinction (between the human world and the animal world) on which our superiority and power is based (*ES* 119).

Thus, questions arise, from the antipodes, about "'undisclosed connections" and "alternative possibilities," and eyes are turned to "beginnings," in an all-inclusive gaze.

2. In *East, West,* Rushdie explores what Naipaul has so appropriately defined "the enigma of arrival." Stories of cultural distance succeed one another in a truly brilliant programmatic order. In the "East" section, two stories set in India narrate, in a sober, realistic style, single human cases against the background of multitudes. A third story follows, "The Prophet's Hair," which introduces a note of magic realism: just because they have spent a few minutes in the same environment as the prophet's hair, four lame beggars are healed (and the narrator ironically comments: "They were, the four of them, very properly furious, because the miracle had reduced their earning power by 75 per cent, at the most conservative estimate: so they were ruined men," *EW* 58), and their mother regains her sight.

In the "West" section, Rushdie carries out the far more refined experiment, with a devastatingly parodic effect on present-day stylemes of Western literature, of constructing two post-modern *caprices,* with all the ingredients—including the rewriting of a historical figure (Columbus) and of a canonic literary text (Hamlet), a desecrating intertextuality, a mixture of genres, some Sternian lines ("..../...../...../...../...../," in order to represent "by each dot [...] the conjunction of one toe-tip with the floor," in the stride of young Hamlet, *EW* 74)—amid which he interpolates another typically Western text, the dystopic fanta-sociological tale, "At the Auction of the Ruby Slippers." Nothing is saved here, of the future which hangs inevitably over Western society: in a not-too-distant future, the real world is completely dominated by the fictitious world, and this is "a symbol of the moral decay of our post-millennium culture," says the anonymous narrator (*EW* 94). Individuals who rarely venture out, and live their lives closed inside bunkers, throng to the auction selling "memorabilia junkies" (*EW* 88). "Imaginary beings" are also present here:

> a large majority of us opposes the free, unrestricted migration of imaginary beings into an already damaged reality, whose resources diminish by the day. After all, few of us would choose to travel in the opposite direction (though there are pervasive reports of an increase of such migrations latterly) (*EW* 94-95).

The ruby slippers are highly desirable

> because we believe they can make us invulnerable to witches (and there are so many sorcerers pursuing us nowadays); because of their powers of reverse metamorphosis, their affirmation of a lost state of normalcy in which we have almost ceased to believe and to which the slippers promise us we can return (*EW* 92).

They also promise to take the wearer home, but

> 'Home' has become such a scattered, damaged, various concept in our present travails. There is so much to yearn for. There are so few rainbows anymore. How hard can we expect even a pair of magic shoes to work? They promised to take us home, but are metaphors of loneliness comprehensible to them, are abstractions permissible? Are they literalists, or will they permit us to redefine the blessed word? (*EW* 93)

It is the auctioneers who establish the value of things, of the past, the future and life, and, after this one of the ruby slippers, the following week's auction is to be dedicated to family trees and pedigrees:

> Family trees, coats of arms, royal lineages will be up for sale, and into any of these one may insert any name one chooses, one's own, or one's beloved [...] Thanks to the infinte bounty of the Auctioneers, any of us, cat, dog, man, woman, child, can be a blue-blood; can be—as we long to be; and as, cowering in our shelters, we fear we are not—*somebody* (*EW* 102-03).

The third section is "East, West," and unlike the verse "Oh the East is the East / and the West is the West / and never the twain shall meet, it contains two stories which describe meetings between young people from different backgrounds. In the first one, there is a search for harmony which subsequently proves to be ephemeral, or even dangerous. In the words of one of the two friends, it is a question of trying to find "a [...] way of making a bridge between here-and-there, between my two othernesses, my double unbelonging" (*EW* 141). In the second story, a friendship is compromised by history and politics. In the third story, a young Pakistani in London observes the two worlds pulling the old nurse Certainly-Mary, in opposite directions:

> It was England that was breaking her heart, breaking it by not being India. London was breaking her heart by not being Bombay [...] was it that her heart, roped by two different loves, was being pulled East and West, whinnying and rearing, like those movie horses being yanked this way by Clark Gable and that way by Montgomery Clift [...]? (*EW* 209)

and in spite of the fact that he has acquired British citizenship, he is, in turn, torn in two directions. In his case, however, the verse "home is best" does not work.

> I, too, have ropes around my neck [...] pulling me this way and that, East, West, the nooses tightening, commanding, *choose, choose.*
>
> I buck, I snort, I whinny, I rear, I kick. Ropes, I do not choose between you. Lassoes, lariats, I choose neither of you, and both. Do you hear? I refuse to choose (*EW* 211).

We find here the "double unbelonging," and the need for a "bridge," the refusal to choose between alternatives *as if* they were mutually exclusive, and the much-desired redefinition of "home."

3. It is the relationships on the synchronic level that interest Rushdie in these stories: he deals with current affairs, history and politics.

It is the relationships on the diachronic level that interest Malouf: "beginnings," and alternative possibilities, as well as relationships between the infinitely large and the infinitely small (the stars and insects in the pond), between so-called highly-developed languages and primitive languages, between human and animal languages, between worlds.

Both Malouf and Rushdie, however, work on edges, borders, thresholds, and boundaries, looking for "links," "bridges," something that will allow them/us to share, instead of dividing, what is on either side. In the last few lines of *The Moor's Last Sigh,* the final words of dying Moraes confirm

> our need for flowing together, for putting an end to frontiers, for the dropping of the boundaries of the self.[5]

It is "gateways" that are of interest for Harris: "the elaboration of gateways into the largely submerged territory of the imagination" (*WS* XIX). In order to go beyond "thresholds," "break polarisations," and make a connection, 'melting pots' or 'mosaics' are not sufficient; what is needed is "a body of harlequin features rooted in many cultures" (*WS* 3), from one ocean to the other.

Once all signs of fragmentation, division, separation, opposition and drifting have been excluded, the continuity-contiguity between men, and between men and the created world, favours metaphors that are not based on scraps of reality, but on a fabric without "seams," not on drifting fragments, but on the totality: "the seamless whole."

To begin with, Harris's imagination is always at work amid "the living museum of creation" and "aeons of matter and space" (*WS* XVII), observing "the live tapestry of the universe" (*WS* XVI), in search of "secrets of potentiality" which may reveal "a universe composed of fabrics of mobility akin to thought" (*WS* XVI). His is a "pilgrimage toward forgotten origins."

The *Womb of Space* is a text made up of critical readings which Harris defines as "explorations": the writers that he "explores" are Faulkner, Poe, Jean Toomer, Juan Rulfo, Jean Rhys, Patrick White, etc., and what interests him is the "thread [...] woven into potential heterogeneity, and arching through European, African and pre-Columbian hidden antecedents" (*WS* 6).

With Harris, a completely 'original' language is born: his critical and his creative languages share in an identical, systematic disruption of binary polarisations and are based on metaphors that all tend towards "disrupting symmetries" (*WS* 18), and thus on paradoxes that unite apparently incompatible elements, in search of a "dialogue" (*WS* XVII), "a doorway *into* a break*through* from tragedy"—the tragedy of twentieth century nihilism—(*WS* 45, my italics)—and the prepositions 'into' and 'through' are frequently, almost obsessively, found on every single page.

Harris follows an "irrational coherence" [...] that breaches conventional logic," moving "against the narrowness of simple logical patterns" (*WS* 4): this is a defence of what Harris calls "asymmetrical" discourse, not because symmetries are false, but because they claim to be universally valid, when instead they are only useful, and at times brilliant, extensions of a superimposed order that reduces the most contradictory phenomena "within patterns of elegant tautology" (*WS* 17). In practice, it is the "symmetrical thinking" which Matte Blanco studies for the unconscious, and whose laws he identifies in *The Unconscious as Infinite Sets, an essay in bi-logic,* that is presented as a language capable of expressing the coexistence of and interaction between two "modes of being" of man: the asymmetrical and the symmetrical, what we use in order to put an order into the organisation of knowledge, but at the same time, more or less unwittingly, to divide and construct rigid boundaries—"obdurate frontiers [...] we must learn to cross," says Harris (*WS* 150)—and the mode of being—"before syntax," as Malouf says—through which we are in contact with the *continuum* of our psychic life.[6] While Matte Blanco claims that symmetrical language is enclitic, in the sense that it needs the support of logical language in order to express itself, in order to express contents that are foreign to rational logic (but in so doing, it uses generalisations, condensations, and all the paradoxes that spring from an absence of the principles of contradiction and of negation), Harris suggests that language should make use of paradoxes (typical of Matte Blanco's 'symmetrical' thought) in order to overcome the resistance of so-called logical language.

> Imaginative sensibility is uniquely equipped by [...] paradox to mirror the inimitable activity of subordinated psyche; inimitable in that no art of total capture or subordination of originality within formula exists despite appearances. Thus the unity or density of *original* expression, in a work of profound imagination, is paradox (*WS* XVII, my italics).

While "the post-modern temperament [...] is committed to dead myth and tamed metaphor" (*WS* 47), it is necessary

> to release profound metaphors [...] to uncover a bridge of forgotten associations between diversity and mutuality, mutual heights/depths, mutual skies/earth, mutual cultures that civilisation has grossly married or eclipsed (*WS* 48).

Clearly, we are in need of "untamable metaphor and myth" (*WS* 47). The metaphor that appears most frequently "to bridge a divide"(*WS* 51) is that of the "rainbow bridge between cultures" (*WS* 29), "rainbow arcs or bridges between cultures" (*WS* 31, 33, 49), which is also "a rainbow arc or bridge of psyche" (*WS* 46), and takes the name of an "alchemical *coniunctio* or true and productive union between man and woman, between one and the other, between culture and culture" (*WS* 37), "between sky and earth" (*WS* 50).

With Harris, we arrive at the re-semanticisation of old metaphors by means of paradox: the river has four banks, and it is not the flow of time that is associated with the flow of its water, but space. In *The Four Banks of the River of Space,* there is one river of the living and one of the dead, and space is a womb.

It is not a question of reconciling opposites:

> not simply a reconciliation of opposites. Such a formula was too uncreative or mechanical. Not just a mechanics of psyche. But a *gathering* up of all that had been experienced in every condition of existence (my italics).[7]

What we are required to do is not to be "blind to originality," "to re-imagine the past, to enter changed spatialities in the past," to enter into "moral twinships with all species and things." There is the metaphor or "overlapping," of "gathering," and above all, of "salvaging," as the "capacity to convert rather than to succumb to, deprivations."[8]

4. In modernism, the dominant metaphor was the fragment, indicating discontinuity and separation. Fragments, ruins, the single occasions, the intermittent moments: pieces that are foreign to one another, and no force exists that can hold them together, except, perhaps, the Form of Art. Henry James distils them, Robert Browning lets them roll down a grassy slope ("Two in the Campagna"), or tries to melt them with gold into a ring, which is, however, the product of art (*The Ring and the Book*). T.S. Eliot piles them up on the shore, James Joyce inserts them into the nostalgia of an ancient form, and, later on, Malcolm Lowry attaches them to the big wheel of a fairground, which moves without making any progress (*Under the Volcano*), and heterogeneous fragments go "slipping past one another" in his story "Through the Panama," which is already a great post-modern experiment.

After the fragment, the drifting, of which *Waterland*, by Graham Swift, may be taken as a representative text: "the fens" are "a low-lying region [...] formed by silt [...], a slow, sly, insinuating agency [...] which shapes and undermines [...], simultaneously accretion and erosion; neither progress nor decay."[9] The protagonist does not expect, or require, a future, and all meaning is absent.

But, while we thought we were in the post-modern era, something new was happening: from the shores of other oceans, we were offered the surprise of "overlapping" connections,[10] of osmosis and metamorphosis, and the thought of the Origin, the origins, of possible, potential alternatives, abandoned but still coexistent.

For the new *topoi* to take shape, a sense of contiguity with the created world and with the Other needed to be revived; observation needed to go beyond the solipsistic boundaries that have made it so arid, settling again with a sense of wonder on the external world; the Other's gaze needed to turn to the Other. East and West, and the antipodes were being connected. The contribution came from far away oceans.

In my opinion, the expressions of originality are to be found in the new dominant metaphors of "links," "bridges," "gateways" ("pushing off the edges," "crossing borders"), which become *topoi* forming the basis for the many stories of relationships between what is on either side of the borders (for example, the only man that Morag can love, in Margaret Laurence's unforgettable novel *The Diviners*, is a métis, while the only man that Ammu can love in Arundathi Roy's novel *The God of Small Things* is an untouchable); other metaphors are those of "overlapping" and sharing, "salvaging" and "gathering," which are at the basis of the many stories about communities (for example, the new community that is reconstructed after the landslide, at the end of Jack Hodgins' *The Resurrection of Joseph Bourne*, etc).

Contiguity with the non-human is presented in various ways: in Robert Kroetsch's *What the Crow Said*, the young Vera is made pregnant by bees, by means of a literalised metaphor; in *The Carpathians*, by Janet Frame, the old Maori woman explains to the protagonist that it is impossible to work with flax if you don't know it, if you don't know how to talk with it; in Malouf's *An Imaginary Life*, Ovid gets lost and finds himself in the countryside:

> We are continuous with earth in all the particles of our physical being, as in our breathing we are continuous with sky. Between our bodies and the world there is unity and commerce.[11]

Continuity with origins it to be found in the revival of contact with ancient myths, no longer exclusively Biblical or Greek, in search of truths of the imagination which have been lost: "Myth [...], like all the past, real or imaginary, must be acknowledged," as Strabo Becker said in Jack Hodgins' *The Invention of the World*, "even if not believed."[12]

"Untamed potential for rebirth in the womb of space" is the formula used by Wilson Harris, to be activated by means of synchronic and diachronic contact, in a constant crossing over and back, through and into.

"Cross-culturalism" goes beyond mere multiculturalism, once again in the metaphor of "crossing": "cross-pollination," according to Rushdie. This is a crossing which takes place in both directions: it is not only Shakespeare familiarised (and parodied) in the tale of Rushdie, or Greek tragedy revisited in a play of the Nigerian Soyinka, or the Dantesque journey of the protagonist of *The Four Banks of the River of Space* by the writer from Guyana, Wilson Harris. It is also the need for Westerners to read the Koran and its commentaries in order to appreciate a book by Nuruddin Farah, or Rushdie's *Satanic Verses,* the ability to read the Mahabharata and classical Indian literature that is being acquired by my colleagues who are experts in English literature produced in India, the usefulness of translating into English the legends of the Canadian Indians, as the poet Robert Bringhurst is doing, before the last elderly Indian who knows them dies.[13] We need to move "through" these oceans, to "open doors" and share cultures.

Notes and References

1. David Malouf, *An Imaginary Life* (London: Chatto and Windus, 1978) 135; Jack Hodgins, *The Resurrection of Joseph Bourne, or AWord or Two about those Port Annie Miracles* (Toronto: MacMillan, 1979).
2. Fay Zwicky, "Talking Mermaid," *Poems 1970-1992* (St Lucia: U of Queensland P, 1993) 232.
3. Salman Rushdie, *East, West* (London: Jonathan Cape, 1994), henceforth *EW*; David Malouf, *Antipodes* (London: Chatto and Windus, 1985), henceforth *A*; *12 Edmonstone Street* (1985; London: Penguin Books, 1986), henceforth *ES*. This essay was first published in *Africa, America, Asia, Australia* 22 (1998): 7-18.
4. Wilson Harris, *The Womb of Space: The Cross-Cultural Imagination* (Westport, USA: Greenwood Press, 1983), henceforth *WS*.
5. Salman Rushdie, *The Moor's Last Sigh* (London: Jonathan Cape, 1995) 435. In the best paintings of the Moor's mother, "the vision [...] in fact was a vision of *weaving* or more accurately interweaving (227); "a land-sea-scape in which the land could be fluid and the sea stone-dry was her metaphor [...] of the present, and the future she hoped would evolve" (227), and on the water's edge "strange composite creatures slithered to and fro across the frontiers of the elements" (226).
6. Ignacio Matte Blanco, *The Unconscious as Infinite Sets, an Essay in Bi-logic* (London: Duckworth, 1975).
7. Wilson Harris, *The Four Banks of the River of Space* in *The Carnival Trilogy* (London: Faber & Faber, 1993) 317.

8. Wilson Harris, *Jonestown* (London: Faber & Faber, 1996) 133, 137, 166, 168, 189, 194, 214, 223.
9. Graham Swift, *Waterland* (1983; London: Picador, 1992) 8-9.
10. I noticed this metaphor for the first time in a short story by Jack Hodgins in the collection *Spit Delaney's Island* (Toronto: MacMilland, 1976) 15.
11. Malouf 147.
12. Jack Hodgins, *The Invention of the World* (1977; Toronto: Macmillan of Canada, 1978) 316.
13. Robert Bringhurst, *A Story as Sharp as a Knife: The Classical Haida Mythtellers and their World* (Vancouver/Toronto: Douglas & McIntyre, 1999).

3

Acid in the Nation's Bloodstream: Satire, Violence, and the Indian Body Politic in Salman Rushdie's *The Moor's Last Sigh*

JOHN CLEMENT BALL

In *The Moor's Last Sigh* (1995), Salman Rushdie explores the tensions between inclusive and exclusive forms of Indian nationalism through the dynamic interplay of inclusive and exclusive forms of satire. Rushdie has been called a satirist in many discursive contexts, from jacket copy to critical articles and books, but the transforming effects of satiric modes of writing on his novels have yet to be fully linked to his political vision of the nation. This paper draws on Mikhail Bakhtin's theories of satire and the grotesque to show how generic strategies work in tandem with political ideas in *The Moor's Last Sigh.*

Since the publication of *Midnight's Children* in 1981, Rushdie's novels have been celebrated and interrogated as much for their portrayals of Indian and Pakistani politics as for their adventurous refashionings of the Indian novel in English. Recent criticism continues to emphasize the nation as a primary thematic focus and ontological category for Rushdie. Josna Rege argues that *Midnight's Children*'s primary achievement was that it offered post-Emergency India "a new literary and conceptual model that opened new worlds of possibility for re-imagining and representing enabling relationships between individual and nation" (Rege 349). For Jyotsna Singh, Rushdie destabilizes and pluralizes the category of "nation-in-formation" in *Midnight's Children*, and continues this project in *The Moor's Last Sigh*, where he "lays to rest all the comforting myths of postcolonial Indian nationalism" (Singh 169, 174). Paul Cantor argues that, by modelling Indian society through the lens of Moorish Spain in the latter novel, Rushdie "condemns efforts to impose a uniform culture on a nation and celebrates instead cultural hybridity" (Cantor 325). The tensions between unity and multiplicity (or consolidation and fragmentation) that animate Rushdie's two major novels of India have both political and aesthetic dimensions: nation and novel are pulled in contradictory directions by opposing forces.

In its idealized form, Rushdie's India resembles Jawaharlal Nehru's vision of an inclusive, pluralist secular democracy. For Rushdie, India's strength is its multiplicity, its impurity, its ability to contain diverse and contradictory realities. His beloved Bombay, the nation's most cosmopolitan city, exemplifies these qualities; in *Midnight's Children* he coins the term "Bombayness" to encapsulate a whole value system (Rushdie, *Midnight's* 301). Hinduism with its millions of gods, its fluid mythology and absorptive, transformative energies also serves as a touchstone for India's inclusiveness—conceptually if not always in practice. In the realm of politics, inclusivity is the principle by which Rushdie judges things. The usual targets of his satire are movements, people, or conditions given to coercion, tyranny, hierarchic exclusion, or a simplifying search for purity. Hillel Halkin writes that in its critique of "the perils of monism," *The Moor's Last Sigh* is "a thematic sequel to *The Satanic Verses*" (Halkin 58) but he could have named any of Rushdie's other novels, whose satiric targets are as varied as Indira Gandhi's Emergency (in *Midnight's Children*), elite Pakistani patriarchies (in *Shame*), and those who would censor stories (in *Haroun and the Sea of Stories*). In addition to being exclusive, self-serving, and ideologically narrow-minded, Rushdie's satiric targets are also typically shown to be violent.

Satire is itself a kind of representational violence. And the dualistic rhetoric through which satirists most often (mis)represent the world is more inclined to judge and banish than to accommodate and include. Rushdie's satire, especially in *Shame*, may therefore be seen to replicate textually the very qualities it critiques referentially. But Rushdie's handling of satire is complex, and his political vision can be best understood if we see his novels as energized by two countervailing forms of satiric energy. One is the conventional "negative" kind of satire mentioned above: satire as attack, as distorting critique of one or more referential somethings (or someones) located outside the text, fixed in (and by) the satirist's hostile gaze. The other is Menippean satire as Mikhail Bakhtin defines it: a dialogic, radically inclusive form marked by outrageously diverse combinations of things, ideas, people, societies, ontologies, narrative styles, and voices.

Bakhtin theorizes Menippean satire through his socially inclusive notion of carnival, from which he also develops his theory of the grotesque body. For Bakhtin, the grotesque offers an optimistic, enabling image of incompleteness; the physiological self transgresses its boundaries, becoming blended with the world and renewed. Bakhtin sets his rhapsodic view against traditional theories of the grotesque as embodying the alienating vision of what he calls the "negative" satirist; for Bakhtin, images of the grotesque body and its open apertures convey hope through the productive intermingling of realms. By grafting Bakhtin's concept of the grotesque onto his related but separately theorized idea of Menippean satire, we can generate a useful hybrid model which I have named "the Menippean grotesque." As the positive counterpart of "negative" satire, it helps open up the political and generic tensions of inclusion and exclusion in Rushdie's novels.

Midnight's Children, for instance, has the sort of fantastic, free-ranging plot and mixed style identified with Menippean satire. And as it inscribes India's history onto Saleem's body, it uses body images to suggest inclusive openness: Saleem as a "swallower of lives" has "consumed multitudes" (*MC* 11); history leaks into him, and his "mighty cucumber of a nose" (*MC* 152) leaks into the world in the early years when he has the greatest power and stature; these are also the years when India inspires the greatest optimism. When his nose becomes a conduit for the Midnight Children's Conference, it offers great hope and potential to the nation, but it ultimately fails. Eventually, the enabling idea of leaking gives way to the imposed, unnatural assaults of draining. When Saleem's nose is surgically drained he becomes disconnected from the multiple voices of community. Moreover, his body is increasingly "buffeted"; as history inscribes his body, it destroys his body. The most brutal bodily assault is the enforced sterilization of the midnight children during Emergency, which Saleem calls "the draining-out of hope" (*MC* 421) for the nation. All of this is part of the satiric darkening of tone in Book Three. The novel traces several linked processes: post-independence optimism leads to authoritarian betrayal; valorized grotesque intermingling gives way to imposed violations of the body's boundaries; the Menippean spirit wanes before the onslaught of a reality that no longer suits it, and a negative, attack-oriented satire takes its place. In terms of politics, imagery and genre, the inclusive is overcome by the exclusive.

The Moor's Last Sigh brings *Midnight's Children*'s politics up to date. While reaffirming the Nehruvian idea of India as secular democracy, it moves past the crisis of governance of the 1975-77 Emergency and into the ideological crises of the 1980s and 1990s. For Rushdie, the rise of the religious right in that period is like "corrosive acid [...] poured into the nation's bloodstream"; it violates "the old, founding myth of the nation" (*MLS* 351) just as the Ram cult reduces polytheistic Hinduism to a religion in which "only one chap matters" (*MLS* 338). In his satire of an exclusive Hindu nationalism, Rushdie again makes the human body the main site where literal and metaphoric versions of the national health (or disease) are enacted. And again the body's fluid dynamics (blood, food, poisons, breath) serve as markers of both an esteemed intermingling and the invasive, "purifying" violence that opposes admixture.

It is mainly through the narrator, Moraes, and his mother, Aurora, that these ideas are inscribed and negotiated. Moraes ages at double-speed, his rapid growth a metaphor for post-independence India (both in terms of population and development), and specifically Bombay: "Like the city itself," he says, "I expanded without time for proper planning" (*MLS* 161-62). By birth, Moraes is a "mongrel" (*MLS* 172); a hybrid blend of Christian, Jewish, and possibly Arabic Muslim ancestry, he belongs to a demographically tiny minority. But if he can be seen as "a freak blond hair plucked from a jet-black (and horribly unravelling) plait" (*MLS* 87), Moraes uses his marginality to make an ideological point. He resists essentialist group identities defined by "majority" and "minority" status: "Majority, that mighty elephant, and her sidekick, Major-Minority, will not crush my tale beneath her feet. Are not my personages Indian, every one?" (*MLS* 87).

Bakhtin's notion of the unfinished body blending into the world is contained in the novel's title image: for the wheezy, asthmatic Moraes "A sigh isn't just a sigh. We inhale the world and breathe out meaning. While we can" (*MLS* 54). The inclusive interchange between realms is often translated from somatic to topographical space. "Bombayness" is conveyed here with the *Haroun*-like image of "an ocean of stories" (*MLS* 350): "In Bombay," Moraes says, "all India met and merged. In Bombay, too, all-India met what-was-not-India, what came across the black water to flow into our veins [...]. Bombay was central; all rivers flowed into its human sea" (*MLS* 350). The novel is full of enabling images of opening up and interpenetration: teenage Aurora opening windows to "let in" Cochin's multifarious world, however "dirtyfilthy" it may be (*MLS* 9); the Alhambra palace of Spain as a "testament [...] to that most profound of our needs, to our need for flowing together, for putting an end to frontiers, for the dropping of the boundaries of the self" (*MLS* 433).

Aurora embodies many traits valorized in the novel. Having invited "the torrential reality of India to awaken her soul" (*MLS* 45) in Cochin, she responds to Bombay with a similar openness: "she sucked in the city's hot stenches, lapped up its burning sauces, she gobbled its dishes up whole" (*MLS* 128). Moraes begins to see her as the human "incarnation of the smartyboots metropolis" (*MLS* 139); in her carnivalesque annual performance on Chowpatty Beach she dances satirically against fundamentalist elements in Hindu culture from a position clearly aligned with inclusive, cosmopolitan "Bombayness." Still, Aurora is not unequivocally idealized: as a mother she shows insufficient love, and in this novel the idea of love is overtly identified with Rushdie's value system: "I wanted to cling to the image of love as the blending of spirits, as mélange, as the triumph of the impure, mongrel, conjoining best of us over what there is in us of the solitary, the isolated, the austere, the dogmatic, the pure; of love as democracy, as the victory of the no-man-is-an-island, two's-company Many over the clean, mean, apartheiding Ones" (*MLS* 289). The actuality of Aurora's love eventually fails to meet these standards: Aurora the "natural soloist" (*MLS* 159) makes her most profound impact on Moraes through an act of exclusion, irrevocably banishing him from her love and from the family when she and Moraes fall victim to Uma's devastating trick.

Nonetheless, it is in Aurora's paintings that Rushdie's pluralist values find their most elaborate and original expression. Through *ekphrasis*, Rushdie puts into (or pulls out of) her images the aesthetic and moral perspectives from which he would have us read his novel. Full of grotesque figures fusing human and animal parts, with breasts for buttocks or whole bodies made from urban rubbish, Aurora's teeming canvases signify a grand, all-encompassing vision. Her blending of realities is geographic as well as social. A key stage of her work's development involves the Bombay landscape blending into an Arabian Sea-scape, with "strange composite creatures slither[ing] to and fro across the frontier of the elements" (*MLS* 226). As chief moral touchstone, Aurora's canvases not only seem to be the visual equivalent of Rushdie's encyclopedic, grotesque, magic-realist novels, but they also help explain a unique feature of this particular novel. Her blurring of "the dividing line between two worlds" (*MLS* 226) is part of a grand merging and palimpsesting of worlds that both she and Rushdie perform to advance their more-or-less mutual idea of contemporary India as a type of Moorish Spain.

Before the tumultuous events of the late fifteenth century—the Inquisition, the expulsion of Jews, and the end of Moorish rule in Granada—the Iberian peninsula had for some time harboured a heterodox, accommodating society. Indeed, in its day medieval Spain comprised Western Europe's most multiracial and religiously pluralist populace. Under tolerant Christian kings, three monotheistic groups (Christians, Muslims, and Jews) had coexisted, convinced that by believing in the same God they could live in peace. But from the thirteenth century on, they became increasingly segregated and hostile. An idea of *limpienza de sangre*, or blood purity, took hold; although its origins have been traced to orthodox Jewry's prohibition against mixed marriages, the idea was appropriated by Christians as a weapon against Jewish and Mudjehar (Moor) minorities (Read 202-07). The purist idea of Christian Spain promoted so fiercely by Ferdinand and Isabella identified the interests of the nation-state with those of a single religious group.

Such an identification is anathema to Rushdie in the Indian context. But when he, like Aurora, starts "using Arab Spain to re-imagine India" (*MLS* 227), the parallels enable a prophetic critique. As J.M. Coetzee notes in his review of the novel, they suggest "that the Arab penetration of Iberia, like the later Iberian penetration of India, led to a creative mingling of peoples and cultures; that the victory of Christian intolerance in Spain was a tragic turn in history; and that Hindu intolerance in India bodes as ill for the world as did the sixteenth-century Inquisition in Spain" (Coetzee 14). Overlaying the context of 1492 on 1992 invokes an historical process of national "purification" through which Rushdie can mirror and satirize an event still *in process* in India. Medieval Spain offers the positive parallel to the older, pluralist nationalism of Gandhi and Nehru, while the ascendant Christian Spain of the late Middle Ages and early Renaissance—a fractious, coercive society—forecasts the course India could take under the sway of Hindu nationalism. As in *Midnight's Children*, Rushdie conveys through imagery the historical shift from a normative, inspiring national condition to a satirized, dangerous one. And again the Menippean grotesque gives way to a more "negative" satire aimed at the very social forces that threaten inclusiveness.

As before, the difference between the earlier and later national conditions is based on a discrepancy between benign interminglings (of realms, fluids, bodies, and peoples) and invasive penetrations or poisonings-in other words, between a voluntary opening up *to* and an unwanted assault or infection *by*. Here is how Moraes first describes the historical process: "What started with perfume ended with a very big stink indeed ... there is a thing that bursts out of us at times, a thing that lives in us, eating our food, breathing our air, looking out through our eyes, and when it comes out to play nobody is immune; possessed, we turn murderously upon one another" (*MLS* 36; original ellipsis). In this passage the nose is invoked to suggest a movement from pleasant to unpleasant bodily intake, leading immediately to a frightening image of parasitic contagion. Forces allied with "purity" are identified with the most damaging and monstrous of impurities. Even in this early foreshadowing the satiric reversal is established. The associations are made more explicit later on with references to acid in the nation's bloodstream, to "the plague-spores of communal fanaticism" (*MLS* 208), and to Uma, whose enticing appearance of affirming pluralism masks a reality of self-seeking devastation: she sows "pestilential seeds" to produce a "menu" of "misery, catastrophe, grief" and division for Moraes's family to consume (*MLS* 320). After the destruction of the Ayodhya mosque in 1992, with fundamentalist ideologies on the rise and Bombay blowing apart, Moraes describes the national condition in a brilliant, multilayered image: "the barbarians were not only at our gates but within our skins. We were our own wooden horses, each one of us full of our doom [...]. [T]he explosions burst out of our very own bodies. We were both the bombers and the bombs" (*MLS* 372). This description is interesting not only for its transhistorical fusions of military and body imagery, but also for its insistence on the collective "we" in assigning responsibility. Even as he laments the violence of divisive forces Moraes adheres to his vision of himself as part of the crowd.

This is appropriate, since he has indeed been part of the problem. Rushdie does not exclude his protagonist from the condition he critiques. Like his forebear Boabdil the Unlucky, whose secret alliance with the Christians helped end Moorish sovereignty in Granada (Harvey 301), Moraes spends time as an agent of the intolerant enemy. He may embody and advocate multiplicity through his ancestry, his professed beliefs, and his "metaphorical rôle" in Aurora's paintings as "a unifier of opposites, a standard-bearer of pluralism, [...] a symbol [...] of the new nation" (*MLS* 303), but when is employed as a thug by Raman Fielding, or Mainduck, he is co-opted by the novel's main exemplar of the new fundamentalism. Admittedly, Moraes does so after the shock of Uma's duplicity, his ostracism from family, his imprisonment in Bombay Central prison ("the stomach, the intestine of the city," *MLS* 287), and his rescue by Mainduck. But he does not feel torn about the betrayal that his job as bully represents. In fact, he relishes the new life: "Unhesitating, I embraced my fate [...]. I would become this man. I studied Fielding closely. I must say as he said, do as he did. He was the new way, the future" (*MLS* 295, 300). Thereafter Moraes features in his mother's paintings only as "a semi-allegorical figure of decay"; she has "apparently decided that the ideas of impurity, cultural admixture and mélange which had been [...] [her] notion of the Good, were in fact capable of distortion, and contained a potential for darkness as well as for light" (*MLS* 303). The inclusive, in other words, can include and then be overcome by powerful forces of exclusiveness.

What is the significance of Moraes's complicity and Aurora's disillusionment to the novel's satiric strategies? Do these developments blur or undermine the idealized moral vision of the nation from which Rushdie's critique is launched? There are two perspectives from which one might answer these questions, which get at the heart of the novel's ideological and generic conundrums.

From the first perspective, Moraes's years with Mainduck serve Rushdie's satiric agenda in a conventional way. Like Saleem's stint in the Pakistani army, they give Moraes access to the primary target so that he (and Rushdie) can really show its deformities. Up close, Mainduck can be described in all his repulsive physicality: "And in his low cane chair with his great belly slung across his knees like a burglar's sack, with his frog's croak of a voice bursting through his fat frog's lips and his little dart of a tongue licking at the edges of his mouth, with his hooded froggy eyes gazing greedily down upon the little beedi-rolls of money [...], he was indeed a Frog King" (*MLS* 232). This is conventionally "negative" grotesque imagery; it is Wolfgang Kayser's alienating satiric grotesque (Kayser 186-87), not Bakhtin's optimistic one. Up close, too, we encounter Mainduck's reactionary public policies: anti-union, anti-immigrant, anti-working women, pro-sati, pro-caste. And we observe the private man, who resembles a coercive and decadent Mafia Don. Besides the grotesque, Rushdie uses many of satire's traditional strategies of representational violence to critique fundamentalists: reductive metonymy (the BJP, RSS and VHP as "Alphabet-soupists," *MLS* 363); analogy (Mainduck as a "little Hitler," *MLS* 297); mechanization (Tin-man Hazaré's robotic appearance); understatement (Moraes's eerie descriptions of beatings); and the appropriation of a satirized discourse as the narrator's own: "Muslims and Hindus had, for a time, shared [Ayodhya] without fuss ... but to the devil with such old news! Who cared about those unhealthy, split hairs?" (*MLS* 363; original ellipsis).

Satiric horror is registered through the image of the violated body that becomes the lowest common denominator of Mainduck's political agitation; assaulting people is the main thing Moraes and the other *goondas* do. As in *Midnight's Children*, imposed transgressions of bodily boundaries signal "negative" satire, not the positive interminglings of the Menippean grotesque. Here blood-letting takes on additional ironic meaning when identified with Hindu nationalists: though they advocate the integrity and purity of blood as metaphor, they violate the integrity and cause impurity of blood in its literal form.

From this first perspective, Moraes's time with Mainduck is a device to facilitate satire of fundamentalist thinking *through* Moraes. The fact that Moraes himself administers beatings, breaks unions, and enforces sati and caste discipline is just a convenient (and powerful) way of displaying a satirized condition in all its nauseating detail. Moraes is thus a target only insofar as he becomes a temporary synecdoche for activities and ideologies attributed to others. In this reading his primary function is as window on, not exemplar of, the religious right; he is exempt from the novel's critique. But is he really? I would like to suggest a second, more allegorical reading, which sees Moraes's involvement as sign of a new satiric despair in Rushdie and of a more all-embracing pessimism about India.

The gloom with which *Midnight's Children* ended was based on a feeling, in the aftermath of the Emergency, that democracy and human rights had been betrayed by the prime minister and her loyalists. There was treachery at the highest level, and citizens (like Saleem and the midnight children) had been victimized. The Emergency's most visible challenge to the secular democracy of India was to its legitimacy as a democracy. Although Rushdie has written that "it was during the Emergency that the lid flew off the Pandora's box of communal discord" (Rushdie, "Imaginary" 41-52), and while Indira Gandhi's politics had always been divisive and factionalizing by comparison with Nehru's, as long as the Congress party was dominant, some version of the secular principle remained officially in place. She may have fostered Hindu nationalist sentiments, especially from 1980 on, but Indira Gandhi continued to advocate secularism until the day she died (Malhotra 18, 229-31). In the 1980s and 1990s Rushdie sees Hindu nationalism (along with other ethnically and religiously based movements) gaining an increased profile and influence among India's people. He shows the secular-pluralist ideal underlying the nation's democracy to be taking a beating, so to speak, and even dying a painful death. Unlike the brutally top-down nature of social upheaval during the Emergency, the rise of the religious right is a function not just of charismatic leadership but of mass participation. It is both a top-down and a grass-roots movement. To Rushdie it therefore represents a greater national crisis than the Emergency.

From this second perspective, then, Moraes's complicity is very significant to the novel's satiric orientation. He starts out, both in the novel and in Aurora's "Moor" paintings, as an allegorical embodiment of India as pluralistic, hybrid, gentle giant. He may grow too fast and get too big, he may be deformed, but he is not a monster. In Mainduck's service, however, he betrays his roots and his ideals. Disillusioned from the fallout of his relationship with the divisive Uma, he lets himself become an agent of the very forces that would deny him-as individual and as national principle. Moreover, he takes pleasure in his new role, administering beatings with cool efficiency, relieved that he can give up his old confusing complexity for the "simplicity" and "straightforwardness" of Mainduck's brutal program (*MLS* 305). His unapologetic embrace of an alien cause suggests that Moraes, the "semi-allegorical figure of decay" (*MLS* 303), now represents a nation increasingly detached from its origins and willing to violate its founding principle of pluralistic secularism. The satiric critique is not just of extremist leaders, but of the body politic that responds to their factionalizing message-hence the insistence on the inclusive "we": "A tragedy was taking place all right, a national tragedy on a grand scale, but those of us who played our parts were-let me put it bluntly-clowns. Clowns! Burlesque buffoons, drafted into history's theatre on account of the lack of greater men" (*MLS* 352).

This sense of societal guilt is echoed numerous times by Moraes. He says, "they are not inhuman, these Mainduck-style little Hitlers, and it is in their humanity that we must locate our collective guilt" (*MLS* 297); "The best, and worst, were in us, and fought in us, as they fought in the land at large" (*MLS* 376); "the barbarians were [...] within our skins [...].

We have chopped away our own legs, we engineered our own fall" (*MLS* 372-73). Rushdie's satire is at its most multi-directional in this novel. The informing principle of its critique is Aurora's pessimistic idea that mixture and mélange can breed darkness and distortion, that inclusiveness can breed exclusiveness. Even "Bombayness" is not powerful enough to overwhelm negating energies: "the great city's powers of dilution" (*MLS* 351), Moraes says, cannot weaken the "rivers of blood" (*MLS* 350) that run through it after Ayodhya. In this key merging of the somatic with the topographical, the whole body-river-street network of arteries and exchanges is infected and polluted. Ideologies of purity and exclusion overrun the systems that used to guarantee impurity and inclusion; such a "disease" (*MLS* 208) could not spread without enormous popular support. Civic nationalism framed by the land—India as territory with all its diverse groups—is undermined by an insurgent ethnic nationalism of the majority peoples-those whose "Hindu blood" prompts them to claim special entitlement over the land.

The result is that Rushdie challenges more strongly than ever the moral and generic dualities he has always invoked-of enabling Menippean multiplicity as the normative position from which violent exclusivity is satirized. If one can turn into the other-not just at the level of genre or textuality as in *Midnight's Children,* but on the societal level too-the distinction becomes impossible to maintain. As "the [apparently] pluralist Uma, with her multiple selves, [...] turned out to be the bad egg" (*MLS* 272), and as the mongrel Moraes, excluded from love, is co-opted by those who would reverse the principles of secular-democratic tolerance, so India as a whole is increasingly hijacked by forces that would deny it.

The novel's all-embracing pessimism is felt at the level of genre and tone. Despite its valorizing of intermingling and impurity, *The Moor's Last Sigh* is rather anemic in the spirit of joy, carnival, regeneration, and optimism that marks the Menippean grotesque. Though it covers much the same history as *Midnight's Children,* it lacks the sense of celebratory hope associated with India's and Saleem's early years. At independence, instead of Nehru's inspirational "tryst with destiny" speech, we hear Vasco Miranda drunkenly prophesying the triumph of Hindu gods over Nehru's secular-socialist ideals: "Minority-group members. Square-peg freaks. *You don't belong here*" (*MLS* 166; original emphasis). Where Saleem as allegorical baby is pampered and loved and celebrated, Moraes's babyhood is erased from the narrative, which leaps immediately to a childhood characterized by a divided family, insufficient love, and by his isolation as a perceived misfit. In this novel division and negativity seem to be pervasive; the seeds of ruin, however dormant, are often shown to have been planted all along. As with the needle buried in Vasco Miranda's circulatory system-the time-bomb that will eventually and without warning kill him-we are encouraged to see, within every enabling system and process, an alien but intrinsic "thing" (*MLS* 36) that will violently destroy it.

This gloomy fatalism is reflected structurally; the ending is contained in the beginning. Where *Midnight's Children* begins with an announcement of birth and ends with a prophecy of death, *The Moor's Last Sigh* is framed by the same moment of exile, despair, and premature death. The shadow of loss and exclusion-from normality, community, from life itself-hangs over the whole book. Perhaps that is not surprising. While writing the novel Rushdie was alienated from his national communities by the *fatwa*, which itself imposed a state of paradoxical inclusion and exclusion: "yes, you are one of us," it said, and then: "but we reject you."

While *The Moor's Last Sigh* may display the fertile storytelling and polyphonic voice that have become Rushdie's signature, it nonetheless seems dominated by a weary satiric detachment and resignation. Though he still waves the flag of the secular, heterogeneous India, Rushdie knows before he starts that it is faded and tattered. That vision, like the Congress party that once advocated it, is wasting away. In the new India, principles of exclusion are gaining more inclusive acceptance; the heterogeneous crowd is embracing those who would divide it. As the nation is infected, so is Rushdie's novel.

However predictably it may espouse a Menippean grotesque, the "negative" satirist's dismay wins out.

Notes

1. For discussions of *Shame*'s exclusive satire, see Harrison (5, 18-24, 70) and Ahmad (123-58).
2. Among those who have theorized satire as referential attack are Edward Rosenheim, Charles Knight, George Test, and Northrop Frye.
3. For Bakhtin's theories of Menippean satire, see Bakhtin (*Problems* 112-22). For his theories of the grotesque, see Bakhtin (*Rabelais* 303-436). For a fuller discussion of the theoretical combination, and of the reading of *Midnight's Children* in the following paragraph, see my article, "Pessoptimism: Satire and the Menippean Grotesque in Rushdie's *Midnight's Children*" in Volume I of this book.
4. Cf. Rushdie, *Haroun.*
5. For a good reading of Rushdie as a magic realist, and of *The Moor's Last Sigh* as a pessimistic parody of *Midnight's Children*, see Moss (121-39).

Works Cited

Ahmad, Aijaz. *In Theory: Nations, Classes, Literatures*. London: Verso, 1992.

Bakhtin, Mikhail. *Problems of Dostoevsky's Poetics*. Ed. & trans. Caryl Emerson. Minneapolis: U Minnesota P, 1984.

____. *Rabelais and His World.* Trans. Hélène Iswolsky. Bloomington: Indiana UP, 1984.

Cantor, Paul A. "Tales of the Alhambra: Rushdie's Use of Spanish History in *The Moor's Last Sigh*." *Studies in the Novel* 29.3 (Fall 1997): 323-41.

Coetzee, J.M. "Palimpsest Regained." *The New York Review of Books* 21 Mar. 1996: 13-16.

Halkin, Hillel. "Salman Rushdie Surrenders." *Commentary* 102 (1996): 58.

Harrison, James. *Salman Rushdie.* New York: Twayne, 1992.

Harvey, L.P. *Islamic Spain 1250-1500.* Chicago: U Chicago P, 1990.

Kayser, Wolfgang. *The Grotesque in Art and Literature.* Trans. Ulrich Weisstein. Gloucester, MA: Peter Smith, 1968.

Malhotra, Inder. *Indira Gandhi: A Personal and Political Biography.* London: Hodder & Stoughton, 1989.

Moss, Laura. "'Forget Those Damnfool Realists!': Salman Rushdie's Self-Parody as the Magic Realist's 'Last Sigh.'" *ARIEL* 29.4 (Oct. 1998): 121-39.

Read, Jan. *The Moors in Spain and Portugal.* London: Faber & Faber, 1974.

Rege, Josna E. "Victim into Protagonist? *Midnight's Children* and the Post-

Rushdie National Narratives of the Eighties." *Studies in the Novel* 29.3 (Fall 1997): 342-75.

Rushdie, Salman. *Haroun and the Sea of Stories.* London: Granta, 1990.

____. *Imaginary Homelands: Essays and Criticism 1981-1991.* London: Granta, 1991.

____. *Midnight's Children.* 1981. New York: Alfred A. Knopf, 1984.

____. *The Moor's Last Sigh.* Toronto: Alfred A. Knopf, 1995.

Singh, Jyotsna G. *Colonial Narratives/Cultural Dialogues: "Discoveries" of India in the Language of Colonialism.* London: Routledge, 1996.

Originally published in *The International Fiction Review* 27.1-2 (2000): 37-47. Reprinted with permission.

4

A Post-modern, Provocative, Metropolitan Mother India: Aurora Zogoiby of Rushdie's *The Moor's Last Sigh*

P. BALASWAMY

"Nobody ever made a movie called 'Father India'" derisively comments the narrator-protagonist, Moreas Zogoiby, of *The Moor's Last Sigh*, "'Bharat-pita'? Sounds all wrong." What is right, according to Moreas, the 'Moor,' as well as his creator, Salman Rushdie, is equating one's native land with one's mother, resulting in the image of 'Bharat- mata'/ 'Mother India'. Elsewhere Rushdie declares: "Motherness [...] is a big idea in India, maybe our biggest: the land as mother, the mother as land, as the firm ground beneath our feet" (137). In his other novels on the Indian subcontinent also one can find this concept reiterated, sometimes in a serious vein, but more often in a mocking tone, in tune with his post-modernist ludic sense and irreverence. In Aurora (Da Gama) Zogoiby, the flamboyant mother of the Moor, however, Rushdie goes further and supplants the traditional image of the kind, compassionate, rural, heroic Mother (courtesy Nargis of Mehboob Khan's movie classic "Mother India") with, to put it in his own words, his "own sort of Mother India [...] metropolitan, sophisticated, noisy, angry and different" (Nair XII). A bitchy, Goan Catholic/Jewess substitutes the kum-kum-clad, devout and divine Hindu female in Rushdie's love/hate novel on India, *The Moor's Last Sigh*. This paper aims to analyze this "dark, bloody mother India" (5) image splashed throughout this epic novel, with the trappings of his usual, brilliant "chutnification" of contemporary history. It leads us to a vital revelation about Rushdie's art as well as his deep concern for the country of his origin.

Salman Rushdie, the expatriate enfant terrible of Indian Writing in English in its post-modern, post-colonial phase, had always been obsessed with a femme fatale in each one of his Indian subcontinent trilogies.

Midnight's Children, highly autobiographical, unraveled the horrors felt in the Indian national consciousness due to the travails of the Independence struggle, the Partition of India, and the Emergency era. Even though the Saleem Sinai picaresque adventures, "chutnified" with the historical events from 1916 to 1980, were the high spots of that novel, a major part of it was, however, hogged by the 'Madam,' Mrs. Indira Gandhi, the femme fatale of the Indian politics and Government in the 1960s and 1970s. At one end of the spectrum of Mrs. Gandhi's public life was her image as a noble, valiant and idealized/idolized Jhansi Rani; and at the other end was perceived an image of the ego-maniacal demoness who devoured her own folks. Rushdie focussed on Saleem Sinai's plight of dispossessedness, impotency and homelessness as a typical condition of the Indian during Mrs. Gandhi's rule. Ironically, even such a Bhadra Kaali figure was assigned motherness by Rushdie, despite the terrible nature of her motherhood as perceived by him. Mrs. Gandhi's followers proclaimed that "India was Indira, and Indira was India" during her heyest of heydays, a sentiment the Moor echoes in The Last Sigh, when he describes "Indira-Mata" as "the living mother-goddess of us all" (137).

No less devastating is the femme fatale of his second historiographic meta-fiction *Shame*, Sufia Zinobia, the personification of shame visited upon this subcontinent when partition between India and Pakistan was effected. Another devouring monster, Sufia is the feminine embodiment of the nightmare that millions of people went through in Pakistan and India. The horror of Sufia was emphasized by Rushdie in his pointed references to the unmotherly, unfeminine and irrational deeds indulged in by her in her metamorphosed state.

The Moor's Last Sigh, the last of the triptych, an allegory of India in the 1990s, has the surface structure of the Zogoiby-Da Gama saga stretching from 1900 to 1993. Briefly stated, the novel traces the Jewish and Goan-Christian ancestry of Abraham Zogoiby, a billionaire Bombayite and his famed artist-wife, Aurora (Da Gama) Zogoiby, and their rise to fame and riches from the pepper estate of Cochin to their fabulous Malbar Hill residence and the Zogoiby enterprises—'Ziodi Corporation'—the third richest of Indian enterprises. A multi-layered epic novel which performs with astonishing brilliance at various levels, it paints (no other imagery will suit this scorching tale of a painter protagonist!) 1) the Oedipal mix-up involving Aurora Zogoiby, her son Moreas ('Moor') Zogoiby and his mistress, Uma Sarasvati!; 2) the underworld operations of the Big Business Houses in Bombay and their devastating gang wars; 3) the alarming rise to power of the Hindu, Muslim fundamentalist groups, their fanning of communal fires (one cannot resist the temptation to mention their much-publicized ire over the movie *Fire*!) and its impact on the Indian society, economics, politics, arts, sports and other invisible spheres all over the country, especially in Bombay. Breathtaking in its multivalent dimensions, *The Moor's Last Sigh* is the 'sigh' of a non-Hindu about the catastrophic Ayodhya events and their poisonous aftermath. Instead of adopting a polar opposite viewpoint of a Muslim victim, the novel objectifies the suicidal track chosen by our nation, through a Jew victim/victimizer's point of view, not sectarian anyhow, but with a pluralistic and multicultural ethos.

In the India of the last four decades, in its pluralistic, modern, malleable, multilingual and multicultural phases, the *idee fixe* about Mother India has to undergo a radical change. Rushdie catches on this need for a revolutionary re/vision of a commonly accepted opinion by presenting the fiery and flamboyant Aurora Zogoiby as the typical Mother India. What a yawning contrast she is to the image fostered by Nargis in the 1950s! In a true post-modernist fashion, Rushdie provides blaring references to his readers to start this comparison game, not the subtle, mild hints of the traditional story-tellers. In fact, the narrator and the other characters lead the readers to this critical practice. The Moor comments: "The year I was born, Mehboob Productions' all-conquering movie Mother India—three years in the making, three hundred shooting days, in the top three all-time mega-grossing Bollywood flicks—hit the nation's screens. Nobody who saw it ever forgot that glutinous saga of peasant heroinism, that super-slushy ode to the uncrushability of village India made by the most cynical urbanites in the world. And as for its leading lady—O Nargis with your shovel over your shoulder and your strand of black hair tumbling forward over your brow!—she became, until Indira-Mata supplanted her, the living mother-goddess of us all (137).

A fictional, stormy meeting between the real-life Nargis Dutt and imaginary Aurora Zogoiby takes place on the semi-realistic terrace of the Malabar Hill palace, Elephanta, in which, a legendary, sacred mother-son relationship is demolished by the rambunctious, wildly funny narrator/ author. The remarkable passage provides a vital clue to our argument: "In Mother India, a piece of Hindu myth-making directed by a Muslim socialist, Mehboob Khan, the Indian peasant woman is idealized as bride, mother, and producer of sons; as long-suffering, stoical, loving, redemptive and conservatively wedded to the maintenance of the social status quo" (138-39).

There can be no doubt about this image of the 'Bharat Nari,' fostered for ages by writers, artists and our popular media. Manu's Smiruthi had codified it, the great Indian epics, the Ramayana and the Mahabharatha have shown ideal figures of women in Sita, Savithri et al in glorious light, and our popular media have nourished this image over the decades. Some positive features of this image notwithstanding, this patriarchal concept, oppressive and imprisoning, is getting to be increasingly objected to and rejected by the modern Indian females.

Indian society, in its globalization, MNC phase, seeds of which were sown in the 1950s themselves, has witnessed far-reaching changes being effected not only in its social and economic spheres, but in the psychological, cultural, ethical makeup of the individuals, too. The changes are more daringly and glaringly adopted among the Indian women in their outlook, behaviour and attitude. The 'Bharat Nari' image, in particular, has received many severe beatings, the ramifications of which are yet to be felt on a large scale.

Rushdie, a novelist with his sharply sensitive antenna, also perhaps the physical distance he has to keep from the Indian society making his vision clear in its contours, unerringly captures these sea-changes in the Indian woman's psyche. The British-fed and expatriate Bombayite he is, some kind of westernization ('Westoxication' as he would like to call it [178]) in his conceptualization and execution process is rather inevitable. Despite such minor aberrations, Rushdie is not wide off the mark in his portrayal of a metropolitan and provocative Mother India in Aurora Zogoiby. As his protagonist puts it rather bluntly, it is "[...] an image of an aggressive, treacherous, annihilating mother who haunts the fantasy life of Indian males" (139).

Reverting to the traits mentioned earlier, of a traditional Mother India, one can find that Rushdie's story systematically breaks that image when it provides the characteristics of this radical, urban Mother India. Aurora Da Gama, from her girlhood, proves herself to be a ruthless, exploitative, calculative and even cruel female. Aurora's mother Isabella had run a cold war with her mother-in-law, Epifania, from the moment Cameons chose to marry, in the old lady's opinion, a "hussy from somewhere" (23). Isabella's only child Aurora also harbours a deep hatred and ill will towards her grandmother. Her reactions to Epifania's last, dying moments on the chapel floor on the Christmas eve of 1938 are so cold and calculated that they would have horrified any other family member present there. Epifania is struck by a fatal paralysis as she is praying alone in the chapel into which Aurora, the sixteen-years-old girl looking for a diversion from her monthly pains, accidentally peeps. Quickly grasping the situation, the young one sits down on the floor, cross-legged, and watches on, not even lifting a single finger to help the suffering old lady. It is cold-blooded murder, if one admits that murder can be committed by inaction. A chilling scene (62-64) that shows Aurora to be some kind of demoness, equaled in horror only by Sufia Zinobia in her tearing moments.

Nargis's Mother India is a coy mistress, an ideal bride, subdued and subjected, a true 'Bharat Nari' on her nuptial night. Aurora Da Gama's "marriage" with Abraham Zogoiby, in contrast, is a public scandal, since the girl is just fifteen, fresh and innocent, and Abraham is her father's age—thirty-five. Add to that the fact that Aurora is the rich Christian heiress, and Abraham is a poor, inconsequential Jewish employee of her father's spices' company. Accidentally meeting him in a pepper godown, Aurora instantly falls in love with the handsome Jew, draws him "by the chin" literally and fornicates with him then and there high up on pepper sacks stacked up to the godown roof (88-90). She even defies her Uncle Aires and Abraham deserts his old mother Flory, to the chagrin of the elders, all for the sake of their mad, "pepper love." In true Shylock fashion she demands that he become a Christian in order to marry her. Aurora is thus "a shameless hussy," as her grandmother would put it, in going through her stormy marriage with a scandal to boot at every stage—in stark contrast to the soft, demure bride of tradition who marries a man even without looking at his face.

One aspect of the conventional bride/wife, celebrated in literature and movies, is her steadfast love, devotion and fidelity to her husband. The heroine of Mother India demonstrates these qualities in an admirably slushy manner. Aurora's score on these counts is not only dismal, but scandalous, too. Her love for Abraham evaporates after a few years' of conjugal life, especially when she learns that Abraham has started fooling around with girls during her absences. She pays him back in his own coin—by launching her own extra-marital affairs: one of them, the Moor audaciously reports, is with the first Prime Minister of India—Jawaharlal Nehru. In fact, the boy Moreas strongly suspects that Nehru might have sired him (176-77). Uma, the Moor's mistress, accuses that Aurora had three affairs, which every Bombayite knew, with "that retard Kekoo Mody," "Vasco Miranda, the fat fraud," and "Mainduck Raman Fielding" (256). Quite strangely, Abraham, perhaps out of a guilty conscience, never acts the role of a righteously angry husband, allowing and suffering her indiscretions silently, all because of his love for her: "The greater, the more public her betrayals, the more overwhelming, and secret, grew his love" (170). This "bitchy, cosmopolitan, Westoxicated" Aurora Zogoiby is the Moor's concept of a metropolitan Mother India!

If Mother India projected an ideal mother as "producer of sons"(139), the Moor's Mother India begets three daughters—Christina, Inamorata, and Philomena—and one son, Moreas; of these four children, only one survives. Aurora outlives her children and, in a sense, contributing to, at least two deaths. In a prophetic statement much earlier in the story, she proclaims: "We all eat children [...]. If not other people's, then our own" (125). Reputed for her "legendary stubbornness [and] determination" (125), she refuses to breast feed her daughters and agrees to do it for the Moor, as he is an abnormal child.

The fact that the Moor is "the only child she suckled at her breast" (129) has Freudian implications, overtly and covertly scattered throughout the novel, and also in the movie Mother India, as well as in the lives of its stars. Fascinating and intricate weaving of the elements of real and imaginary lives—both on screen and off, and in the novel—has been handled in a masterly manner by Rushdie. That Nargis (who played the role of the mother in Mother India) married Sunil Dutt (who played the bad son's role) in real life is everybody's knowledge; but transforming this Oedipal element into the celluloid story, by finding a couple of apt references in the naming process in the movie, has been a masterly stroke of Rushdie's.

The mischievous mix up between f(l)iction and real life is worth quoting in full.

> Aurora has invited Nargis and Sunil Dutt to her Malabar Hill residence: "The first time I saw that picture," she confided to the famous movie star on the high terrace at Elephanta, "I took one look at your Bad Son, Birju, and I thought, O boy, what a handsome guy—.... And now look—you have gone and marry-o'ed him! What sexy lives you movie people leadofy: to marry your own son, I swear, wowie" (emphasis added). When Sunil Dutt tries to explain that she is mixing up fact and fancy, life and movie, Aurora persists: "Even in the picture.... I knew right off that bad Birju had the hots for his gorgeous ma. Nargis stood speechless, open-mouthed. Vasco Miranda, who could never resist a bit of trouble-making, saw the storm brewing and made haste to join in. "Sublimation," he offered, "of mutual parent-child longings, is deep-rooted in the national psyche. The use of names in the picture makes the meaning clear. This 'Birju' moniker is also used by God Krishna, isn't it, and we know that milky 'Radha' is the blue chap's one true love. In the picture, Sunil, you are made up to look like the god, and you even fool with all the girls, throwing your stones to break their womby water-pots; which, admit it, is Krishna-esque behaviour. In this interpretation," and here clowning Vasco attempted unsuccessfully to convey a certain scholarly gravitas, "Mother India is the dark side of the Radha-Krishna story, with the subsidiary theme of forbidden love added on. But what the hell, Oedipus-schmoedipus! Have another chotta peg" (138).

In her remarks here, the daring Aurora seems to express a hidden longing for her own handsome, hefty son Moreas. (Owing to a freakish genetic factor, the Moor grows faster than normal children. By age ten, he had grown into a full-fledged adult of great proportions. His big sister Ina comments: "You have become Mr Gulliver-Travel and we are your Lilliputs" [188]). This Oedipal element has been dormant in her probably from the day she suckled her only son. One way of sublimating her original sexual impulse is seen in her artistic endeavours, which result in the famous 'Moor paintings.' In two of her sketches, the Oedipal element is revealed, though in a reversed manner. In the first picture, Aurora paints "herself as the young

Eleanor Marx and me as her father Karl. Moor and Tussy was a rather shocking idea—my mother girlish, adoring, and I in patriarchal, lapel-gripping pose [...]. 'If you were twice as old as you look, and I was half as old as I am, I could be your daughter,' my forty-plus mother explained [...]"(224). The second painting "To Die upon a Kiss" is more revealing of the hidden impulses: she portrayed herself as murdered Desdemona and son Moreas as Othello! (224-25) Shocking though these Freudian explications are, Rushdie seems to be more amused at the parallels with Mother India movie's stars proving the point in an ironic life-imitates-art fashion.

Not only is Rushdie's Mother India figure the anti-thesis of the popular image in her roles as bride, wife and mother, Aurora is never "redemptive" nor "conservatively wedded to the maintenance of the social status-quo": on the other hand, she is a sharply-retaliating, vindictive woman in many of her reactions. Once again Rushdie is particular in portraying the modern Indian woman as not tolerant anymore (of her husband's sins, for example), retaliatory and furious. Gone is the tendency to treat the husband with reverential acceptance even if he were to be metaphorically "a stone or a blade of grass." When Aurora learns that her husband had agreed to give up their first born to his angry and demanding mother Flory, she simply shuts him out of her bedroom and vows not to indulge in conjugal love as long as her mother-in-law is alive (114-15). To spite her mother-in-law's effort to snatch her first born, Aurora launches herself on the national scene.

Rushdie has often resorted to a device in his earlier novels, too, of linking the personal life of his protagonist with the historically famous events, for it is one technique which he employs to burlesque history. A critic has observed: "Narrative never follows the emotional logic of the characters' lives, but the brittle, externally determined contours of 'current events'. Rushdie deliberately prevents his readers from being caught up in a story with its own 'organic' life, that progresses uninterrupted, and that creates a completely imagined world" (Brennan 84-85). Thus we find that Rushdie presents an amusing mixture of the personal perversities of his protagonist with her glorious public career/life as part of the Independence struggle: [...] Aurora Zogoiby grew into the giant public figure we all know, the great beauty at the heart of the nationalist movement, the loose-haired bohemian marching boldly alongside Vallabhai Patel and Abdul Kalam Azad when they took out processions, the confidante—and according to persistent rumours, mistress—of Pandit Nehru, his 'friend of friends,' who would later vie with Edwina Mountbatten for his heart. Distrusted by Gandhiji, loathed by Indira Gandhi, her arrest after the Quit India resolution of 1942 made her a national heroine [...]. People began saying that Aurora Zogoiby was the new Chand Bibi, standing up against a different and even more powerful Empire [...](116).

A brilliant instance of Rushdie's 'chutnification' of history, this parodic exercise of turning gossip into history serves a vital function for the creator. It is a stroke of genius to refashion "Mother India as a bitch-goddess." As a critic has pointed out, "It creates exactly that ironic gap for post-Rushdie postcoloniality to manifest itself—the gap between the stodgy, unidimensional portrait of a traditional Mother India beloved of the early days of Nehruvian nationalism and the multivalent image of a mother whose wandering sons are as unpredictable and ambiguous as herself" (Nair XII).

The Bharat Nari portrait Rushdie presents in *The Moor's Last Sigh* has yet another dimension in the character of Uma Sarasvati, his love, who is supposed to look like his mother, Aurora. Rushdie's penchant for stealing contemporary personalities for making them figures of his fiction reaches its most controversial point in his turning Bal Thackeray, the maverick Siva Sena leader of Bombay, and Uma Bharati, another irrepressible leader of a political party wedded to Hindu fundamentalism, as Raman Fielding and Uma Sarasvati, respectively, in his novel. In Uma Sarasvati, the enigmatic Mata Hari, for whom the Moor develops a grand and tragic passion which leads to his fall, Rushdie paints a radical whose commitment to her cause matches her histrionic and chameleon talents to maintain an incredibly deceptive façade. Convinced that the Muslims, the Christians and other minority communities are harming the interests of the majority community of Hindus, Uma Sarasvati plots to destroy the Moor, the only male heir of the fabulously rich Jew. But, a ludicrous, last minute farce, a slapstick clash of heads reverses their roles, and consequently, their fates, whereby she ends up as the dead. The predator that Uma is, she makes terrible, unimaginable use of Moor's passion for her to poison his parents' minds against him. The Moor's final evaluation of Uma is striking: "I imagined a chameleon-like creature, a cold-blooded lizard from across the cosmos, who could take human form, male or female, as required, for the express purpose of making as much trouble as possible [...]. Turbulence, disruption, misery, catastrophe, grief—all these were on the menu of its preferred foods" (320).

The advent of persons like Uma Sarasvati on the Indian political scene forebodes a disastrous phase, not only for the Indian polity, but for its society too, which had practiced pluralism in an exemplary manner all along. "Turbulence, disruption, catastrophe, grief" are the outcome of the actions/reactions of Uma Sarasvati/Raman Fielding group's activities and attitudes, as well as the underground workings of the mafia men like Scar (a Muslim fanatic) or even Abraham Zogoiby. One evil does not justify another evil—the thesis of *The Moor's Last Sigh* emphasizes this age-old maxim. What is quite intriguing, according to Rushdie's portrayal of the tragic events of Ayodhya and its aftermath, is that the traditionally marginalized, oppressed women of India might have a key role to play in the new Indian society that is emerging at the end of the millennium.

The emergence of a fiery substitute for the traditional image of Mother India in the character of Aurora Zogoiby is accomplished in a truly post-modern mingling of Roman, Zudaic-Christian and Hindu myths of goddess icons. The pastiche begins at the earliest point in the novel (5) when Aurora, the Roman goddess of dawn/gardens, is hinted at—"Paradise of Aurora." This classical Paradise is turned into Biblical Heaven, the seat of God Almighty, when Vasco Miranda compares the Moor to Lucifer "hurled from that fabulous garden and plunged towards Pandaemonium" (5). The point, however, is stressed that this Edenic paradise contains in itself an "infernal private universe" (5). Aurora, in another context, is "a godless madonna" in her own painting (220). The madonna being a metropolitan dame, unhesitating in passing a severe sentence on her own offspring for his evil deed, metamorphoses into a "monster": "O, an age of monsters is come upon us. Kalyug, when cross-eyed red-tongued Kali, our mad dame, moves among us wreaking havoc" (288). The mythic references, however, have a contradictory portent in typical post-modernist spirit.

Rushdie's iconoclastic exercise, its satiric and cynical tone and tenor notwithstanding, reveals his deep concern about the catastrophic path chosen by his country of his origin in recent times. In Rushdie's reckoning, the image of Mother India as a "bitch goddess" projected through the two female protagonists of this novel calls for a deep and sustained introspection. Following the footsteps of his literary ancestors, Jonathan Swift and Alexander Pope, he has drawn a bitter and scorching painting of the country which he has left, but cannot forget, and which has deserted him under various compulsions. (One may add here that he had indulged in similar satiric exercises earlier in his second and third novels, too). This way leads you to disaster, he seems to be warning Indians, if Aurora Zogoiby is the kind of mother that modern India nurtures. Though he zooms upon the nihilistic aspects quite often, Rushdie, being a true artist with a passion for the truth, admits the greatness of the nation amidst this gloom. Aurora's paintings, often used as metaphors and commentaries of/on reality, show that there is yet a saving grace available in the nation's plurality: "[...] that exploration of an alternative vision of India-as-mother, not Nargis's sentimental village-mother, but a mother of cities, as heartless and lovable, brilliant and dark, multiple and lonely, mesmeric and repugnant, pregnant and empty, truthful and deceitful [...]"(204).

One of the characters in Benengeli village in Spain (where Vasco Miranda had fled to with Aurora's 'Moor' painting) utters the following words to Vasco: "Men and women who leave their natural places are less than human. Either something is lacking in their souls or else something surplus has gotten inside—some manner of devil seed" (327). One may view this comment as the tragic, self-deprecatory words of Rushdie himself, who has been under the double fate of expatriation and a fatwa. It seems to indicate the "twice-doomed"(in contrast to the "twice-born" status that he should enjoy) condition of Rushdie. Whatever factors drove a person out of his native land, his love for his mother country will surface quite often, despite the hostile poses he may adopt. Rushdie's art is allegorical in its most sophisticated garb, very effectively hiding his motives. *The Moor's Last Sigh* is yet another demonstration of his love for India under the guise of a parodic allegory.

Works Cited

Brennan, Timothy. *Salman Rushdie & the Third World: Myths of the Nation.* London: Macmillan, 1989.

Nair, Rukmini Bhaya. "What did Rushdie Mean and Why?" *The Hindu Literary Review* 17 Aug. 1997: IX, XII.

Rushdie, Salman. *The Moor's Last Sigh.* London: Vintage, 1996. Parenthetical page references are to this edition.

5

The Subversive Sub-text of Spices in Salman Rushdie's *The Moor's Last Sigh*

CELIA M. WALLHEAD

1. Introductory

Salman Rushdie's recent writing reveals that he has not given up his continued exploration of the human desire for broad unity and a diversified wholeness. Commentators have insisted that Rushdie's work is "intensely political" (González 41), and this is so in at least two ways. It is political in that his major novels contain the political history of the Indian sub-continent from time immemorial, taking "political" to include the essential religious and mythical basis. It is political in a second sense in that it criticises, both directly and through subversion, the political regimes that are responsible for human division and disorder. Rushdie declared that *The Satanic Verses* was about the protagonists' "search for wholeness" (Rushdie 393-414). In his subsequent book of stories, *East, West* (1994), Rushdie questioned the strict dichotomy of East and West, bringing the two together in the third and final section (Section One: "East," Section Two: "West," Section Three: "East, West"). Rushdie's reviewer, Homi Bhabha, had noted that here he explores those "most contentious fault-lines of cultural debate-metropolis periphery, atavism/modernity, fundamentalism/multiculturalism" (Bhabha 1994).

In his longer work, the 1995 novel *The Moor's Last Sigh*, Rushdie continues his exploration of the putative East/West divide. He shows how divides can have bridges, and how the centre shifts. In English literature, the West is central, but as Rushdie writes himself into the English canon, he shows us other centres and other peripheries. His human and political longings for unity in diversity are expressed in his creation, in this novel, of four Utopias or Edens, the first three in India, which is central for the protagonists, and the last in Spain, a sort of marginalised exile. Spain's past as the crucible of Western and Eastern culture obviously interested Rushdie, especially the medieval Granadan kingdom of the three religions and the Renaissance meeting-place of the Old and the New Worlds, the "fabulous multiple culture of ancient al-Andalus" (Rushdie, *Moor's* 398). Like true Edens, they are flawed, they have a serpent lurking at their heart, and in his novel, Rushdie explores the nature of the serpent, of atavistic evils.

His novel ends as the narrating and creating hero, the Moor (who has been locked up in a tower, reminiscent of his own author), has just written of "that most profound of our needs, [to] our need for flowing together, for putting an end to frontiers, for the dropping of the boundaries of the self" (433). The fulfillment of this desire has been, and is, prevented by the serpent, which is not prominent as a symbol, but is ever-present as evil. An easy answer to the identification of the source of this evil is to be found in perversity, both natural and human. It is particularly prevalent in fanaticism about owning a monopoly of the truth, and is incorporated by Rushdie into the iconic aggressive features of the game of chess: "[T]hat lozenged, particoloured Moor whose tragedy—the tragedy of multiplicity destroyed by singularity, the defeat of Many by One—" (408). An insignificant character towards the end of the novel (an anti-Nazi German, who is perversely called "the Nazi" just because he is German) says: "How to forgive the world for its beauty, which merely disguises its ugliness; for its gentleness, which merely cloaks its cruelty; for its illusion of continuing, seamlessly, as the night follows the day, so to speak-whereas in reality life is a series of brutal ruptures, falling upon our defenceless heads like the blows of a woodman's axe?" (391)

The protagonist, the Moor, is a miraculous reincarnation and also descendent of Boabdil, the last of the Nasrid kings in Granada, who went down in history, as Rushdie reminds us (315), as being chided by his (battle-axe) mother for weeping like a woman for what he could not defend as a man. The Moor ends his life in exile in Granada, by the Alhambra, unlike his forebear, who died as a mercenary, having been exiled from Granada. The Moor is in exile from Bombay, the centre of his life, at a time when, after the violence erupting upon the assassination of Indira Gandhi, India seemed set yet again, upon a course of internecine strife:

> Bombay was central, had been so from the moment of its creation: the bastardchild of a Portuguese-English wedding, and yet the most Indian of Indian cities. In Bombay all Indias met and merged. [...] Bombay was central; all rivers flowed into its human sea. It was an ocean of stories; we were all its narrators, and everybody talked at once. [...] Bombay was central. In Bombay, as the old, founding myth of the nation faded, the new god-and-mammon India was being born. The wealth of the country flowed through its exchanges, its ports. Those who hated India, those who sought to ruin it, would need to ruin Bombay: that was one explanation for what happened. [...] And if Bombay was central [...] (350-51)

What happened in Bombay, the end of an era, is compared to the end of the Nasrid dynasty in Granada (its seriousness albeit subverted by the intertextual references like *O Calcutta!* an airline advertising):

> Bombay was central: had always been. Just as the fanatical "Catholic Kings" had besieged Granada and awaited the Alhambra's fall, so now barbarism was standing at our gates. O Bombay! *Prima in India! Gateway to India! Star of the East with her face to the West!* Like Granada-al Gharnatah of the Arabs-you were the glory of your time. But a darker time came upon you, and just as Boabdil, the last Nasrid Sultan, was too weak to defend his great treasure, so we, too, were proved wanting. (372)

The Moor diagnoses an internal evil, and in his condemnation of fanaticism of any kind, Rushdie shows that evil is born from the desire for wealth and for power over others:

> For the barbarians were not only at our gates but within our skins. [...] The explosions were our own evil-no need to look for foreign explanations, though there was and is evil beyond our frontiers as well as within. We have chopped away our own legs, we engineered our own fall. And now we can only weep, at the last, for what we were too enfeebled, too corrupt, too little, too contemptible to defend. (372-73)

The pursuit of wealth and power has long been a bridge that unites East and West. In this novel, which lays bare many things, there are two major factors-commodities even-which Rushdie employs to deconstruct political and cultural history. On the political plane, he lays bare the East-West power axis based on the age-old spice trade, and shows that while spices have undergone certain vicissitudes, the axis remains in place. On the cultural plane, he unveils, albeit a more recent, but equally bilateral interchange, based upon art, broadly seen as art works and the cinema and television. A Rushdie hallmark is the choice of a polyvalent concept which gives much mileage. We could say that in this novel, he gets much mileage out of spices, and we will see in turn, how he mixes a hot sauce from spices and all of the following: wealth, history and politics, race and identity, the arts and love.

2. Spices

Spices mean different things to East and West. In the East, they are enjoyed for themselves, as part of the Oriental identity. At one point in the story, the Moor (who is half Jewish, on his father's side) becomes a cook, learning from Ezekiel, the family's "ageless cook". From the very beginning, Rushdie exploits the metaphorical meaning of "cook up," or create, that is, applied to life itself, or history, art or identity:

"Baba sahib, sit only and we will cook up the happy future. We will mash its spices and peel its garlic cloves, we will count out its cardamoms and chop its ginger, we will heat up the ghee of the future and fry its masala to release its flavour. [...] We will cook the past and present also, and from it tomorrow will come." So I learned to cook Meat Cutlass (spicy minced lamb inside a potato patty) and Chicken Country Captain; to me the secrets of prawn padda, ticklegummy, dhope and ding-ding were revealed. I became a master of balchow and learned to spin a mean kaju ball. I learned the art of Ezekiel's "Cochin special," a mouth-wateringly piquant red banana jam. And as I journeyed through the cook's copybooks, deeper and deeper into that private cosmos of papaya and cinnamon and spice, my spirits did indeed pick up; not least because I felt that Ezekiel had succeeded in joining me, after a long interruption, to the story of my past. (273)

The fragmented protagonist finds satisfaction in a sense of history and this is given to him through food and spices. In the West, however, the huge demand for spices was not explained by their desirability in themselves, but in their power to transform bad into good. From the Middle Ages, they were used to transform bad meat into good, edible meat. Their desirability remained high until the advent of canning and freezing. But as Rushdie shows, the trade route opened up by spices was kept open even as other valuable commodities came to replace them.

2.1 Spices and Wealth

The Moor begins his story with reference to his lineage: "Moraes Zogoiby, called 'Moor', for most of my life the only male heir to the spice-trade-'n'-big-business crores of the da Gama-Zogoiby dynasty of Cochin" (5). His mother's family, the da Gamas, are said to trace their lineage to Vasco da Gama, who blazed the pepper trail that opened up the spice route. In an early passage, we see the versatility of the concept of pepper, as it points to the source of wealth and power, to history and to language games:

> I repeat: the pepper, if you please; for if it had not been for peppercorns, then what is ending now in East and West might never have begun. Pepper it was that brought Vasco da Gama's tall ships across the ocean, from Lisbon's Tower of Belém to the Malabar Coast: first to Calicut and later, for its lagoony harbour, to Cochin. English and French sailed in the wake of that first-arrived Portuguese,

so that in the period called Discovery-of-India-but how could we be discovered when we were not covered before?-we were "not so much sub-continent as sub-condiment," as my distinguished mother had it. "From the beginning, what the world wanted from bloody mother India was daylight-clear," she'd say. "They came for the hot stuff, just like any man calling on a tart." (4-5)

From pepper, the business grew to include nuts: cashews, pistachios, and also coffee beans "and the mighty tea leaf itself," but pepper was the "coveted Black Gold of Malabar" (6). Like their ancestor Vasco da Gama, who sought out "whatever was spicy and hot and made money" (59), the da Gamas are like alchemists, they practise "the age-old da Gama art of turning spice and nuts into gold" (17). With the Moor's father, Abraham Zogoiby, the Jews of Cochin enter the story, as his mother Aurora da Gama, heiress to the family fortune, falls in love with her Jewish duty-manager, possibly (in one version), descended from the Muslim Boabdil! As Abraham's mother dreams of "Jewish cashews and areca-nuts and jack-fruit trees [...] Jewish oilseed rape [...] Jewish cardamoms [...] the basis of the community's prosperity" (71), she considers the da Gamas as Johnny-come-latelies and bitter rivals:"(And what did Muslims and Jews fight over in the *cinquecento*?-What else? The pepper trade)" (73). The meeting of Aurora and Abraham the "Jewish Muslim" comes about because she notices that a pepper shipment has not gone off because the ships are retained in Cochin harbour on account of the outbreak of war in 1939. From here, we see the versatility of spices, how they metamorphose into other forms of currency, and how they unite the historical, mythical and purely fictional.

In one mythical version of his history, the Moor was told that the Jewish line in Cochin was founded by an exiled Jewess who had been Boabdil's mistress. She fled to India, taking with her Boabdil's emerald crown, and gave birth to a male child. The crown was hidden for centuries, and was lately found in Abraham's mother's "treasure chest." So Boabdil

"El-zogoybi," "the Misfortunate," unwittingly bequeaths his blood, his cursed name and his emeralds to his descendants. Abraham obtains the emeralds from his mother in a *Rumplestiltskin* (111), or Abraham-Isaac, arrangement, in exchange for his firstborn child. The pepper/straw-into-gold idea mixes with the Old Testament, with *Treasure Island* and even Shakespeare, as the mother is frustrated like Shylock (112). These emeralds are used to bribe ships' captains and other necessary officials after several spice-laden ships have gone to the bottom of the sea. The attempt is to "corner the British market as compensation for loss of German income" (108), and as, much later in the novel, the mad villain Vasco Miranda was to define democracy on the night of India's independence: "one man one bribe" (167), corruption was rife the world over. As a two-edged sword, it is suggested that corruption is the only answer to fanaticism.

The spices/gold having temporarily metamorphosed into emeralds, they now remetamorphose into all kinds of commodities, given the vulnerability of spices: "The family business diversified triumphantly in a hundred and one directions, as the treasure-mountains grew from mere Gama-Ghats into Zogoiby-Himalayas" (107). A serious sub-text to this is that the Jewish-Muslim-Christian diversified union can only be to the good, while at the same time, any rapid enrichment smacks of corruption. Perhaps sleaze is the answer to the Middle East's troubles. Abraham Zogoiby builds up a "huge corporate entity, the 'Siodi Corp' from C.O.D. or Cashondeliveri, a decaying financial empire of Hindu grandees he had bought out" (240). His son, the Moor, speculates upon the new diversification of the spice trade:

> Corrupt global-scale banking schemes, stockmarket fixing at the super-epic Mogambo level, multi-billion-dollar arms deals, nuclear technology conspiracies involving stolen computers and Maldivian Mata Haris, export of antiquities including the symbol of the nation itself, the four-headed Lion of Sarnath [...]. (250-51)

As Moor is forced into working for his father, he finds that the spices have metamorphosed yet again, this time into "rather more lucrative white powders" (332), known officially as "Baby

Softo Powder" (251), so the spice route has become the "talcum powder route" (333) or drugs route. Moor survives drugs and armament trafficking and money laundering, but draws the line at contributing to the build-up of "large-scale nuclear weaponry" for the Muslims (335). As Abraham's empire begins to fall apart, he is arrested, and he uses the spice trade as a front, ironically going back to the origins: "To make bail, the title-deeds to the original spice-fields of the da Gama family had to be given in surety" (361). As the end comes for Abraham, and Bombay goes up in smoke, Rushdie paints a "Towering Inferno," as in the film, with the sky-rise empire raining down not only water, but spices, and especially pepper:

> Peppercorns, whole cumin, cinnamon sticks, cardamom mingled with the imported flora and birdlife, dancing rat-a-tat on the roads and side-walks like perfumed hail. [...] Fenugreek and nigella, coriander seeds and asafoetida fell upon Bombay; but black pepper most of all, the Black Gold of Malabar [...]. (375)

2.2 Spices, History and Politics

The concept "history" is never innocent in the work of Rushdie, the trained historian. His work has introduced us to a subaltern historiography of India and has foregrounded the problematization of historiography. History, in all its senses-important events, majority views, minority views, subjective and objective views, the political, the individual-comes under Rushdie's scrutiny in his novels. The history of India, indeed, of the West's relationship with India, is tied up with commodities like spices. To illustrate his ideas and to offer the reader great feats of story-telling, Rushdie incorporates views of history into the story of four generations of an Indian family, taking us from pre-Independence days down to the present. Glimpses of their forebears also take us back to the great discoveries of Vasco da Gama.

Momentous events are conveyed through their relation to the spice trade. The outbreak of the Second World War sees a temporary halt through the German menace to shipping. On the eve of Independence, Vasco Miranda holds out no hope for "blankety blank Pandit Nehru and his blankety blank protection-of-minorities Congress watch-wallahs" (166), and recommends that the family get on their spice boats and leave the country before it eats them up (167).

For six years after his banishment by his parents, Moor works for his father's enemy, the fanatical Hindu Raman Fielding, "Mainduck," a hybrid name from cricket and English literature. His new work is the perpetration of violence and terror: "O *baby.* Violence today is *hot.* It is what people *want*" (306). With his fellow-worker, the Tin-man, a Wizard-of-Oz-cum-Terminator figure, he uses his hammer-fist to put down Communist and other activism. The details of a putting down of a revolt of female workers, where "the freshly gathered hot chillies stood around the houses in low hills of colour and spice," cannot be told, as it is "such hot stuff" (308). Rushdie intermingles personal histories of fictional characters reaping "a rich harvest" with reports of true momentous events like the Sikh massacre at the Golden Temple and the assassination of Mrs Gandhi:

> And events on a greater stage also played their part in the bloody game of consequences that our history has a way of becoming. A golden temple harboured armed men, and was attacked, and the armed men were slain; and the consequence was, armed men murdered the Prime Minister; and the consequence was, mobs, armed and unarmed, roamed the capital and murdered innocent persons who had nothing in common with any of the armed men except a turban; and the consequence was, that men like Fielding who spoke of the need to tame the country's minorities, to subject one and all to the tough-loving rule of Ram, gained a certain momentum, a certain extra strength. (309)

What Aruna Srivastava wrote of *Midnight's Children* and its views of history is also true of *The Moor's Last Sigh*:

> *Midnight's Children* points to the fact that history is a method of fictionalizing experience, as is the telling of lives-biography and autobiography. For Saleem, irreality and truth are not quantifiable and not ascertainable. They are constructs of imagination and experience, and of language. For him, the truth of a story lies in its telling and

> is a reflection of the idiosyncratic process of selecting events from memory [...]. (Srivastava 67)

The imposition of an imperialist view of India's history, inevitably repressing the Indians' own versions of their history has made "the Empire write back" as Rushdie playfully puts it. Rushdie and other post-colonial writers offer their versions, revealing how history is a construct, made up of many contributing factors. In the same article, Aruna Srivastava indicates how Rushdie sympathises with Mahatma Gandhi's transcendental view of history which is called "inner history" (Srivastava 68). Gandhi believed truth transcended history and eluded the mere chronicler of quantifiable time of dates and events. He added myths and mythologies to the realm of conventional history to aim at a truer and more complex version of historical movements. Internecine strife between the different religions and factions dividing India's "three hundred million people" (39) is encapsulated in the legendary internal strife seen in the history of the da Gama family. Forever tongue-in-cheek, Rushdie begins an early chapter: "What started with perfume ended with a very big stink indeed [...]" (36). Carmen da Gama, née Lobo, Moor's great aunt, sends her family to the Spice Mountains, described as a fruitful paradise of rice-paddies, carpets of green and red capsicums, cashew and areca-nut orchards, cardamom and cumin, coffee and tea plantations, only to raze it to the ground:

> The unmistakable odour of burning spices, cumin coriander turmeric, red-pepper-black-pepper, red-chilli-green-chilli, a little garlic, a little ginger, some sticks of cinnamon. It was as if some mountain giant were preparing, in a monstrous pan, the largest, hottest dish of curry ever cooked. (38)

Even when the Communists infiltrate, Rushdie jokes: "with a garnish of Red Sauce" (39). In an uneasy truce between the two brothers, Carmen's husband Aires da Gama and Camoens da Gama, Moor's grandfather, spices are used yet again, this time like sand-bags: "She had sackfuls of spices piled high along her newly established frontier [...]" (42).

As India sinks into conflagration after Mrs Gandhi's assassination, this violent spice-related background is ever present. Rushdie achieves the union of the mythical, the factual, and the partial by creating a palimpsestic text. He refers explicitly to the synchronic and the diachronic, of the historical event also being its steady accumulation of factors, through the idea of layers of time or civilization. He has the Hindu Fielding say "This true nation is what we must reclaim from beneath the layers of alien empires" (299). Raman Fielding, the fanaticist, is violently against colonial power in India, but he is "intricate," he will defend "the culture of Indian Islam that lay palimpsest-fashion over the face of Mother India" (299). Religions, civilizations, even time itself, lie superimposed, revealing glimpses of the former self.

Moor's father, Abraham Zogoiby finds "age had painted a palimpsest-image over the memory of the man" (241). He has become the big boss of the strongest mafia in Bombay. His spice trade is just a front, a cover, for his other, illicit dealings. As Moor talks of the "Over World" (317), the top of his father's high-rise luxury tower, the centre of his empire, he also has had personal experience of the Underworld, or Hell (317), Bombay's prison. The palimpsest-image recurs in the novel in relation to art works, another wealth-related, identity-related commodity.

2.3 Spices, Race and Identity

In his article "Cultural Identity and Diaspora," Stuart Hall, while speaking of Caribbean identity and uniqueness, articulates the general problems associated with attempts to search for, define or depict identities. He says that cultural identity is a matter of becoming as well as being:

> It belongs to the future as much as to the past. It is not something which already exists, transcending place, time, history and culture. Cultural identities come from somewhere, have histories. But, like everything which is historical, they undergo constant transformation. Far from being eternally fixed in some essentialised past, they are subject to the continuous "play" of history, culture and power. Far from being grounded in mere "recovery" of

> the past, which is waiting to be found, and which when found, will secure our sense of ourselves into eternity, identities are the names we give to the different ways we are positioned by, and position ourselves within, the narratives of the past. (Hall 394)

The creation of Moor in Rushdie's novel is an excellent example of a writer attempting to lay bare the complexities of cultural identity as theorised by Hall. As Rushdie writes from within otherness, he shows how identity is constructed through non-factual factors such as memory, fantasy, narrative and myth. Moor has no unproblematic, transcendental "law of origin," but recovers with difficulty, and not much pride, a past which grounds him (!) in spice. He is positioned by the East-West axis of the spice trade, as we have seen. Then he goes on to position himself, through choices available to him or situations forced upon him, within the narratives of the past. Moor's story gives him an identity, just as Martin Luther's ninety-nine theses pinned to the church door at Wittenberg gave him identity, and Scheherazade's tales night after night gave her a place in mythical history. Moor is forced by Vasco Miranda to recount the "sinful saga" like Scheherazade under menace of death (421), and when he escapes, he goes round the Andalusian and Alhambra woods pinning the pages of his story (*the* story of the novel) to the trees (3 & 6).

Moor can trace his history to fixed points of departure: Vasco da Gama's historically recorded travels eastwards; fantasy narratives of Boabdil's Jewish mistress escaping to India and the more historical diaspora of the Jews. But the points of arrival are in cultural flux, so the search for steady points of reference by which to make critical decisions in life is very difficult. Kinship and ethnicity function as identity markers, but there too, the ground is not solid. Kinship in the spice trade has given Moor roots: "(Great family trees from little 'corns': it is appropriate, is it not, that my personal story, the story of the creation of Moraes Zogoiby, should have its origins in a delayed pepper shipment?") (68) His ethnicity, his alterity through the colour black is thus also associated with spices in the sense of *black* pepper, though as his mother said: "we have red chillis in our veins" (5). There is no denying Moor's black skin: "my South Indian dark skin (*so* unattractive to society matchmakers!)" (162), but he ardently believes race is only skin deep, and if only he could be peeled like certain spices, even flayed alive, a basic sameness or Oneness would be found underneath: "the naked unity of the flesh" (414). Then he would be no more black than the Anglican priest Oliver D'Aeth, who through a photophobic allergy peels all over (92), and also dreams of being flayed and finding "the oneness of mankind" (95). The matriarch Epifania, Moor's grêat grandmother, was allergic to "the sources of her family fortune" (9), and Moor's great aunt Carmen had dreamed the same dream in her misery of "unbeauty" when rejected by her homosexual husband (47).

Thus flesh is also history and identity, and Rushdie continues the idea begun with the Pakistanis in *Shame*: "All migrants leave their pasts behind, he writes; it is the fate of migrants to be stripped of history." (Rushdie, *Shame* 63). Unity is a false and impossible dream. The "Moor-figure," an invention, loses his "previous metaphorical rôle as a unifier of opposites, a standard-bearer of pluralism [...] a new imagining of the idea of the hybrid" (Rushdie, *Moor's* 303). He stands for many things; he is also Othello (225), involved in a reverse murder attempt by his white lover Uma. But as he pieces together his fragmented self, he finds nothing but abjection in hybridity. Being neither a Catholic nor a Jew, his parents having turned their backs on their religion, postmodern word-play is made with "cashew nuts": "I was both, and nothing: a jewholic-anonymous, a cathjew nut, a stewpot, a mongrel cut. I was—(what's the word these days)—*atomised*. Yessir, a real Bombay mix." (104) Moor is a doubly hybrid character, not only racially, but in terms of literature, he is at once Boabdil himself and Othello. As Paul Gilroy says:

> Multiple meanings have grouped around the central symbol of racial alterity—the colour black-and it is difficult to anticipate the outcome of the political struggle between the different tendencies they represent-ethnic absolutism on the one hand and a utopian democratic populism on the other. (Gilroy 416)

Rushdie rejects the former of these two ideas, especially through Moor, a symbol of nothing at all, a symbol of polyvalence created through the hybridity in Bombay stemming from the spice trade. Rushdie explores the second idea, that of multi-racial utopias, but as we said before, all the utopias are flawed. *The Moor's Last Sigh* covers most of the twentieth century:

> At the dawn of the century she came on Great-Grandfather Francisco's arm to Cabral Island, the first of my story's four sequestered, serpented, Edenic-infernal private universes. (My mother's Malabar Hill salon was the second; my father's sky-garden, the third; and Vasco Miranda's bizarre redoubt, his "Little Alhambra" in Benengeli, Spain, was, is, and will in this telling become, my last). (15)

The paradise of Cabral Island is divided into East and West, according to the division between the son who favours Home Rule for India and the one who does not, both of whom end up in prison. Rushdie has a not yet famous Le Corbusier come and build two "follies" or garden houses, one in each style. It was Belle (Isabella Souza), wife of one of the brothers, who played a Queen Isabella of Spain rôle in presiding over a house divided by spice bags (41). The second Eden, founded after the war in 1945, is a large bungalow on the slopes of Malabar Hill, Bombay. This Edenic-infernal private universe is more inferno than Eden. It is the place of Moor's birth and childhood. Here, over a period of forty years, his mother Aurora produced her paintings and held court in her art salon. She takes on a painter who is infatuated with her and later becomes a traitor, turning into Moor's would-be executioner as in *Alice in Wonderland*. He can create a "spiced-up re-hash of the European surrealists" (148), and creates a "Paradise" bedroom of Disney characters (150). Jawaharlal Nehru (who ends up in the novel as a stuffed dog dragged from pillar to post) is made to visit this Eden. He has to recite a poem from *Alice in Wonderland*, "The Walrus and the Carpenter," about eating children. Moor describes the begetting and consuming of her own children by their mother:

> She had four of us. Ina, Minnie, Mynah, Moor; a four-course meal with magic properties, because no matter how often and how heartily she tucked in, the food never seemed to run out. For four decades, she ate her fill. (126)

Like the turn-taking game their names allude to as well as the Disney characters, they are each eliminated. When she dies, or is killed by her own husband, as we later learn, in turn, the sea eats her: "A thin, salivating tide washed over her body, as the black jaws went to work" (126). By the time of her death, all the children had left or been thrown out of the "paradise." The first daughter, Ina, dies of cancer: "The lymphoma developed quite suddenly, and gobbled up her body like a beggar at a feast." (216) The second daughter, Minnie, becomes a nun, Sister Inamorata, "the wearer of the roughest and itchiest undergarments in the Order, which she had sewn for herself out of old jute sacks stinking of cardamoms and tea" (238-39). The third daughter, Mynah, an activist working to denounce her father's corruption is ultimately murdered by him while investigating maltreatment of the female workforce in a chemical factory. She dies of chemical poisoning, "a shortage of breath," which ties in with Moor-Boabdil's sighs and breathing problems, with their intertextual word-play:

> I am what breathes [...] suspiro ergo sum. I sigh, therefore I am. The Latin as usual tells the truth: suspirare=sub, below; + spirare, verb, to breathe. (53)

Moor himself is thrown out of paradise on account of a woman, his chameleon-lover Uma. His mother had warned him about her falseness:

> That little fisherwoman had her hook in you and like a stupid fish you think she only wants to play. Soon you will be out of the water and she will fryofy you in ghee with ginger-garlic, mirch-masala, cumin seed, and maybe some potato chips on the side. (246)

He is rescued from the Under World of Bombay's prison by his father, who introduces him to the third Eden, his Bombay high-rise paradise. As he moves between this and the headquarters of his father's enemy, Raman Fielding, Moor is in a Wizard of Oz world with the violent Tin-man. In terms of his own identity, he is still in an Alice in Wonderland world, as, from his very conception, he has been characterised or marked by a peculiar disability. He is a freak of nature, because, like Alice, who eats the mushroom and grows into a giantess, he is growing at an accelerated rate. He is television's "Incredible Hulk" (188), or the grown-up man in the film with the mind of a child. He grows too fast, like the city of Bombay itself (161). He seeks his identity in his genealogy, and Moor's contribution to this has been hurried up. Thus his youth and early adulthood in this third Eden are marred by the fact that he looks as old as his father. His life-span is coming to a rapid end, as is his story. In this, he is like Saleem Sinai of *Midnight's Children*, whose bodily decay is correlated with the progress of his written novel. With both protagonists, when they finish writing, the process of decay will be complete.

Aruna Srivastava reminds us of the parallels between Foucault's thinking on history and the examples Rushdie invents in his novels:

> Foucault opposes conventional history to the search for genealogy, or the analysis of descent, which he also shows to be a very disquieting alternative, for "it disturbs what was previously considered immobile; it fragments what was thought unified; it shows the heterogeneity of what was imagined consistent with itself" (147). (Srivastava 70)

Although descent attempts to attach itself to a body, the body is not a unity, but the site of a disassociated self, often in perpetual disintegration, as in the cases of Saleem Sinai and Moor. Left-handed because of a mutilated right hand, Moor was always "imperfect" in Eden. Identity is therefore sought by him outside his individual self and in his genealogy, with the articulation of the body and history, the result being a patchwork figure. In *The Moor's Last Sigh*, Rushdie gives us the twentieth century speeded up into the reading space of the time it takes each reader to read the novel. Moor's body reflects this speeding up process, and as Foucault said, the body is imprinted by history and the process of history destroys the body (Srivastava 70).

The fourth paradise-hell sees the end of the process for Moor. In a way, he has come full circle, as in returning to the Iberian Peninsula, he returns to the point of origin of Vasco da Gama's spice route. The would-be executioner calls himself Vasco too, and he has an even shakier identity: "he was his own invention" (157), having fled from Goa when the Indian army put an end to Portuguese colonial rule. Moor comes full circle in a literary sense too, as the village is called Benengeli, reminiscent of the Moor who narrated *Don Quixote,* the father of novels.

2.4 Spices and the Arts: Painting, the Cinema, Television and Advertising

In this last paradise-hell, the theme of art comes to the fore. Abraham's vigilant and successful administration of Aurora's money in the spice trade, and its later ramifications, had enabled her to dedicate herself to painting. Through her painting she became famous, but Vasco Miranda, who lacked her genius, became an "airport painter" and through the commercialisation of his art became even more rich and famous. At the end, he has had two paintings of Aurora's stolen from Bombay, both on the same subject of *The Moor's Last Sigh* (415), and both painted over another painting underneath. In the first, Aurora paints over Vasco's portrait of her, which was not to Abraham's liking, and in the second, Aurora has painted over a picture she has done of her husband as the clue to the secret identity of her future murderer. Thus in this, Rushdie continues the idea of palimpsest art (416), like the layered art of the old masters. Aurora even calls the "hybrid fortress" (227) in Benengeli "Palimpstine" and "Mooristan" (235), and the invisible varnish between the two superimposed pictures divides "two worlds" (427). The layered approach is therefore applied to the recovery of the past and of personal history, also to the creation of new art, eternally responding agonistically to that which has gone before. The spice empire can be glimpsed at all times. Moor's fellow captive in this final paradise-prison is a Japanese art expert, who is being forced by Miranda to chip away at Aurora's painting to lay bare the commissioned portrait he painted of her. As Moor looks on, it occurs to him that by this chipping away and the X-ray investigation, Vasco may be trying to discover the secrets of Aurora's artistic genius. In this novel, Rushdie, in postmodern fashion, meditates not only upon how history and cultural identity are created, but also upon how art is created, be it painting or writing.

It has already been shown that in some of Rushdie's novels there lies beneath the surface text a sub-text significant only to those in the know. Cricket, India's most popular sport, is one such sub-text, and it frequently puts in an appearance in this novel, for example, in the figure of Raman Fielding and in the "mean kaju ball" Moor spins. But the cinema is the most obvious of these sub-texts. Vijay Mishra and Bob Hodge have commented on this sub-text in *The Satanic Verses* in their scrutiny of the seminal work *The Empire Writes Back* (*EWB*) (Ashcroft et al 1989):

> Thus if one were to read the song of Gibreel in Rushdie's *The Satanic Verses* through *EWB*, its effect within the context is all that would really matter to the reader. The fact that beneath the song is an entire text of Bombay cinema which, to the bilingual reader, would recall, more specifically, Raj Kapoor's *Shree 420* (1955) is knowledge that *EWB* must either ignore or relegate [...]. This supplementarity, however, even in terms of *EWB*'s own design is counter-discursive in a radically different fashion. The supplement, the anecdotal invasion or culture-specific power, is, however, a form of intervention that questions, as supplements always do, the very adequacy of a theory of the centre and its periphery. At the very moment that the narrative is invaded by an intertext from a different centre—the centre and the centrality of the Bombay commercial cinema, India's pre-eminent contemporary cultural form—the focus shifts from a fixed centre and its satellite system to a multiplicity of centres in the culture itself. (Mishra and Hodge 280)

Mishra and Hodge emphasize in their article the counter-discursive nature of postcolonial literary practice as opposed to a more central, homologous one. As in *The Satanic Verses, The Moor's Last Sigh* makes both explicit and implicit reference to the cinema, and Rushdie shows that, in a way, the cinema functions like the articulations of the spice trade, only in reverse. The source product is found in the West, with Hollywood being the model. We saw how Aurora was so fascinated by Disney characters that she named her children after them, and had Vasco paint a magic, ever-changing Disneyland children's bedroom for them. Disney's version of *Alice in Wonderland* has given Rushdie not only the accelerated growth of Moor, but also the pepper that makes the Duchess's baby cry. Moor turns into an "Incredible Hulk," bursting out of his clothes; his father's empire comes crashing down like "The Towering Inferno"; and at the critical moment in which Vasco Miranda is about to kill Moor, he just bursts open and blood pours out, as the Ice Queen's splinter reaches his heart. *The Empire Writes Back* is also in fact a brainchild of Rushdie, a cinematic image for discussing postcolonial writing. In this novel, the sinister sub-plot is Moor's father's involvement in the creation of Star Wars type armaments aimed at the destruction of the world. So even the narrative depends upon the cinema, not just special effects. Rushdie shows how the media mediate events and phenomena for us. Thus Disney's version of *Alice* is the only one most people know. The media reporting of Mrs Gandhi's death is what the vast majority believe. With spices, the home market also consumes, and with the cinema, Bombay has made itself a new centre in its own right. The West kept on importing spices, but Bombay created the home-grown product: "Bollywood."

The Indian film industry is now the world's largest, and according to Tim McGirk, it is fifty per cent controlled by organised crime. McGirk reported from Bangalore in collaboration with Meenakshi Ganguly in Bombay for an article in *Time* magazine. They show how the top mafia dons of Bollywood, like Abraham and Raman Fielding in Rushdie's novel, find the film industry "a safe way to launder loot gained from extortion and smuggling gold and drugs" (McGirk 46). The gangsters look upon film not as a work of art, but as yet another commodity, and in order to win wider audiences, they want more action and vulgarity. They force film directors to make dialogue and action more risqué, and in a country that is supposed to worship women, on screen women are now subjected to abuse as the criminals impose their violent tastes to the point of repulsion. McGirk and Garguly report that two years before, an uncooperative starlet was forced to dance and sing in public, and this reminds one of Moor's mother Aurora dancing, albeit voluntarily, but in protest and in a public spectacle, and eventually dancing to her death. Even if Aurora is not a sly hint at the pressurising of the film mafia, two other factors are certainly true. At the time of writing of the novel, Bombay was still reeling from the Hindu-Muslim clashes of 1992 and 1993 that left hundreds dead, and Rushdie has portrayed these events in the final showdown between Abraham and Raman Fielding. The Wild West, mythologised by the American cinema is a subtext here. These events have been made into a film by a leading non-mafioso film director, and his life has been threatened if he goes ahead for fear of stirring up more unrest. He has to take these threats seriously, since a few years ago, another Indian director had his house bombed for breaking the screen taboo of showing a Muslim woman marrying a Hindu. Rushdie himself suffers the consequences of breaking taboos, but he does it in the name of non-violence. The second factor is that much as Moor says that violence is "hot" and the mafia are all for it, the customers who previously were all in favour are beginning to reject it, and McGirk reports that the biggest hits over the last few years have been not violent films but romance and family dramas, which is what *The Moor's Last Sigh* purports to be, albeit in postmodern guise.

Before he became famous as a novelist, Rushdie worked in advertising. His interest in this field has not waned. He shows himself equally master of the four hundred-page saga as of the thirty-second, impact-making commercial. Towards the end of his life in Bombay, Moor discovers he has a rival, an adopted brother. Needless to say, he is identified, in a wonderful thumbnail sketch, through spices:

> Since then the boy had been raised in a pink skyscraper at Breach Candy by two elderly Goan Christian ladies who had grown wealthy on the success of their popular range of condiments, Braganza Pickles. He had taken the name of Braganza in the old ladies' honour, and, after they passed

> away, had taken over the factory itself. Soon afterwards, as smartly turned out and slick-styled at seventeen as many executives twice his age, he had come to Siodicorp in search of expansion capital, hoping to put the old ladies' legendary pickles and chutneys into the world market under the snappier brand name of *Brag's*. On the modernised packaging which he brought in to show Abraham's people was the slogan, *Plenty to Brag about.* (342)

The young fellow's "sloganising touch": "*Not Ram but RAM*" (343) is Rushdie linguistic brilliance. Language itself, "modern lingo" (343), stories themselves, can all be "hot like spices". Moor compares Bombay to Cochin and shows how it is central in exciting event, incredible story:

> No matter what pepper 'n' spices goings-on there might have been or have been in Cochin, this great cosmopolis of ours was and is the Central Junction of all such tamashas, and the hottest tales, the juiciest-bitchiest yarns [...] are the ones walking our streets. In Bombay you lived crushed in this crazy world [...] your own story has to shove its way through the throngs. Which was fine by Aurora Zogoiby; never one for a quiet life, she sucked in the city's hot stenches, lapped up its burning sauces, she gobbled its dishes up whole. (128)

2.5 Spice 'n' Sex

Part of the meaning of hot and spicy comes from a sexual dimension. From the beginning of the novel, passionate love is related to spices: "Pepper love: that's how I think of it. Abraham and Aurora fell in pepper love, up there on the Malabar Gold" (90). Not puppy love (Aurora was just fifteen), but *pepper* love, and Moor's parents had first made love high up on the pepper sacks in the warehouse. Aurora said that from then on: "that stink of grinding spices, my *dears*, it makes him paw the ground" (90). When Aurora closed her bedroom door to Abraham and refused to bear a child until her mother-in-law had died, because of the Rumplestiltskin-cum-Abraham and Isaac pact, Abraham began to look elsewhere for sex. At about the same time, he began to diversify his business, moving from spices into prostitution. When the merchandise happened to be virgin, it was known as "Extra Hot Chilli Peppers: Green" (183).

Passionate love, "the thing that made you sweat beads of coriander juice and breathe hot-chilli flames." as Moor calls it (221), is one of the factors involved in the flawed nature of the different Edens. The other factors involve beauty, its opposite, "unbeauty," and revenge. Carmen Lobo, deserted by her homosexual husband, is jealous of her beautiful sister-in-law Belle, at once Beauty of Beauty and the Beast and Queen Isabella of Spain. Carmen burns for revenge "let [...] *the spices wither in the sun* [...] she howled *revenge*" (47). Moor is thrown out of *Elephanta*, the second Eden, because of the treachery of Uma. He had been torn between his mother and her in a sort of Oedipal struggle taken literally. Moor meditates on the "*amours fous*" (289) within his genealogy and is disappointed that the ideal of love in all its senses: individual, bilateral, national, supranational, appears impossible:

> I wanted to cling to the image of love as the blending of spirits, as mélange, as the triumph of the impure, mongrel, conjoining best of us over what there is in us of the solitary, the isolated, the austere, the dogmatic, the pure; of love as democracy, as the victory of the no-man-is-an-island, two's company Many over the clean, mean apartheiding Ones. (289)

In the third Eden, there is treachery too, as Abraham apparently murders his wife Aurora after many years of frustration, thus avenging her infidelities. Vasco Miranda's evil designs in the fourth Eden also have passion as a motive. His frustrated love for Aurora and jealousy of her husband make him seek revenge on her son, but not before the whole spicy, bloody saga has been written down by him.

3. Conclusions

In choosing the format of the family history for his novel, Rushdie has given us an action-packed story, with excitement from beginning to end. There is no slow build-up to a climax here, this wealthy family gets up to tricks which propel them from drama to drama. Larger-than-life, they have talents and opportunities within each generation that poorer families would not see in all their generations put together. They are central to their world, but also, through the source of their wealth, the spice trade, they conduct a life that moves along the axis uniting East and West. Through this axis, which manifestly explores the external world of the physical, the exchange of colourful, strong-smelling spices for Western money or other goods like film culture, Rushdie is able to suggest other submerged axes uniting East and West, also, for example, chess moving westwards and cricket eastwards. Through the image of the palimpsest, he suggests there are layers of time, of experience, of truths and lies to every aspect of our lives, be they our personal lives, our history, or commerce or art. Indian nationalists located Indian subjectivity in the spiritual domain of culture, as opposed to Western materialism. One could say that Rushdie embodies Western materialism and fortune-seeking in the original commodity of spices. Then he explores the inner truths of East-West relations. He suggests that there are always two ways of looking at the problem, as expressed by the patriarch Francisco and his rebellious wife and son:

> (Francisco): "The nation's wealth is being shipped off, madam, at home our people starve, but British Tommy is utilising our wheat, rice, jute and coconut products."
>
> (Epifania): "What are we but Empire's children? British have given us everything, isn't it?-Civilisation, law, order, too much. Even your spices that stink up the house they buy out of their generosity, putting clothes on backs and food on children's plates." (18)

Rushdie questions both sides, even the Indian belief in cultural superiority, embodied in the ideal of the Indian woman. The ideal of the Western-educated woman upholding traditional Indian values is seen in Aurora and her dance of protest, but she is also a mother who eats her own children.

Rushdie uses postmodern metafictive techniques to subvert not only the "myth" of the colonisers' view, but also the myths created by postcolonial writers themselves. India's political struggle is verbalised by Rushdie on an East-West axis in order for it to escape being marginalised. He subverts everything, from "Mother India" to deconstruction itself: "*Imperso-Nation and Dis/Semi/Nation: Dialogics of Eclecticism and Interrogations in A.Z.*" (329). But his dream of a multi-coloured, spicy, hybrid

Eden, described in the novel by Camoens, the brother named after the Portuguese poet, remains just a dream for a dying beautiful woman:

> [T]he *dawning of a new world, Belle, a free country, Belle, above religion because secular, above class because socialist, above caste because enlightened, above hatred because loving, above vengeance because forgiving, above tribe because unifying, above language because many-tongued, above colour because multi-coloured, above poverty because victorious over it, above ignorance because literate, above stupidity because brilliant, freedom, Belle, the freedom express, soon soon we will stand upon that platform and cheer the coming of the train,* and while he told her his dreams she would fall asleep and be visited by spectres of desolation and war. (51)

Works Cited

Bhabha, Homi K. "Exploring the Place of Silence." *Guardian Weekly* 16 Oct. 1994: 29.

Gilroy, Paul. "Urban Social Movements, 'Race' and Community." In Williams and Chrisman. 404-21.

González, María Luz. "Subversion of History and the Creation of Alternative Realities in Salman Rushdie." *Revista Canaria de Estudios Ingleses* 28 (1994): 41-53.

Hall, Stuart. "Cultural Identity and Diaspora." In Williams and Chrisman. 392-404.

McGirk, Tim. "Mob Scene." *Time* 19 May 1997: 46-47.

Mishra, Vijay and Bob Hodge. "What is Post(-)Colonialism?" In Williams and Chrisman. 276-91.

Rushdie, Salman. *Midnight's Children*. London: Pan, 1982.

____. *Shame*. London: Jonathan Cape, 1983.

____. *The Satanic Verses*. London: Viking, 1988.

____. *East, West*. London: Vintage, 1995.

____. *The Moor's Last Sigh*. London: Jonathan Cape, 1995.

Srivastava, Aruna. "'The Empire Writes Back': Language and History in *Shame* and *Midnight's Children*." *Past the Last Post: Theorizing Post-Colonialism and Post-Modernism*. Ed. Ian Adam and Helen Tiffin. New York: Harvester Wheatsheaf, 1991. 65-79.

Williams, Patrick and Laura Chrisman, eds. *Colonial Discourse and Post-colonial Theory: A Reader*. New York: Harvester Wheatsheaf, 1993.

6

RUSHDIE'S UN-INDIAN MUSIC: *THE GROUND BENEATH HER FEET*

CHRISTOPHER ROLLASON

> "This book[1] is not a novel about rock'n'roll, but an attempt to respond to the evolution of world culture in the last half-century."
>
> (Rushdie to *Le Monde*, 1999[2])

Prologue

In 1968, from the symbolically radical location of the French capital's *rive gauche*, no less a critic than Roland Barthes proclaimed the death of the author.[3] Following on from the "death of God" announced by Nietzsche close on a century before, the iconoclastic Gallic philosopher laid the "Author-God" to rest,[4] arguing that the literary text henceforth belonged not to its writer but to its readers, who now had the right to interpret its words multiply and at will: "the birth of the reader comes at the price of the death of the Author."[5] This gesture ushered in an era of text-centred, anti-intentionist, anti-biographical criticism, the underlying tenet being that the reader's dynamic appropriation and rehandling of the text necessitated no reference whatever to the details of the writer's life.

Twenty-one years later, in Tehran on 14 February 1989, the death of the author, or, at least, of one individual author, was decreed in a rather less symbolic fashion by Ayatollah Khomeini: "[...] the author of the book entitled *The Satanic Verses*, which has been compiled, printed and published in opposition to Islam, the prophet and the Qur'an, as well as those publishers who were aware of its contents, have been declared [...] those whose blood must be shed,"[6] Khomeini thus unwittingly countered Barthes' anarchic radicalism with a stern return to tradition. The English translation of his fatwa seems to imply that a text—in this case, Rushdie's novel—has only one meaning ("opposition to Islam") and is "compiled" by its author with a single intention that is totally consonant with that one meaning; and that the author bears full responsibility for his or her text—a responsibility that may light an unfortunate author all the way to dusty death. The Shi'ite cleric's edict unleashed a battle of the books—indeed, a war that involved not two but three texts—*The Satanic Verses*, the Koran, and his own fatwa. Few observers noticed a certain curious detail—the incontrovertible circumstance that the Ayatollah could not, when he made his ruling, possibly have read *The Satanic Verses*, a book which then existed only in English, a language in which he could not have handled a complex and allusive postmodernist novel. Similarly, only a minority of the neo-Zhdanovite,[7] pro-censorship lobby in Britain who subsequently demanded the banning of Rushdie's novel had actually read it—though that small matter did not stop them calling for its suppression in the name of political correctness, in an epidemic of moral absolutism worthy of their Puritan forbears. It appeared that Roland Barthes' notion of an infinitely fecund text, permanently reinterpreted by its readers, was in serious danger of succumbing to a rigid, theocratic notion of a text which, imbued with a single, self-evident, and authorially signified "meaning," manifests itself in identical fashion to all, readers and non-readers alike.

Another decade passed, and while Khomeini was now dead, Salman Rushdie was still alive. Political correctness had continued its advances in the West, but no OECD country, with the predictable exception of Turkey, had banned *The Satanic Verses*—not even Britain, despite the best efforts of certain politicians on the left.[8] In 1999, Rushdie published *The Ground Beneath Her Feet*, a novel in which he visibly aims to revisit the theme of the death of the author—this time, by drinking from the wellsprings of Western culture, from the Greco-Roman tradition and the myth of Orpheus, the archetypal poet-musician. For that tale ends with the spilling of a poet's blood: Orpheus is killed by a vengeful band of would-be followers. Such is the mythical destiny around which Rushdie has consciously woven this new fiction, ten years on from the fatwa.

1

From this point on, I shall return to Barthes, as far as is still possible today, and endeavour to read and interpret *The Ground Beneath Her Feet* with only incidental reference to the fatwa or to Rushdie's personal life, although I shall take due account of certain of the author's opinions, as expressed in articles and interviews, as well as of his other literary works. As the French critic Guy Astic stressed in 1996, "the Indo-British writer is not an individual defined by a single work, nor is he just the face of a fatwa [...] we have to examine Salman Rushdie's work as a whole."[9] I shall take it as axiomatic that a literary text is to be read primarily as text—as a piece of writing that exists in dialogue with other texts, as well as with the wider series of texts surrounding it that we know as history—a history that, obviously, does not exclude Khomeini's edict or the PC lobby's burn-it-and-ban-it campaign, but also ranges far deeper and wider in time and place, transcending all such narrow ideological concerns.

The Ground Beneath Her Feet (hereinafter referred to as *GF*) is based on what might be called a literary-musical conceit: the reader is asked to suspend disbelief and accept the notion that—to quote Rushdie himself, from an interview with the Madrid daily *El País*—"the world's two most famous rock stars are both Indian,"[10] Rushdie's two fictional stars are Ormus Cama, born into an old Bombayite Zoroastrian family in 1937, and Vina Apsara, born in the US in 1944 to an Indian father and a Greek-American mother, raised there till her parents die in 1956, and then sent "home" to India. She and Ormus, then aged nineteen, meet in a Bombay record shop. The two migrate in the 60s to London, where they form the group VTO (the reader never learns what those initials stand for) and achieve stellar success. Ormus writes the lyrics; both sing. The two megastars fall in and out of love, move to the US and go on notching up superplatinum sales worldwide through the

70s and most of the 80s, in VTO until the group breaks up and afterwards as solo artists. After Vina's death in 1989, in an earthquake in Mexico, Ormus carries on, despite increasing psychological instability, until one winter's morning when a crazed woman fan kills him in New York. The whole saga is narrated in the first person by another Bombayite, Rai Merchant, an internationally known photographer of secular Muslim origins who bears within himself a second, secret identity as Vina's occasional non-platonic confidant.

One of the distorting effects of the *Satanic Verses* controversy has been to cast Rushdie as a writer defined essentially in relation to Islam. This is, in reality, only partially the case if we consider his fictional work as a whole. *Shame*, certainly, is a novel about Pakistan, and the protagonists of *Midnight's Children* (hereinafter *MC*) and *The Satanic Verses* (hereinafter *SV*), and, indeed, the narrator of *GF*, are of Muslim origin, albeit secularised to a greater or lesser degree. However, it is far more illuminative to view Rushdie less as a product of Islam than as the chronicler in fiction of the Indian subcontinent in the twentieth century—and of that subcontinent's relations with the wider world.

Rushdie's fictional production thus far may be roughly classified into two modes, magic-realist and fantastic, with the former predominating. His first novel, *Grimus* (1975), set in the imaginary location of Calf Island, is cast in the fantastic mode throughout, and he revisits that dimension in the central part of *Haroun and the Sea of Stories* (1990) and in the final section of *The Moor's Last Sigh* (1995; hereinafter "*Moor*"), whose nominal Spanish setting reads more like an arbitrary dream-world. For the rest, Rushdie's writing is magic-realist with the main emphasis on the realist component, located either wholly or mostly in the Indian subcontinent and with the explicit presence of real, if partially distorted historical events. This is the pattern established in *MC* (1981) and repeated in *Shame* (1983), *SV* (1988), and the first three-quarters of *Moor*. The subcontinent is narrated, not as a closed-in, autarkic universe, but in its dynamic interaction with the rest of the world—with the West and beyond—from the colonial period through Independence and Partition to the era of globalisation:

MC, *Shame* and *Moor* all range in chronology from the Raj-era early twentieth century to the actual time of writing, a pattern which is repeated in *GF*. The action of *MC* takes in India, Pakistan and Bangladesh, and while not straying topographically outside the subcontinent, introduces British and American colonials and expatriates; *Shame* focuses on Pakistan but includes episodes in Britain; *Moor* is set in its first three sections in India, again including turn-of-the-century colonials in its cast, before spiralling out at the end to an invented Spain. A somewhat different logic is followed in *SV*, which, based squarely in the contemporary world and centred on Indian characters, situates the bulk of its action in London, with forays to Bombay and, briefly, to Argentina, while also, crucially, featuring a series of dreams: some located in an Indian village, others—as, notoriously, even the book's non-readers know—set in a simulacrum of the Hejaz in the time of the Prophet; while the short stories collected in *East, West* (1994), read in order, take the reader from the subcontinent to an Asian émigrés' London. In all Rushdie's fictions other than *Grimus* and *Haroun*, invented characters coexist with historical figures; the latter appear either under their own names, or disguised and satirised but still clearly recognisable (the Gandhis in *MC*, the Bhuttos and Zia Ul-Haq in *Shame*, Bal Thackray in *Moor*). All in all, Rushdie's fictional production prior to *GF*, taken as a whole, may be read as constituting an imaginative model of the Indian subcontinent within twentieth-century history, a latter-day Asian equivalent, albeit on a smaller scale, to what Honoré de Balzac did for nineteenth-century France in his monumental *Comédie Humaine*.

GF follows the pre-established pattern—up to a point, and with significant divergences. The two protagonists and the narrator are, as before, Indian, or at least half-Indian, while Rushdie pays obeisance to his own previous work by discreet use of the device (again harking back to Balzac) of recurring characters: the Englishman William Methwold, who plays a key part in *GF*, has walked in from *MC*, and Homi Catrack, also from that novel, and Aurora Zogoiby, from *Moor*, are resurrected for bit-parts. In terms of fictional chronology, *GF* begins, like its predecessors, in the Raj of the early twentieth century; in narrative sequence, however, it opens in 1989, in Guadalajara, Mexico, with the earthquake and Vina's dramatic disappearance, before shifting back, in reverse mode, to the characters' Indian past. The bulk of the novel does, however, approximately observe a linear chronology, with the notable circumstance, new in Rushdie, that halfway through the action moves definitively to the West—to Britain, then the US—with virtually no subsequent revisiting of the subcontinent (Vina, Beatles-like, spends a brief spell in an ashram;[11] a planned tour of India by Ormus falls victim to a government ban[12]). The East-West alternation model of *SV* has been ditched in *GF*, in favour of a sequential model: the reader watches East being replaced by West as the epicentre.

2

This change in spatial priorities has been admitted by Rushdie himself, with specific reference to Bombay, the city which has been so important to his writing in the past. Bombay, or as we now have officially to call it, Mumbai (the recent, ideologically-motivated change of name was actually predicted by Rushdie himself, in his quasi-historical account of the Hindu-particularist "Mumbai's Axis" movement in *Moor*) has played a part in his work which may be compared to that of Paris in Balzac. *MC* opens with the narrator, Saleem Sinai, declaring: "I was born in the city of Bombay [...] in Doctor Narlikar's Nursing Home on August 15th, 1947,"[13] *SV* ends with Saladin Chamcha's return to the Maharashtran metropolis: "He stood at the window of his childhood and looked out at the Arabian Sea";[14] the narrator of *Moor*, Moraes Zogoiby, laments the decline of his once-latitudinarian home city into shallow sectarianism: "Bombay was central; had always been. [...] now barbarism was standing at our gates. O Bombay! Prima in Indis! Gateway to India! Star of the East with her face to the West!"[15] Of course, other contemporary Indian or "Indo-Anglian" writers as well as Rushdie have centred their fictional imaginings around Bombay-Mumbai: notable examples include Anita Desai's *Baumgartner's Bombay* (1988), Vikram Chandra's *Love and Longing in Bombay* (1997), and, indeed, the best-selling Shobha Dé's Bollywood saga *Starry Nights* (1991). However, the city returns in Rushdie's pages with a special insistence, as the symbol of a specifically Indian version of multiplicity, tolerance and (in the subcontinental sense) cosmopolitanism; as Roshan G. Shahani put it in 1994, "Bombay's infinite variety, its paradoxes and contradictions [...] mirror and account for the heterogeneous presence and the polyphonous voices of the 'Bombay writers'"[16]—among whom Shahani highlights Rushdie, for whom the city "had encapsulated this country's multicultural diversity and its secular ideology."[17] In *GF*, we find Rushdie re-treading the city's streets—indeed, Rai Merchant's father turns out to be an amateur Bombayologist: "Bombay. Don't ask. I could pass any exam you care to set [...] My father liked digging into place names, so allow me to inform you, just off the top of my head, that Chinchpokli is 'tamarind hollow' and Cumballa Hill is named after the lotus flower and Bhendhi Bazaar is situated where once the ladies'-fingers grew."[18] In the end, however, this evocation of Bombay comes over as a valediction, as the centre of gravity of Rushdie's world shifts (irrevocably?) to the US: Rushdie, indeed, has said as much, in an interview with Laura Miller in the on-line magazine *Salon*:[19] "I think I really have said what I had to say about that city, and I don't want to repeat myself [...] I think I've done it." Whether this apparent abandonment of his subcontinental roots for the glittering surfaces of globalisation makes for a real gain is an open question. Shahani states that "by writing about Bombay, writers like Rushdie have charted anew the cultural map of the world;"[20] it remains to be seen if those who cut loose from India can still keep their bearings, or read that global "cultural map" with their old acuity.

3

Throughout *GF*, Rushdie deploys his customary artillery of literary, historical and intellectual references, from Karl Marx and Charles Baudelaire through to William Faulkner and Jorge Luis Borges, but, at the same time, gives centre stage to a form of popular or mass culture, namely rock music. His reasons for choosing this theme are no doubt multiple. One is that as a long-standing rock'n'roll fan (from the moment when, as a Bombay adolescent, he bought a much-prized copy of Elvis Presley's 45 rpm record "Heartbreak Hotel"[21]), he has an expert's knowledge of the field. Another may be, as Carla Power hypothesised in *Newsweek*, the circumstance that Rushdie can himself be considered "a household name [...] literature's first global celebrity—as famous as a pop star."[22] In addition, there are partial precedents in his earlier work. Specifically subcontinental popular-cultural forms are present in *MC*, where Saleem's sister, the "Brass Monkey," becomes, as Jamila Singer, a highly-regarded popular vocalist in post-independence Pakistan, and another of Saleem's relatives works in the Bollywood film world; while in *SV*, Gibreel Farishta is one of India's greatest celluloid heartthrobs, and, indeed, the all-too-controversial dreams that haunt him when he undergoes psychiatric treatment have the unfortunate star imagining himself playing the lead role in a filmic reinterpretation of the founding years of Islam.

If we step outside the subcontinental mass-cultural orbit and enter that of the West, we discover a fair number of rock-music allusions in Rushdie's writing prior to *GF*. In *Grimus*, one of the main characters is called Bird Dog, after an Everly Brothers hit from 1958: "When I was your age I went into the town, she said, and listened at a window outside an eating-place. There was a singing machine there. It sang about a creature called a bird-dog, clever, fiendish.."[23] An article of 1990 on the novelist Thomas Pynchon (reprinted in the essay collection *Imaginary Homelands*) features the phrase "days of miracle and wonder," which comes from "The Boy in the Bubble," a song by Paul Simon from his *Graceland* album of 1986.[24] In "The Courter," the concluding story of *East, West* (1994), the narrator, an Indian adolescent growing up in London in the 60s, listens avidly to rock'n'roll on the radio, and, in an ironic detail, confesses: "London, W8 was Sam Cooke's country that summer. Another Saturday night [...] I was down with lonely Sam in the lower depths of the charts [...] How I wish I had someone to talk to,/I'm in an awful way"[25]; it so happens that Cooke's hit, "Another Saturday Night," returned to the charts in the 70s, in a cover version by Cat Stevens—a Anglo-Greek singer who later abandoned international stardom, converted to the Muslim religion, changed his name to Yusuf Islam and [...] became a particularly virulent defender of Khomeini's fatwa.

To mention Cat Stevens in this way is not purely anecdotal, for it is this kind of surprising connection that illuminates the globalised nature of culture today. Rushdie, as an émigré writer with a foot in both Eastern and Western worlds, is himself clearly both product and exponent of that globalisation; and that phenomenon affects, not only (and as is notorious) mass culture, but high culture too. If both high and mass culture now operate on a planetary scale, their inevitable interaction can only become more intricate and more complex. In this context, a prominent aspect of Rushdie's writing in *GF* is his endeavour, on the level of the text, to confer a degree of solidity and credibility on that rock music world which some olympian intellectuals would dismiss as, always and necessarily, innately trivial and insubstantial. Rushdie explained his position to *Le Monde* on 1 October 1999: "Most pop music is purely intended to make money and then disappear. [...] But if you take the other end of pop music, the best of the last forty years [...] you have to take it seriously,"[26] similarly, in the *Salon* interview he stated: "I wanted to take this [rock'n'roll] world and treat it seriously as a vehicle to examine our life and times."[27] With this in view, he adopts two main strategies: the dignification of his subject through the Orpheus myth; and the incorporation of a rock'n'roll sensibility into the texture of his writing, via wholesale quotation from song lyrics.

4

To take the second-named strategy first, a close reading of Rushdie's text reveals a remarkable density of song references. Song titles, album titles, individual lines and phrases from songs: all abound in this book's pages. Some are quoted au pied de la lettre, others are reshaped; some are attributed to their historical authors, some are deliberately misattributed, others still are left unflagged. To these real or modified-real song texts should be added the imaginary lyrics of Ormus Cama's songs, extracts from which are "quoted" at length. The heterogeneous nature of these quotations and allusions fits in with Rushdie's general method in *GF*: throughout, literary texts and authors, historical events, etc., are alluded to with a magpie eclecticism that by no means always recognises the dictatorship of fact. In

Rushdie's reordered universe, John and Robert Kennedy are killed together by the same Palestinian gunman;[28] Britain's Labour government sends troops out to Vietnam;[29] and The Garden of Forking Paths is not an imaginary novel existing only in Borges' story of that name, but a real book, Vina's "favourite nineteenth-century novel."[30] The same rewriting of history applies to the novel's rock'n'roll world. The song "Feelin' Groovy" is attributed not to the real Paul Simon and Art (Arthur) Garfunkel, but, punningly and absurdly, to an invented duo of the real (but female) Carly Simon and the non-existent Guinevere Garfunkel.[31] Again, we are told that in a series of "solidarity concerts" held circa 1974 to protest Ormus' threatened deportation from the US, "Dylan, Lennon, [Janis] Joplin, Joni [Mitchell], Country Joe and the Fish turn up to sing for Ormus,"[32] although, even had Ormus Cama really existed, one of those artists, Ms Joplin, could hardly have turned up, as she had died of an overdose in 1970.

The song micro-texts that are embedded in Rushdie's macro-text, wherever they stand on the real-to-imaginary spectrum, are clearly offered as an integral part of this novel's global textual project—and, as such, call for detailed elucidation. Their presence is already announced in the book's chapter-headings: chapter 10, "Season of the Witch," takes its title from a 60s song by Donovan, and the title of chapter 13, "Transformer," is also the name of a Lou Reed album from 1972. The rock-generation singer-songwriters whose words or titles are quoted, straight or askew, across Rushdie's text include Paul Simon, Joni Mitchell, Carole King, Randy Newman, Tom Waits and, notably, Bob Dylan (in view of the central issues it raises, I shall consider Rushdie's use of Dylan in a separate section[33]). To cite examples, the phrase "the hissing of summer lawns"[34] is the title of a 1975 album (and song) by Joni Mitchell, while "I feel the earth move under my feet"[35] quotes the title and first line of a 1972 song by Carole King. At one moment, Vina and Ormus (accurately) quote, paraphrase and dissect Randy Newman's song " Sail Away," also from 1972.[36] At another, Vina puts on a disc: "This is the CD she plays: Raindogs, the honky-tonk blues as reinvented and growled out by Lee Baby Simms. She starts singing along with Simms, long and slow, and the hair rises on my neck. Will I see you again/on a downtown train."[37] Here, rock fact and fiction intertwine: the lines Vina sings are slightly misquoted from "Downtown Train," a song which indeed appears on an album called *Rain Dogs* (spelt thus), released in 1985 not by the non-existent Lee Baby Simms, but by Tom Waits.

On occasion, Rushdie steps back in time to raid older songwriting traditions. Vina recalls the blues singer Ma Rainey ("I go back a century to ugly Ma Rainey preaching Trust No Man"[38])—but gets her chronology wrong, since the historical Rainey flourished in the 1920s; and when Ormus declares: "Like a mole in the ground I will root this mountain down," his words are virtually a direct quotation from the traditional song "I Wish I Was A Mole in the Ground," recorded in 1928 by an obscure Appalachian folk-blues singer, Bascom Lamar Lunsford.[39] The text even once quotes from the repertory of French-language chanson, with a pun ("she was predictably called the pornographer of the phonograph"[40]) which must have come from Georges Brassens' song of 1958 "Le Pornographe" ("J'suis l'pornographe/Du phonographe/Le polisson/De la chanson"). Despite these instances, however, the great majority of Rushdie's song quotations and references are to Anglo-American lyrics of the 60s and 70s.

5

Nonetheless, if Rushdie's musical vision is largely bound to a particular time, place and genre, he still wishes to claim universality for it: and here his reanimation of the Orpheus myth comes into action. The reader may not object to being reminded of the story, in the refined form which it eventually assumed in the ancient world and which has provided the "Orpheus template" for later generations in the West. Orpheus is the archetypal poet and musician of the Greco-Roman world, begotten by the god Apollo, himself famed for his prowess on the lyre, on Calliope, the Muse of epic poetry. Orpheus' haunting voice and plangent lyre had the power to subjugate nature: as Shakespeare put it centuries later, he "made trees/And the mountains that did freeze/Bow themselves when he did sing."[41] Soon after the poet's marriage to Eurydice, his young bride died from a snake-bite as she was fleeing the unwanted advances of Aristaeus, a bee-keeper. The inconsolable Orpheus went down into Hell to get her back, and charmed the powers of the underworld into accepting his outrageous demand, subject to one condition: he must walk out of Hell ahead of her, and must not look back till both of them were safely within the sunlight. He looked back at the very last minute, and lost her forever. Inconsolably mourning his twice-lost bride, he vowed never to touch a woman again. This incurred the wrath of the Maenads, the crazed women devotees of the god Dionysus, and one day, feeling provoked beyond endurance, a band of them seized on the recalcitrant poet and tore him to pieces. They cast his limbs and head into the river; and yet the severed head went on singing. The Muses gathered his remains and buried him; the gods placed his lyre in the stars as a constellation. The martyred poet lived on posthumously into recorded history, as the inspirer of a devotional cult, whose initiates were called the Orphics; at some point in the sixth to fourth centuries BC, there emerged from their circles the "Orphic hymns," a set of panegyrics to the gods which remain extant today.

Only two full versions of this legend have come down to us from the ancient world, both by Roman poets—Virgil in the *Georgics* (29 BC; Book Four),[42] and, later, Ovid in the *Metamorphoses* (8 AD; Books Ten and Eleven).[43] There is a very clear latter-day summary by the American Thomas Bulfinch, in *The Age of Fable*[44] (1855), and a more speculative modern synthesis, with analytic commentary, by Robert Graves in *The Greek Myths*[45] (1955). I shall use Virgil's version—the one essentially followed by Rushdie—as my reference point. Although Orpheus is most certainly a figure of Greek origin, associated with Thrace, no complete account of his story by an ancient Greek writer has survived; passing references appear in, for instance, Euripides' *Alcestis* (438 BC)[46] and Plato's *Symposium* (c. 370 BC).[47] Euripides speaks of "the Thracian inscriptions/Written down from the voice of Orpheus,"[48] a handful of these have survived, as have eighty-seven Orphic hymns. This material, all written in Greek, has recently been collected in a French translation, carefully edited by Jacques Lacarrière; only one of the hymns, however, actually mentions the legendary poet's name (as a putative "signature" in the last line,[49] and none tells his story. Graves, while underlining Orpheus' status for the ancients as "the most famous poet and musician who ever lived," notes that "Eurydice's death by snake-bite and Orpheus's subsequent failure to bring her back into the sunlight figure only in late myth."[50] This view is confirmed by Lacarrière, who calls the Eurydice episode as it stands in the *Georgics* (with Aristaeus and the serpent) a "fable invented by Virgil," adding that "the name of Eurydice, as Orpheus' wife, appears only very late in ancient literature" and noting that "Plato and Euripides knew the myth of Orpheus' descent into hell in search of his wife, but did not name her."[51] Virgil's canonic version of the story seems even to be an afterthought—a bypath from the main highway of the *Georgics* (essentially a poetic treatise on agriculture), an interpolation into a digression which may have been dictated less by literary choices than by political events in the Rome of Augustus.[52]

The Orpheus-Eurydice story, with its long history of reverberation across Western culture, seems then, ironically, to have appeared in its now-familiar form almost by chance. Lacarrière does, however, stress Orpheus' key importance to the ancients as the archetype of the artist as initiate, a human in intimate contact with the forces of death and darkness:

> What assured Orpheus his glory and eternity in Greece (and later in the West) was [...] the power he was believed to have of exorcising death by his songs, the power that allowed him to descend alive into hell and then return. Having been able to confront and conquer the darkness, he came to symbolise the initiate, the master of the beyond, the messenger of immortality [...] the poems, the music, the message of Orpheus [had the role of] awakening humans, revealing their true selves by opening up before them the path to immortality.[53]

Across Rushdie's text, references to the Orpheus myth come thick and fast, starting with the novel's very title (which suggests the ground trembling beneath Eurydice's feet as she descends into hell) and the holographic lyre on the front dustjacket of the British edition. Rushdie appears to see his musician protagonists as manifestations of the Orphic principle of the indestructibility of music; in the *El País* interview, he declares: "the myth of Orpheus tells us that you can kill the singer, but not the song."[54] The Ormus-Vina saga is preceded by an epigraph from Rainer Maria Rilke's *Sonnets to Orpheus* (1923)—"Once and for all/it's Orpheus when there's singing";[55] Virgil's "extraordinary" version of the myth is summarised;[56] Plato's commentary, too, is parapahrased, with Orpheus seen by Rai Merchant as "the singer with the lyre or, let's say, guitarist—the trickster who uses his music and wiles to cross boundaries";[57] on stage, after Vina's death, Ormus impersonates Orpheus as part of his act;[58] even his recording studio in New York is baptised "the Orpheum."[59]

Unfortunately, it may be seriously doubted whether very much is achieved by these and the numerous other textual references to the Virgilian myth. The analogy between the Ormus-Vina and Orpheus-Eurydice pairs proves, on closer inspection, to be at best rather forced, and at worst downright vague. Ormus is, certainly, a celebrated musician like Orpheus, but Vina too is a musician—a role which Eurydice is not known to have filled. Vina's earthquake death, however spectacular, scarcely resembles Eurydice's: on her last night in Mexico, she dreams, it is true, of a serpent, but it is the god Quetzalcoatl, "the plumed serpent,"[60] and Raúl Páramo, the ephemeral partner with whom she spends that night, is no Aristaeus-like unwanted admirer, as the relationship, if superficial, is clearly consensual ("she had surrendered herself to this nobody ... had selected him more or less at random from the backstage throng"[61]), and her intimacy with Ormus is by then over. Ormus, does, for a long time after Vina's decease, do his utmost to deny it, but his refusal to accept reality comes over as a near-pathological delusion, not a hero's endeavour to reverse nature's law ("they could see how hard he was trying to get there, maybe some world through a gash in the air, some variant dimension where Vina was still alive"[62]). His denial of death takes on, with this notion of a "variant dimension," a science-fictional aspect which, strangely, has Rushdie returning to the somewhat dubious experimental mode of *Grimus* ("The pain is caused by one's first experience of the Outer Dimensions. Suddenly universe dissolves, and for a fraction of time you are simply a small bundle of energy adrift in a sea of unimaginably vast forces"[63]). The reader will, however, search in vain for an episode that might approximate to Orpheus' descent into hell and his attempt to undo his consort's death; Ormus heals his wounds with generalised denials, searching for substitute Vinas, and bringing fake Vinas on stage. Finally, the Indian star meets his end, not from a group of frustrated would-be admirers, but a single demented fan, "a tall dark-skinned woman with red hair gathered above her head like a fountain"[64]: this could perhaps be a solitary Maenad, but the violent death and the assassin's gender still provide only a sketchy and incomplete parallel with the fate of the Thracian bard.

All in all, if Ormus does in any substantive sense resemble Orpheus, it can only be insofar as the text presents him as the artist-initiate, nourishing his creativity at the fount of dark, mysterious forces—a daemonic element which comes to the fore in the paranormal communication which the patient reader is asked to believe Ormus maintains with his dead twin Gayomart, the alleged ghostly inspirer of some of the most celebrated Anglo-American songs of the 60s. This "Gayomart conceit," which will be looked at in detail below, will itself prove to be far from unproblematic; the alert reader has no choice but to ask whether Rushdie's much-vaunted "rewriting" of the Orpheus myth is in reality little more than a forced, arbitrary and far-fetched set of doubtful part-analogies.

6

If the Ormus-Vina musical couple ostensibly derive part of their energy from the Orpheus-Eurydice dyad, the story does not end there: other analogies, far more recent, also populate the narrative. Those addicted to the *roman a clef* school of criticism have, predictably, had a field day trying to trainspot which Anglophone rock stars Ormus and Vina might be modelled on. In so dense and allusive a text, both can only be composite figures, not fictionalisations of singer X or Y;

nonetheless, a brief consideration of possible models does have its interest, as it may help understanding of the precise nature of the cultural hybridation that Rushdie appears to be propounding in this novel.

For a start, neither is modelled on an Indian singer: I shall return to this point below, in the discussion of "world music," but it may be stressed here that only one rock artist of (ultimately) South Asian origin has ever achieved international stardom, and that was the late Freddie Mercury, the lead singer of Queen, who is mentioned in the novel[65] but whose music Rushdie has explicitly said he detests.[66] Mercury was, in fact, born Farrokh Bulsara in Zanzibar in 1946, to parents who were British subjects but had their roots in Bombay's Zoroastrian community, and spent most of his childhood in Bombay before moving to Britain in 1963: this circumstance may, despite Rushdie's views on Queen's music, have provided a hint for the Ormus idea. Reviewers have tended to see Ormus as a cross between Presley (a raw talent manipulated by the rock business), Lennon (threatened with expulsion from the US; murdered by a psychopath) and Dylan (poet laureate of modern music).[67] Those three giants of twentieth-century song clearly are all there behind Ormus, and I shall examine the particularly important Dylan connection in some detail in the next section.

The case of Vina is actually more problematic: the genius and originality of Presley, Lennon and Dylan is beyond doubt, but Rushdie's fictional diva seems only to have been compared by the reviewers to certain women artists of undoubted commercial projection but zero musical value, whose names are not even worth mentioning. There is repeated stress across the text on the extraordinary quality of Vina's voice ("she was a great river, which could bear us all away"[68]), and it may seem best to conclude that she stands for a female creative principle which has never quite manifested itself in rock music in the shape of a truly talented woman singer as world-famous as Lennon or Presley. Possible models do exist, in the shape of US women singers who have had such a voice: two candidates might be the late Laura Nyro, of Italian-

American origin, and the Mexican-American Linda Ronstadt—both remarkably gifted vocalists in full control of their material, and both hyphenated Americans like Vina, but neither of whose trajectories especially resembles hers. Rushdie himself, in the *Salon* interview,[69] half-suggests Grace Slick, the full-throated lead singer of the 60s group Jefferson Airplane, but again the analogy is not close. A more intriguing possibility surfaces at the beginning of the novel, when, just before the fatal earthquake, the reader learns for the first time of "that celestial voice of hers, that multiple-octave, Yma Sumac stairway to heaven of an instrument."[70] Yma Sumac was a Peruvian singer who claimed to be a lineally-descended Inca princess and achieved major US and international success in the 50s; as a curious intertextual aside, it may be noted that one of her songs bore the title "Earthquake,"[71] while one critic of the time wrote of her four-octave voice: "There is no voice like it in the world today [...] It soars into the acoustic stratosphere, or it plumbs sub-contralto depths of pitch with equal ease."[72] This connection, if developed, could have helped make Vina-the-voice something less of an all-American phenomenon, but, regrettably, Rushdie's text does not—as will be shown below—develop this "world music" dimension to its full potential. For the most part, his Ormus and Vina are stuck firmly within the Anglo-American rock-music mainstream.

7

One key influence on the figure of Ormus remains to be considered, which leads the reader into areas other than rock'n'roll pure and simple, and that is the question of Rushdie's singer-songwriter's resemblances to Bob Dylan. The Jewish-American Dylan (born Robert Allen Zimmerman in 1941, into a family which had left Odessa—then in Russia, now in Ukraine—in 1875) is, beyond doubt, both the most celebrated and the most talented example of the modern singer-songwriter. Dylan's work eludes the category of songwriting pure and simple, to trespass boldly on the terrain of literature: his close associates have included not just fellow popular musicians but writers like Allen Ginsberg and Sam

Shepard, his song texts have been subjected to sustained and detailed literary analysis,[73] and he is the only practitioner of the singer-songwriter genre to have been proposed (in 1997, 1998 and 1999) for the Nobel Prize for Literature—a distinction which, indeed, he shares with Salman Rushdie.

Dylan's presence in *GF* is undeniable: Rushdie explains in the *Salon* interview that he wanted to honour rock'n'roll with its "best-case portrait: Bob Dylan," adding:

> Dylan is very important to me because I think along with Paul Simon he is probably the greatest songwriter [...] other than Lennon and McCartney [...] of the last many decades. I remember first hearing early Dylan when I was still at boarding school in England and being astonished. I'd never heard anyone write like that in a song, this fantastically impressionistic but also savage writing, which was completely complemented by his phrasing and his voice.[74]

Dylan is certainly one of the models behind Ormus: in the *Le Monde* interview, to his interlocutor's assertion that "the character of Ormus borrows a lot from Dylan," Rushdie replies: "If you want to invent a rock God, there are only a limited number of models!"[75] Indeed, several references to Dylan appear in Rushdie's earlier work; the songwriter's influence on the novelist has been pointed out in a critical study, the French-language volume *Salman Rushdie* (1996) by Marc Porée and Alexis Massery.[76] In *The Jaguar Smile*, Rushdie's documentary record of his visit to Nicaragua in 1986, he tells how an acquaintance informs him he has visited Mobile, Alabama—upon which, confesses Rushdie, "Dylan started to sing 'Stuck inside of Mobile' in my head."[77] Dylan reappears in the 1990 essay on Thomas Pynchon (mentioned earlier with reference to Paul Simon), which contains a direct quotation of the songwriter's celebrated line from 1963: "The answer is blowin' in the wind."[78] Most intriguingly, in no less a novel than *SV*, Saladin Chamcha attends an event at the Brickhall Friends Meeting House, London, at which "a pretty young British Asian woman with a slightly-too-bulbous nose and a dirty, bluesy voice was launching into Bob Dylan's song, I Pity the Poor Immigrant."[79]

Given these antecedents, it is neither surprising nor fortuitous that the text of Rushdie's rock'n'roll novel should, on close examination, yield up a whole rich vein of Dylan references, analogies and quotations. Dylan's name appears in *GF* all of three times, all in the book's American section; in the most significant of these, Ormus' ever-more spectacular shows are described as precursors of "the whole multiple-image videorama which is now the staple fare of stadium rock but in those days gave people the kind of shock Bob Dylan did when he went electric" (this is a historically correct allusion to Dylan's electric performance at the Newport Folk Festival in 1965, which famously offended the folk purists).[80] In addition, the text of *GF* reveals a good sixteen Dylan quotations/allusions, culled from eleven different songs. By no means all are openly sourced by Rushdie/Rai, but they give Dylan, all in all, a denser and more copious textual presence in this novel than any other songwriter can claim. The first, implicit allusion comes as early as the earthquake episode: "It [the town] had acquired the quality of brokenness, had become kin to the great family of the broken: broken plates, broken dolls, broken English, broken promises, broken hearts";[81] here, Rushdie is echoing Dylan's "Everything is Broken," from 1989: "Broken bottles, broken plates, broken switches, broken gates/Broken dishes, broken parts, streets are filled with broken hearts." The 1965 song "Mr Tambourine Man" supplies a quintessentially sixties reference when, in the heady incense-and-patchouli atmosphere of Antoinette Corinth's London boutique, we are told that the owner is, in true psychedelic fashion, "disappearing down the smoke rings of her mind" (Dylan's line is "take me disappearing through the smoke rings of my mind");[82] while Rai posthumously names Vina "Death-Vina, the sad-eyed lady of the broken lands,"[83] in a clear reference to "Sad-Eyed Lady of the Lowlands," Dylan's epic song of 1966.

Further Dylan song-references are scattered all across the novel.[84] However, the most significant of these allusions—if not the most conceptually successful—are those to "Blowin' in the Wind" (1963), no doubt the Dylan composition best known to the general public. This song's title phrase—cited earlier, as we have seen, in the 1990 Pynchon essay—crops up three times in Rushdie's text,[85] but the most venturesome instance is in the bizarre "Gayomart episode." This, as already noted, is built around the notion that, in and around 1960, a whole series of what were to become major hit songs of the 60s in the West were "really" (!!) composed in Bombay by Ormus Cama, acting on the supernatural promptings of his dead twin Gayomart. These "songs from the future," the reader is impudently informed, included "Blowin' in the Wind":

> At first Ormus played only the songs he had half learned from Gayomart in his dreams, singing those strange vowel sequences of his that made no sense to anyone, or fitting nonsensical words to them that utterly undermined the mysterious authority of the dream-music [...]. "The dancer is glowing with her sin. The gardener is mowing with a grin [...]," [...] one thousand and one nights later, "Blowin' in the Wind " hit the airwaves in its authentic version [...] and whenever one of Gayomart Cama's melodies burst through from the world of dreams into the real world, those of us who had heard them for the first time in garbled form in a Bombay villa on the old Cuffe Parade were forced to concede the reality of Ormus' magic gift.[86]

This conceit of Rushdie's must be considered as, at best, problematic. It may seem, on the face of it, a liberating gesture to create a reshaped world in which a song like "Blowin' in the Wind" had origins that were not just Orphic, rising up from the depths of the "world of dreams," but Asian too—as if, through the workings of a "magic gift," Indian culture could stake out a claim of authorship in the new global popular culture that came into being in the West in the 60s. However, there is the small question to be considered of the real origins of Dylan's song. The fact is that Dylan based "Blowin' in the Wind" on a nineteenth-century song called "No More Auction Block," in which a fugitive slave who has escaped to Canada celebrates his new-found freedom; in 1978, he told a journalist: "I took it off a song called 'No More Auction Block'—that's a spiritual, and 'Blowin' in the Wind' has the same feeling."[87] There was, then, already a verified historical input into Dylan's song from a non-WASP source; given which, why did Rushdie feel the need to give it a contrived and fantastical origin in Bombay? The reader is entitled to ask whether the "Gayomart conceit," applied to this and other 60s songs, actually has, in its sheer arbitrariness, the effect of trivialising those songs, instead of underscoring their claims to universal significance.

Beyond the specific textual allusions, the reader is invited to see Ormus the songwriter as some kind of fictional Dylan. His career exhibits certain resemblances to Dylan's: Rushdie's star is removed from public view in 1967 by a near-fatal car crash[88] which recalls Dylan's motorcycle accident of 1966; and, later, he takes obsessively to non-stop touring ("For most of 1994 and 1995 he lived exclusively in the world of the tour [...] Rio, Sydney, London, Hong Kong, Los Angeles, Beijing"[89]), mirroring the "Never Ending Tour" that has occupied a large part of Dylan's energies almost constantly from 1987 to the present. As for Ormus' lyrics, their "perceived anti-establishment contents" are, we are told, expressed through a throng of chaotic images: "street entertainers, card-players, pickpockets, wizards, devils, union men, evil priests, fisherwomen, wrestlers, harlequins, vagabonds, chameleons, whores, eclipses, motorbikes and cheap dark rum."[90] For Rai, "Ormus Cama was the greatest popular singer of all, the one whose genius exceeded all others [...] a golden troubadour the jouncy poetry of whose lyrics could unlock the very gates of Hell; he incarnated the singer and songwriter as shaman and spokesman."[91]

All this seems reasonably close to Dylan, at least to certain phases or facets of his career (the anti-establishment position, the troubadour-shaman-spokesman role); Ormus' images and characters, too, resemble their counterparts in the real Dylan songbook. Dylan's work of 1965-1966, notably, offers evil ecclesiastics (the "jealous monk" of "Desolation Row"), vagabonds ("It's All Over Now, Baby Blue"), fishtrucks ("Visions of Johanna"), sex industry workers ("Just Like Tom Thumb's Blues"), an eclipse ("It's Alright, Ma [I'm Only Bleeding]"), a "motorcycle black madonna two-wheeled gipsy queen" ("Gates of Eden"), and even a bottle of "Jamaican rum" ("4th

Time Around"). Ormus might thus appear to have a goodly part of Dylan in him.

An unfortunate problem occurs, however, when Rushdie's text shifts from the evocation of Ormus' lyrics to their (fictional) reproduction. It is difficult to see how these productions, as given, could possibly be thought to come up to the exacting standards of modern poetic song laid down by Dylan. Two examples of Ormus' alleged compositional gifts, as "quoted" in the text, should suffice: "The earth begins to rock and roll, its music dooms your mortal soul, and there's nothing baby nothing you can do;"[92] and again: "Now I know she's kinda crazy and a little too much, but I'm hopin' for the strokin' of her lovin' touch, and I'm really not insistin,' but if we were tongue twistin,' what a twistin' good time it'd be."[93] Against these specimens, it should be enough to quote two examples of Dylan's songwriting, without further qualitative comment: "When you wake up in the mornin,' baby, look inside your mirror/You know I won't be next to you, you know I won't be near/I'd just be curious to know if you can see yourself as clear/As someone who has had you on his mind" ("Mama, You Been On My Mind," 1964); and: "Footprints runnin' 'cross the silver sand/Steps goin' down into tattoo land/I met the sons of darkness and the sons of light/In the bordertowns of despair" ("Dignity," 1994). The reader may justifiably ask whether Rushdie himself really thinks there is any particular merit in Ormus Cama's lyrics, or whether their "reproduction" is, to quote Dylan's words from "Desolation Row," "some kind of joke" [...].

8

Whether or not Ormus and Vina come up to the musical standards of their real Western counterparts, a further question has to be asked concerning Rushdie's claim to have subversively rewritten rock history by inventing two Indian megastars: what, in fact, is Indian about these two—apart from their origins? What, if any, are the specifically Indian elements behind these twain's meteoric careers? The reader will search in vain for any but the most superficial references to any subcontinental musical tradition, be it erudite, folkloric or popular. In *SV*, Rushdie did include a stray mention of the "hindi-pop" scene in London;[94] this is probably a reference to British bhangra (an urbanised version of traditional Punjabi dance music), or to the then-budding "techno-Asian" school—but if Rushdie, as he may do, knows anything about either genre, *GF* finds him keeping that musical knowledge remarkably close to his chest. In recent years in both Britain and the US, fusions of Indian and Western genres have produced interesting and listenable new popular-music hybrids, in the work of artists such as London's Talvin Singh[95] and Sheila Chandra,[96] or the Gujarat-born, California-resident female vocalist Shweta Jhaveri;[97] such musical hybridation might seem in tune with Rushdie's own oft-declared belief in cultural mixity and miscegenation,[98] but there is precious little evidence of any such synthesis in VTO's arch-Western music.

Vina Apsara's professional name, it is true, designates a South Indian instrument (vina) and a mythical female dancer (apsara); but in the music of VTO's heyday any Asian musical influences are minimal. Ravi Shankar gets a brief, rather superficial allusion, when Ormus names him to an ignorant Briton as an example of a famous Indian;[99] but the great Shankar, friend of the Beatles and Yehudi Menuhin, is, as he never ceases to remind the Western press,[100] an Indian classical musician who would not qualify as a direct influence on exponents of more demotic genres. Early on, we are told of Vina: "The music of India, from northern sitar ragas to southern Carnatic melodies, always created in her a mood of inexpressible longing. She could listen to recordings of ghazals for hours at a stretch, and was entranced, too, by the complex devotional music of the leading qawwals."[101] There is, alas, no input into VTO's music from these early influences. They remain promising hints that are never developed: the ghazal and qawwali genres both straddle the subcontinental classical/popular divide, raising possibilities of ground-breaking hybrids and crossovers, and the most famous qawwal of modern times, Pakistan's Nusrat Fateh Ali Khan, actually worked with the British rock musician Peter Gabriel on recordings that fuse devotional tradition with state-of-the-art technology. Jamila Singer from *MC*[102] might have had a word to say here, too, but unfortunately in *GF* Rushdie seems to have forgotten her legacy. Ormus, very late in his career and after Vina's death, does at last begin to integrate something of his origins into his music, evolving towards a "techno-Asian" style: "the tabla rhythms and sitar and yes vina riffs pushed through his sequencers along with pure synthesised sound";[103] but this mutation is little more than a hint, coming so close to the end. VTO's music, and, therefore, the greater part of both Vina's and Ormus' musical production is, from the textual descriptions and the sources and analogies named, clearly a textbook case of mainstream Anglo-American 60s/70s stadium rock, bereft of any "Asian" input other than the two stars' national origins and the piece of trickery that is the "Gayomart conceit."

9

Vina, nonetheless, in the final, solo, stage of her career, does develop artistically, away from mainstream rock and towards something more resembling "world music." Again, though, Rushdie's treatment of a potentially interesting theme proves disappointingly superficial. The term "world music," in the sense that emerged in the late 80s and 90s, deserves some elucidation here. "World music" may be approximately defined as either: traditional-based music from anywhere in the world that makes use of modern recording technology, distribution systems, etc., rather than remaining "ethnic" in a purist sense; or: a fusion of traditional-based musical idioms from more than one culture. Philip Sweeney, compiler of the *Virgin Directory of World Music,* defines the term as "world popular and roots music from outside the Anglo-American mainstream";[104] Ian Anderson, editor of *Folk Roots,* the British magazine that has done much to promote the concept, speaks of a form of crosscultural musical dialogue that "has greatly helped international understanding and provoked cultural exchanges."[105] Outstanding exponents of "world music" in the first sense include Khaled, an Algerian singer based in Paris who performs in both Arabic and French,[106] and Senegal's Youssou N'Dour, who has been described as "Africa's most successful musician [...] thanks to [whom] Senegal is becoming more [...] Senegalese,"[107] and has said that "if a Senegalese musician played a synthesiser or an electric guitar, it became a Senegalese instrument."[108] In the second sense, among the best-known examples are Paul Simon's *Graceland* album of 1986, made largely in collaboration with South African musicians; and the Buena Vista Social Club project, which has engendered a CD (1997) that has sold over two million on the global market, as well as a critically-acclaimed film by Wim Wenders (1999), and involves the Californian guitarist Ry Cooder and an agglomeration of superb Cuban musicians, some of them septuagenarian or even nonagenarian, whom Cooder's musicological researches helped re-emerge from obscurity.[109] Essentially, the notion of "world music" entails an openness to musical dialogue and cooperation on a footing of cultural equality, whether the collaborators are all from third-world or "exotic" backgrounds or, as in the Buena Vista case, hail from both sides of the first/third world divide.

The world music phenomenon is a viable contemporary alternative to the commercial excesses of today's mass-consumption Anglo-American music, and Rushdie certainly seems to be aware of its existence. His familiarity with Simon's *Graceland* is clear, since he has, as already noted, quoted elsewhere from one of that album's songs. Rai-the-narrator himself notes that one of the possible meanings of his own name is—Algerian rai music, the genre of which Khaled is the best-known exponent: "And in another part of the world, Rai was music. In the home of this music, alas, religious fanatics have lately started killing the musicians. They think the music is an insult to god, who gave us voices but does not wish us to sing, who gave us free will, rai, but prefers us not to be free."[110] A rai star, Cheb Hasni, was, indeed, assassinated by fundamentalists in Oran, birthplace of the genre, in September 1994;[111] and the word rai, associated by Rushdie with free will, derives, according to the music critic Ken Hunt, from the Arabic for "opinion."[112] These narratorial insights, of course, approximate the risks facing Algerian performers to Rushdie's own predicament, but, alas, no more is made of the possible connections by either Rai or Rushdie. Nor can it possibly be said of the novel's Indian stars that they send western listeners back to Indian music, as has happened in reality with Buena Vista Social Club and Cuban music (as Ibrahim Ferrer, one of the Buena Vista artists, has rather bemusedly declared: "There is all this music in America and Europe and they come to Cuba for our sound"[113]). The VTO stars' musical trajectory, from Bombay to New York, is, surely, quite the reverse.

Both Ormus and Vina do, admittedly, push their later careers somewhat away from mainstream American rock and more in a world-music direction. One of the later incarnations of VTO is characterised by "un-American sounds" added by Ormus: "Cuban horns," "Brazilian drums," "Chilean woodwinds," "African male choruses," and even "the holy passion of the Pakistani qawwals." The very excess of this hyper-eclectic pot-pourri, however, suggests less a tribute to world music than a superficial travesty of it, while the Ormus/Vina vocal combination clearly remains as American as ever: "more Righteous than the Righteous Brothers, Everlier than the Everlys, Supremer than the Supremes."[114] After VTO finally split, Vina, in 1988, tours Latin America, showcasing self-penned songs with a new backing band ("her three demented Brazilian percussionists and her pair of duelling Argentine guitarists who threatened to end each performance with a knife fight").[115] Here too, the concession to world music does not go beyond the superficial, either on Vina's part (the old VTO hits are still at the heart of her repertoire) or, indeed, Rushdie's: there is no reason why the intentness of Brazilian percussion, with its roots in African ritual, should be dismissed as "demented," while the conceit of "duelling guitarists" (based on a pun on "duel" in the twin senses of musical and physical combat) merely replicates a stereotype of Argentine violence which, if acceptable in a Buenos-Aires born writer like Borges, from Rushdie's pen seems a tired, second-hand cliché. The conclusion seems inevitable that Rushdie has missed a golden opportunity, fluffing the challenge of a sustained literary engagement with the world music phenomenon. We could have had an Indian Buena Vista Social Club; what we get is VTO, playing born-in-the-USA rock'n'roll while laying claim to an Asian "authenticity" that derives from literary sleight-of-hand alone.

10

The critical response to Rushdie's rock-generation odyssey has been mixed. As a novelist (and not just a *cause célèbre*), its author has, among people who read books, a formidable reputation to live up to. Anita Desai, looking back on *MC* in 1995, declared: "It was a very ambitious and bold book. And [...] it led to a whole generation of young writers and gave them the confidence they might not have had otherwise. He can be said to have set free the tongues of the younger writers—a tremendous influence upon their work."[116] Of *SV*, considered as a novel, the Franco-Algerian political scientist Sami Naïr wrote in 1989: "The interpretation of *The Satanic Verses* could be multiplied indefinitely: but this novel is so rich that no such reading could exhaust its meaning [...] This is the birth of a great—of a very great writer."[117]

By no means all reviewers found *GF* up to the standard of Rushdie's earlier fictional production. A representative sample of reviews from various countries suggests an approximately equal three-way breakdown between the eulogistic, the ambivalent and the disappointed or downright hostile. In the first category, Hermione Lee, in the London *Observer*, praised *GF* as "a very exciting novel, hugely ambitious and original," full of "true Rushdiean boldness"—a book "about the making and the meaning of myths," in which "the Orpheus and Eurydice myth gets turned around and upside down";[118] while *Newsweek*'s Carla Power lauded it as "a book about the way we live now," remarkable for its "mythic scope, epic stretch and huge intelligence."[119] In France, *Le Monde*'s reviewer, Raphaëlle Rérolle, read Rushdie's tale as celebrating "the force of dream and imagination" and affirming "music and its power" against "the violence of those who oppose it";[120] conversely, in *Libération* Antoine de Gaudemar found it a "metaphoric and finally pessimistic novel," an indictment of our times in which the musical protagonists are "unreal beings, abstract icons, toys in the hands of a ruthless system and a fiercely volatile public opinion."[121]

A more ambivalent note was struck by the *Economist*, whose reviewer noted the "familiar mix of magical realism, dazzling verbal display, self-conscious fictionality, and allusion," but found the novel rather amorphous: "Designed to mimic the theme of cultural overload in its construction, its narrative shape is on the verge of constant collapse."[122] Similarly, *Time*'s reviewer, Paul Gray, while praising the "energy, intelligence and allusiveness" of Rushdie's writing, concluded that "the parts of this novel seem greater than the whole."[123] Perhaps most tellingly, in *La Quinzaine Littéraire* Marc Porée (co-author, as noted above, of a substantial critical study of Rushdie),[124] found *GF* vitiated by a culpable dose of superficiality, deriving from an excessive fixation on the cult of celebrity ("Has he really striven to de-sacralise Islam [...] only to end up legitimating a latter-day version of the sacred?"), and drew attention to the un-Indianness of Ormus and Vina as musicians: "The idea of having Indian rockers as the main characters succeeds only imperfectly [...] the aficionado inevitably imagines these characters in the skin and the features of stars from the English-speaking world," before nonetheless concluding that the book "may be redeemed if we recognise its extreme darkness, the darkness of a world living on the edge."

Adverse views of Rushdie's novel included one from Italy and two from his native South Asian world. The novelist and critic Silvia Albertazzi, in her review in the Italian magazine *Pulp*, found *GF* markedly inferior to its author's earlier work, simultaneously over-superficial and over-complex: Rushdie, she complained, has "chosen to break with the methods of the Indian oral tradition—stories grafted on to one another, Chinese box-like, spiralling, to be swallowed all together—in favour of a more linear narrative," while "the novel gets tangled up in its own excess of stimuli, metaphors and sets of symbols, losing, above all, its sense of the link with history—hitherto one of the strongest points of Rushdie's narrative." The same critic concluded that nothing in the text justifies the alleged genius of Ormus and Vina, adding the judgment that "Ormus' song texts are of an exasperating banality beneath their rhetoric."[125] C.J. Wallia, writing on the *India Star* website, dismissed the book as a "muddled melodramatic novel," objecting to its "repeated inflictions of mindboggling mythological references" and "long pontifical soliloquies on death and art";[126] while the novelist Pankaj Mishra, in a violent critique first published in the Delhi magazine *Outlook*, accused Rushdie of producing a novel replete with "cartoon-like simplicities," "empty bombast," "pseudo-characters" and "non-events," which is not a critique but a symptom of the processes at work in today's world—and of using "secular radicalism" as a pretext for an uncritical and politically suspect eulogy of "American pop culture."[127]

From the reviews quoted, whatever their evaluation of Rushdie's novel, there emerges a consensus that one of its key themes is the economic and cultural process that has come to be known as globalisation. The critics also recognise that Rushdie's narrative and stylistic strategies—the use of mythology, the East-to-West sweep of the tale, the multi-layered allusiveness—represent an attempt, successful or otherwise, to create a fiction that will adequately reflect that process of globalisation and offer the reader certain possible responses to it. None of the critics cited has, however, looked in detail—as I have tried to do in this study—at those elements in the book (the non-use of the Orpheus myth, the failure to engage creatively with "world music") which fail to satisfy in this respect, and thus cast doubt on the validity and usefulness of Rushdie's social critique; and only Porée has drawn attention to the un-Indian nature of the novel's music, surely one of its most unsatisfactory paradoxes. Nonetheless, the strictures which Wallia and Mishra lay at the door of Rushdie's actual writing in this novel seem less justified than the more substantive faults identified: the allusive density of the text shows beyond doubt that Rushdie has put an enormous amount of work into this novel, and has enriched it at the textual level with a wealth of ideas and information accumulated from his enormously wide reading and his own very specific interaction with history. Whether all this knowledge and effort has given birth to a genuinely useful fable for our times is another matter.

11

Globalisation is a knife that cuts both ways—threatening universal, US-dominated standardisation and the annihilation of cultural diversity, yet also opening up, through the Internet and its limitless resources, unprecedented possibilities of expression, communication and solidarity. The question is whether Rushdie's novel offers an adequate fictional representation of this dynamic contradiction. Certainly, his characters inhabit a world in continual flux, subject to endless shocks and mutations—as symbolised by the earthquake metaphor, and as self-consciously and repeatedly registered in the text: "if the world itself were metamorphosing unpredictably, then nothing could be relied upon any more";[128] "Instability, the modern condition, no longer frightens them; it now feels like possibility."[129] The reader may ask, however, whether Rushdie's Asian protagonists do not end up as largely passive victims of US mass culture—a victimhood disguised only rhetorically, by the box-of-tricks strategy of the "Gayomart conceit." Large parts of the book's second half seem merely to replicate the hollowness of the one-dimensional creations of the entertainment industry, the self-validating procession of surfaces which Rushdie's text itself, in a metalingual flourish of doubtful profundity, calls "that zone of celebrity in which everything except celebrity ceases to signify."[130] It is also disappointing to find the East-West relationship embodied in this novel's narrative structure in such a linear fashion. Instead of East and West alternating, what we get is East in the first half, replaced by West in the second. As far as "Indo-Anglian" writing is concerned, the true continuators of the complex "East-West" narrative structure which Rushdie superbly deployed in *SV* would appear to be not Rushdie's own later novels, but such works as Vikram Chandra's *Red Earth and Pouring Rain* (1995)[131] and Amitav Ghosh's *The Calcutta Chromosome* (1996)—both novels in which a dense, intricate narrative, snaking back and forth in time and place, reflects an awareness of world history and culture in their sheer density which is, sadly, lacking in *GF*.

In 1994, Rushdie closed the final story of *East, West* with a proud declaration of neutrality between East and West—a pregnant manifesto of neither-norness and both-andness, of hybridity and cultural miscegenation:

> I, too, have ropes around my neck, I have them to this day, pulling me this way and that, East and West, the nooses tightening, commanding, choose, choose [...] Ropes, I do not choose between you. Lassoes, lariats, I choose neither of you, and both. Do you hear? I refuse to choose.[132]

Five years later, he chooses to conclude *GF* with the vignette of a New York child:

> Tara's got hold of the zapper. I've never got used to having the tv on at breakfast, but this is an American kid, she's unstoppable. And today, by some fluke, wherever she travels in the cable multiverse she comes up with Ormus and Vina [...] they're just going to go on singing.[133]

Whether this peroration marks Rushdie's final choice of "West"—not just over "East," but, perhaps more significantly, over his earlier, challenging choice of cultural hybridation—whether closing this novel with a child's ersatz journey into the "cable multiverse" means that our novelist has lost the plot, has finally given in to the seductions of transatlantic mass culture—whether the literal death of the author threatened by the fatwa has led to the spiritual death of the author we once knew: all these are enigmas to which only the future, and Rushdie's own future writing, can provide an answer.

Rushdie's sea of stories has certainly not dried up, but it does seem to have become a trifle shallow. My prediction is that *GF* will live less as a rock'n'roll epic than as pure text—in the mercurial play of the words on the page, in the allusive density and resourcefulness of Salman Rushdie's protean, spell-weaving, still-alert writing. It is, however, an open question whether a fiction that relies so heavily for its impact on textual scintillation can, ultimately, allow either writer or reader to gain a full, intelligent grasp on the dynamic and dangerous complexities of today's ever-shifting, globalised cultural universe.

Notes and references

1. Salman Rushdie, *The Ground Beneath Her Feet* (London: Jonathan Cape, 1999). Hereinafter referred to as *GF*.
2. Salman Rushdie, interview with Bruno Lesprit ("Salman Rushdie, enfant du rock"), *Le Monde* 1 Oct. 1999 (review section): VI.
3. Roland Barthes, "La mort de l'auteur" [1968], *Le bruissement de la langue: Essais Critiques IV* (Paris: Seuil [Collection Points], 1984).
4. Barthes 67.
5. Barthes 69.
6. Ayatollah Khomeini (quoted), Malise Ruthven, *A Satanic Affair: Salman Rushdie and the Rage of Islam* (London: Chatto & Windus, 1990) 112.
7. For Zhdanov, see George Steiner, "Marxism and the Literary Critic," *Language and Silence* (1967; Harmondsworth: Penguin, 1969).
8. For the campaign against *The Satanic Verses* in Britain, see Ruthven 4; Marc Porée and Alexis Massery, *Salman Rushdie* (Paris: Éditions du Seuil, 1996) 129-36.
9. Guy Astic, "Rushdie, écrivain laïc? " *La Règle du Jeu* 18 Jan. 1996: 60.
10. Salman Rushdie, interview with John Carlin ("El guardaespaldas de Rushdie"), *El País Semanal* 9 May 1999 <http://www.elpais.es>.
11. Rushdie, *GF* 404-407.
12. Rushdie, *GF* 555-57.
13. Salman Rushdie, *Midnight's Children* (1981; London: Picador, 1982) 9.
14. Salman Rushdie, *The Satanic Verses* (London: Viking, 1988) 546. Hereinafter referred to as *SV*.
15. Salman Rushdie, *The Moor's Last Sigh* (London: Jonathan Cape, 1995) 372.
16. Roshan G. Shahani, "Polyphonous Voices in the City: Bombay's Indian-English Fiction," *Bombay: Mosaic of Modern Culture,* ed. Sujata Patel and Alice Thorner (Bombay: Oxford UP, 1995) 104-05.
17. Shahani 110.
18. Rushdie, *GF* 60-61.
19. Salman Rushdie, interview with Laura Miller ("A touch of vulgarity"), *Salon* 16 April 1999 <http://www.salonmag.com/books/int/1999/04/16/rushdie/index.html>.
20. Shahani 112.
21. See Rushdie, *Le Monde* interview; Rushdie, interview with Antoine de Gaudemar ("Star Traque"), *Libération* 30 Sept. 1999: 48.
22. Carla Power, "Rock'n'Roll Rushdie," rev. of *GF, by Salman Rushdie, Newsweek* (international edition) 19 April 1999: 71.
23. Salman Rushdie, *Grimus* (1975; London: Paladin, 1989) 18-19.

24. Salman Rushdie, "Thomas Pynchon" (1990), *Imaginary Homelands: Essays and Criticism 1981-1991* (1991; London: Granta, 1992) 352. A second Paul Simon reference occurs in the same essay (353): "Paul Simon's girl in New York City who calls herself the Human Trampoline, bouncing into Graceland " (this is a paraphrase of lines from "Graceland," the title song of Simon's 1986 album of the same name).
25. Salman Rushdie, "The Courter," *East, West* (1994; London: Vintage, 1995) 196-97.
26. Rushdie, *Le Monde* interview: VI.
27. Rushdie, *Salon* interview.
28. Rushdie, *GF* 225.
29. Rushdie, *GF* 266.
30. Rushdie, *GF* 351.
31. Rushdie, *GF* 267.
32. Rushdie, *GF* 402.
33. See section 7 below.
34. Rushdie, *GF* 492.
35. Rushdie, *GF* 349.
36. Rushdie, *GF* 330-31.
37. Rushdie, *GF* 459.
38. Rushdie, *GF* 336.
39. Rushdie, *GF* 375.
40. Rushdie, *GF* 385.
41. William Shakespeare, *Henry VIII*, III-I, 3.
42. Virgil, *Georgics* [29 BC], trans. into English prose by H. P. Fairclough, Virgil, *Eclogues. Georgics. Aeneid 1-6* (Cambridge, Mass.: Harvard U.P [Loeb Classical Library], 1916; rev. ed. 1999); *Géorgiques*, trans. into French verse by Jacques Delille [1769], Virgil, *Bucoliques. Géorgiques*, ed. Florence Dupont (bilingual French/Latin edition) (Paris: Gallimard [Folio], 1997).
43. Ovid, *Metamorphoses* [8 AD], trans. into English prose by Mary M. Innes (Harmondsworth: Penguin, 1955) 225-27, 246-48.
44. Thomas Bulfinch, *The Age of Fable* [1855] (London: Dent [Everyman's Library], 1912; rpt. 1948) 190-99.
45. Robert Graves, *The Greek Myths* (1955; rev. ed., 2 vols., Harmondsworth: Penguin, 1960), vol. 1, 111-15; see also Simon Hornblower and Antony Spawforth, eds., *The Oxford Companion to Classical Civilization* (Oxford: OUP, 1998) 504-05.
46. Euripides, *Alcestis* [438 BC], trans. Philip Vellacott, *Alcestis/Hippolytus/Iphigenia in Tauris* (Harmondsworth: Penguin, 1953; new ed. 1974), lines 357-62.

47. Plato, *The Symposium* [c. 370 BC)], trans. as *The Banquet of Plato* by Percy Bysshe Shelley [1818], Shelley, *Selected Poetry, Prose and Letters* (London: Nonesuch Press, 1951) 821-80 (for Orpheus, see 831).
48. Euripides, lines 968-69.
49. Jacques Lacarrière, ed. and trans., *Orphée: Hymnes. Discours sacrés* (bilingual French/Greek edition) (Paris: Imprimerie nationale, 1995). Hymn 59 in this volume ("Aux Moires" / "To the Fates") concludes with the line: "Thus ends this ode to the Fates, composed by Orpheus."
50. Graves 111, 115.
51. Lacarrière, introduction 17, 18.
52. According to Florence Dupont in her 1997 preface, the second half of the fourth book of the *Georgics* originally consisted of a panegyric to the general Caius Cornelius Gallus. However, between Virgil's first and second editions, Gallus had committed suicide after falling out of favour with Augustus, and therefore, says Dupont, "Virgil did not hesitate to replace Gallus by Orpheus" (19). This version of the poem's history is, however, disputed by other modern scholars.
53. Dupont 7.
54. Rushdie, *El País* interview.
55. Rainer Maria Rilke, *Die Sonette an Orpheus* (1923); trans. by Charles Dobzynski as *Sonnets à Orphée* (bilingual French/German edition) (Paris: Éditions Messidor, 1989). The passage quoted in Rushdie's epigraph is from Sonnet V, in a translation by M. D. Herter Norton.
56. Rushdie, *GF* 21-22.
57. Rushdie, *GF* 498.
58. Rushdie, *GF* 561.
59. Rushdie, *GF* 413 and *passim.*
60. Rushdie, *GF* 3.
61. Rushdie, *GF* 4.
62. Rushdie, *GF* 560.
63. Rushdie, *Grimus* 244.
64. Rushdie, *GF* 569.
65. Rushdie, *GF* 517.
66. Salman Rushdie, interview with Philippe Manoeuvre ("Mes disques à moi"), *Rock & Folk* September 1999: 20.
67. For instance, John Carlin, in the *El País* interview, sees Ormus "as a composite of Elvis, Dylan and Lennon."
68. Rushdie, *GF* 124.
69. Rushdie, *Salon* interview.
70. Rushdie, *GF* 8.

71. Yma Sumac, "Tumpa (Earthquake)" (written by Moisés Vivanco); issued on *Voice of the Xtabay*, 1950; CD reissue, "The Right Stuff" (Hollywood, CA), 0777-7-91217-2-4, 1996.
72. Glenn Dillard Gunn, *Washington Times-Herald* 1950; quoted in liner notes, *Voice of the Xtabay.*
73. See, notably, the 918-page study by Michael Gray, *Song and Dance Man III: The Art of Bob Dylan* (London: Cassell, 2000). I have myself published at length on Dylan (from 1998 to the present), in essays collected at the *Bob Dylan Critical Corner*, <http://www.geocities.com/Athens/Oracle/6752/magazine.html>.
74. Rushdie, *Salon* interview.
75. Rushdie, *Le Monde* interview; for Rushdie on Dylan, see also the *Rock & Folk* interview.
76. See Porée and Massery 14-15, 115.
77. Salman Rushdie, *The Jaguar Smile: A Nicaraguan Journey* (London: Picador, 1987) 125.
78. Rushdie, "Thomas Pynchon," *Imaginary Homelands* 352.
79. Rushdie, *SV* 415. The reading of the song which Rushdie's text goes on to offer is rather dubious, but its discussion would take us outside the scope of this study; whether or not Dylan thought it an honour to have his name mentioned in *SV* is not recorded.
80. Rushdie, *GF* 425. The other Dylan references are: "Lennon, Dylan, Phil Ramone, Richards, these old men were still the giants along with VTO themselves" (435); and the invented benefit concert incident (402), as already quoted in section 4 above.
81. Rushdie, *GF* 17.
82. Rushdie, *GF* 286.
83. Rushdie, *GF* 491.
84. Further Dylan allusions in *GF* are to: "The Times They Are A-Changin'" (1964), 435; "With God On Our Side" (1964), 266 and 281; "She Belongs To Me" (1965), 269 and 500; "It's Alright, Ma (I'm Only Bleeding)" (1965), 239; "Like A Rolling Stone" (1965), 183 and 470—another song "attributed" to Gayomart!; "Lay Lady Lay" (1969), 322 and 500; and "Forever Young" (1974), 486. These, together with the four songs discussed in the text, make up eleven Dylan compositions echoed by Rushdie in this novel.
85. Rushdie, *GF* 274, 455.
86. Rushdie, *GF* 141.
87. Bob Dylan, quoted by John Bauldie, booklet notes, Dylan, *The Bootleg Series*, volumes 1-3 (3-CD set), Columbia, 1991, 6.
88. Rushdie, *GF* 307.
89. Rushdie, *GF* 558-59.

90. Rushdie, *GF* 395, 102.
91. Rushdie, *GF* 89.
92. The "rock and roll/mortal soul" rhyme is taken over from a real song, Don McLean's Dylan-influenced "American Pie" (a hit of 1971).
93. Rushdie, *GF* 390, 416.
94. Rushdie, *SV* 291.
95. See Talvin Singh, *OK*, Island/Omni CID 8075/524 559-2, 1998; Pete Lawrence, "Tabla tastemaker," *Folk Roots* (Jan./Feb. 1999) 22-29.
96. See Sheila Chandra, *Moonsung: A Real World Retrospective*, Real World CDR W77, 1999; Ruth Rosselson, "Return of the voice," *Folk Roots* (July 1999) 15-16.
97. See Shweta Jhaveri, *Anahita*, Intuition Music & Media INT 3509-2, 1998; Ken Hunt, "Khyal Creed," *Folk Roots* (June 1999): 34-35.
98. Rushdie speaks of cultural mixity and "métissage" in " L'entretien d'Arte," interview with Bernard-Henri Lévy, *La Règle Du Jeu* 13 May 1994: 28-29.
99. Rushdie, *GF* 284.
100. See, for instance, Eric Dahan, "Shankar, un grand classique" (interview with Ravi Shankar), *Libération* 6 July 1999: 30-31.
101. Rushdie, *GF* 122-23.
102. Cf. section 3 above.
103. Rushdie, *GF* 546.
104. Philip Sweeney, *Virgin Directory of World Music* (London: Virgin, 1991) ix.
105. Ian Anderson, "World Wars," *Folk Roots* (March 2000): 39.
106. For Khaled and the rai genre, see Tewfik Hakem, "L'inventaire Khaled-Mami," *World* (March/April 1998): 86-89; Ken Hunt, "Khaled Comfort," *Folk Roots* (Oct. 1999): 26-27, 41.
107. Lucy Duran, "The Xippi Trail [Youssou N'Dour]," *Folk Roots* (Nov. 1999): 20.
108. Anderson 39.
109. *Buena Vista Social Club*, collective CD produced by Ry Cooder, World Circuit/Nonesuch 79478-2, 1997; Wim Wenders, dir., *Buena Vista Social Club*, Road Movies, 1999; see Nigel Williamson, "The Bolero Boy [Ibrahim Ferrer]," *Folk Roots* (June 1999): 28-29, and "Ry comments [Ry Cooder]," *Folk Roots* (July 1999) 20-27; cf. for a US perspective, Tom Moon, "The Cuban Invasion," *Rolling Stone* 2 Sept. 1999: 29, 40.
110. Rushdie, *GF* 19.
111. See *World* (March/April 1998): 82.
112. See Hunt, "Khaled Comfort" 26. This etymology is confirmed by Sweeney, who explains how young Algerian singers "began to pepper their verses with the phrase 'Ha er-rai' or 'Ya rai,' meaning something like 'it's my opinion'" (9).

113. Ibrahim Ferrer (quoted), Williamson, "The Bolero Boy" 29.

114. Rushdie, *GF* 379.

115. Rushdie, *GF* 8.

116. Anita Desai, "A Sense of Detail and a Sense of Order: Anita Desai Interviewed by Lalita Pandit," Patrick Colm Hogan and Lalita Pandit, eds., *Literary India: Comparative Studies in Aesthetics, Colonialism and Culture* (Albany: State U of New York P, 1995) 163.

117. Sami Naïr, "Comment lire *Les Versets Sataniques*?," Esprit (October 1989); reprinted in the collective volume *Pour Rushdie: Cent intellectuels arabes et musulmans pour la liberté d'expression* (Paris: La Découverte/Carrefour des Littératures/Colibri, 1993) 235. This volume in fact consists not of the contributions of 100 authors, but of 99 essays and one musical score (by a Moroccan composer) by a total of 226 authors, as one item is a collective letter in support of Rushdie signed by 127 Iranian intellectuals.

118. Hermione Lee, rev. of *GF, Observer* (review section) 28 March 1999: 11.

119. Power 71.

120. Raphaëlle Rérolle, rev. of *GF, by Salman Rushdie, Le Monde* (review section) 1 Oct. 1999: VI.

121. Antoine de Gaudemar, "Rushdie, chaos tectonique," rev. of *GF, by Salman Rushdie, Libération* (review section) 30 Sept. 1999: VII.

122. "Boy's toys," rev. of *GF, by Salman Rushdie, Economist* 15 May 1999: 13.

123. Paul Gray, "Ganja Growing in the Tin," rev. of *GF, by Salman Rushdie, Time* 17 May 1999: 62.

124. Marc Porée, "Rushdiessime," *La Quinzaine Littéraire* 16-31 Oct. 1999: 5.

125. Silvia Albertazzi, "Salman Rushdie: *La terra sotto i suoi piedi*," rev. of *GF, by Salman Rushdie, Pulp* 20 (July-Aug. 1999): 29.

126. C. J. Wallia, rev. of *GF, by Salman Rushdie, India Star*, 1999 <http://www.indiastar.com/wallia20.html>.

127. Pankaj Mishra, "Anatomy of an Anti-Novel," rev. of *GF, by Salman Rushdie, Outlook* 9 April 1999, <http://www.wish.u-net.com/roy/pm_rushd.htm>.

128. Rushdie, *GF* 184.

129. Rushdie, *GF* 487.

130. Rushdie, *GF* 425.

131. On Chandra's novel, see Christopher Rollason, "Entwining Narratives: Intertextuality in Vikram Chandra's *Red Earth and Pouring Rain*," *Il Tolomeo* (Venice) IV (1998/1999): 108-13.

132. Rushdie, "The Courter," *East, West* 211.

133. Rushdie, *GF* 575.

7

"Searching for a Sense of Self": Postmodernist Theories of Identity and the Novels of Salman Rushdie

MICHAEL HENSEN
MIKE PETRY

Postmodernism and Identity

Although in one of the founding texts of postmodern cultural criticism Jean François Lyotard claims that a key constituent of postmodernism is an 'incredulity towards' all 'master-narratives'[1] postmodernism continues to tell itself grand narratives habitually. We may even say that a tolerance, or rather an indifference towards the plurality of meta-narratives is postmodernism's paradoxical ideology-the most significant of these grand tales being that about the existence of postmodernism itself.

A somewhat more credible of these great narratives concerns the history of self-identity in the West. Postmodernist histories of personal identity usually develop along these lines: in archaic cultures, writes Douglas Kellner, "the self was basically fixed, solid and stable. Identity was a function of predefined social roles and a traditional system of myths which provided orientation and religious sanctions to one's place in the world."[2] A conscious form of self-reflexiveness was, as Kellner has it, not existent in traditional societies: "individuals did not undergo identity crises, or radically modify their identity. One was a hunter and a member of the tribe and that was that."[3] However, besides Kellner's postmodernist, there is the post*structuralist* position, holding that it is precisely this notion of an earlier, less problematic, stable identity that has always been a myth-a cultural, linguistic construct of Western metaphysics.

The majority of critics writing about self-identity (and those not subscribing to the poststructuralist notion) believes that what we today understand as *self* has its origins in modernity, there being, however, a significant difference between the subject of modernity and that of postmodernity. Whilst the subject of modernity is generally referred to as relatively stable but 'alienated,' the postmodern subject is imagined as highly unstable and 'fragmented.'[4] So while in modernity "identity still comes from a circumscribed set of roles and norms,"[5] there is, in postmodernity, as Terry Eagleton says deliberately polemical, "no longer [even] any subject to be alienated and nothing to be alienated from, 'authenticity' [which both Eagleton (1988) and Jameson (1983) see as an important constituent of modernist aesthetics] having been less rejected than merely forgotten."[6]

But the contemporary subject is of course neither only stable, alienated or fragmented. Rather, it is a mixture of all such aspects. Still we may say that late-capitalist economics, new ways of communication and information, as well as postmodern social and cultural processes avert the subject's psychological and emotional unity and foster its fragmentation.

Postmodernism and Post-Colonialism

Having very briefly presented some key issues concerning postmodernist 'theoretical selfhood,' the question arises in how far a postmodern approach to Salman Rushdie's novels with respect to conceptions of identity is viable in the context of postcolonial literature. In the very special case of Rushdie, however, the supposed gap between postmodernism and post-colonialism is quite easily bridged: as Christoph Reinfandt has pointed out, Rushdie enjoys the status of "one of the cosmopolitan champions of Western postmodernism on the one hand" and, conflictual perhaps, "a Non-Western, postcolonial writer on the other hand."[7]

This is certainly not the place for an in-depth analysis of the compatibility of postmodernist and postcolonial theory.[8] In general, however, we can say that the discourses of post-colonialism and postmodernism need not necessarily be read as strictly opposed to each other. Bernd-Peter Lange is quite right when he makes out major mutual concerns in the two approaches, writing: "both deconstruct the great narratives of modern cultures in the West. While postmodern theory dismantles universalist models of signification, postcolonial theory rejects Euro-centric discourse."[9] Or as Linda Hutcheon says with direct reference to Rushdie in a chapter entitled 'Decentering the Postmodern' in her *A Poetics of Postmodernism*:

> Postmodernism does not move the marginal to the center. It does not invert the valuing of centers into that of peripheries and borders, as much as *use* that paradoxical doubled positioning to critique the inside from both the outside and the inside. Just as Padma, the listening, textualized female narratee of Rushdie's *Midnight's Children,* pushes the narration in directions its male narrator had no intention of taking, so the ex-centric have not only overlapped in some concerns with postmodernism, but also pushed it in new directions. Though I would insist that the ex-centrics' agendas only *partially overlap* and do not coincide with that of the postmodern, it still seems to me that the perspective of these inside-outsiders has added race, ethnicity, sexual orientation and gender to the class analysis of ideology of Althusserian Marxists.[10]

About the fiction that concerns us in this essay, we may generally say that "the location of Rushdie" is pretty much the same as that of Homi K. Bhabha, i.e., at the intersection of theories of the postmodern and the post-colonial. Actually, both the writer of fiction, Rushdie, and the foremost theoretician of *hybridity,* Bhabha, have successfully blended typical issues concerning migrant-identities and cultural diversity with poststructuralist and postmodernist theory. In their respective works, both have pointed to a concept beyond the postmodern and its fragmentation of the personal and the social. This is a concept of fruitful in-betweenness—a powerful "third space" between one's own and an *Other*'s culture, a space that acknowledges a certain "*incommensurability* between cultures."[11] It is, furthermore, a concept that at least tries to use the paradigms of poststructuralist and postmodernist discourses for more satisfactory ends. Thus Bhabha says, for instance, that, "the fragmentation of identity is often celebrated as a kind of pure anarchic liberalism or voluntarism, but I prefer to see it as a recognition of *the importance of the alienation of the self in the construction of forms of solidarity.*"[12] And with respect to Rushdie, Reinfandt has argued that, "the emergence of a *positive concept of cultural hybridity* is one of the most prominent features of Rushdie's *œuvre.*[13] Bhabha, again, has said: "I try to place myself in that position of liminality, in *that productive space of the construction of culture as difference,* in the spirit of alterity or otherness."[14]

It is, in fact, precisely this kind of *productive difference* that links thinkers such as Bhabha, Derrida, Charles Jencks and Paolo Porthoghesi (and thus postcolonial, poststructuralist and postmodernist discourses). Productive difference, however, is also what propels the writings of Salman Rushdie-and what informs his portrayals of our searching for a sense of self.

Identity in the Novels of Salman Rushdie

The foremost question in the present context is of course: how do postmodern theories of subjectivity re-connect to the novels of Salman Rushdie? We shall try to answer this question with the help of three separate, though inter-connected categories: *fragmentation, mutability* and *identity versus alterity.* Those three aspects of personal identity-formation are, in fact, already alluded to in the following central passage from Rushdie's oeuvre: "O eternal opposition of inside and outside! Because, a human being, inside himself, is anything but a whole, anything but homogenous; all kinds of everywhichthing are jumbled up inside him, and he is one person one minute and another the next."[15]

Fragmentation of personal selves is a recurring theme in Rushdie's novels. Physical fragmentation, for example, is particularly significant as a central metaphor for psychic fragmentation in *Midnight's Children*. Apart from Aadam Sinai's "fragmented" views of his future bride through the perforated sheet at the outset of the novel and the "symbolic hole" inside of him (expressing Aadam's religious disbelief), there is further textual evidence regarding Saleem Sinai's bodily mutilation. For example: Saleem's hair is torn out by a teacher (*MC* 232), a part of his middle finger is cut off in a struggle with other pupils about a girl (*MC* 234-35), he is sterilised (*MC* 439), throughout the narrative he discovers "cracks in his body" (*MC* 179).

The physical mutilations thus point towards Saleem's split identity, his schizophrenia,[16] an aspect underscored by the frequent mistakes Rushdie's narrator deliberately implants in his tale.[17] Saleem's psychic split is formally emphasised by him continually speaking of himself in first *and* third person (see, for example, *MC* 167, 309, 419). Thus he is presented, interestingly, as having (and providing the reader with) a double perspective which makes him a seemingly omniscient *and* limited first-person narrator at the same time.[18]

Furthermore, Saleem's psychological fragmentation is symbolised by the famous pickling of his life in jars, each jar of pickles "containing one year of his life" (*MC* 460-61). A similar metaphor for '(identity-)conservation' is employed in *The Moor's Last Sigh* (Moraes has to write down his story in order to prolong his life), and in Rushdie's novel, *The Ground Beneath Her Feet* (Rai takes photos in order to be able to structure and understand a chaotic world). Rushdie seems to be saying: life becomes understandable only retrospectively, by putting together various pieces of the 'puzzle of life,' thus, ultimately, trying to find coherence. But the protagonists of Rushdie's novels most often cannot actively build up a coherent picture of self-identity themselves. Accordingly, some characters (like, for example, Saleem in *Midnight's Children*) admit that it is rather others who may determine "who he really is" (cf. *MC* 192), feeling like a "person to whom things *have been done*" (*MC* 237).

The Moor's Last Sigh and *The Ground Beneath Her Feet* share yet another feature of identity-fragmentation—a feature that is symbolised, in both novels, by a broken mirror. After 'the Moor' is thrown out of his parental home he laments:

> I stumbled through them [the gates], giddy, disoriented, lost. I was nobody, nothing. Nothing I had ever known was of use, nor could I any longer say that I knew it. I had been emptied, invalidated; I was, to use a hoary but suddenly fitting epithet, ruined. I had fallen from grace, and the horror of it shattered the universe, like a mirror. I felt as though I, too, had shattered; as if I were falling to earth, not as myself, but as a thousand and one fragmented images of myself, trapped in shards of glass.[19]

And the mirror image is also to be found in a passage where Rai, the photographer and narrator of *The Ground Beneath Her Feet*, describes the rock-star Vina Apsara:

> To her last day, I could always see in her the skittish, disintegrated creature she'd been when she first came to us, looking as if she might run away again at any moment. What a piece of jetsam she was then, what a casualty! Literally selfless, her personality smashed, like a mirror, by the fist of her life. Her name, her mother and family, her sense of place and home and safety and belonging and being loved, her belief in the future, all these things had been pulled out from under her, like a rug. She was floating in a void, denatured, dehistoried, clawing at the shapelessness, trying to make some sort of mark. [...] She was a rag-bag of selves, torn fragments of people she might have become.[20]

This last quotation also introduces the second aspect of our analysis: identity's *mutability*. In most of Rushdie's novels, the main characters are set off against strong *alter egos*. In *Midnight's Children*, for example, Saleem Sinai's antagonist is Shiva who in fact is the very child Saleem believes to be. Shortly after their birth, the nurse Mary Pereira had swapped the two babies so that Saleem is in reality Shiva and Shiva is Saleem. In the context of the novel this means that Saleem is neither the "inspirational force" nor the "mirror-image to India" as the Prime Minister foretold him (*MC* 122).[21] Instead, he becomes the destroyer which the antagonist's and archrival's name "Major Shiva" (*MC* 407), as well as his mostly evil actions so aptly depict. However, although Saleem knows about the swapping (*MC* 118), he rather continues to believe that Ahmed and Amina Sinai (and not Vanita and William Methwold) are his real parents.[22] This might be read as yet another indication for the process of the oscillation between different parts of self.

Saleem also has various names that stand for the different roles he has to act out in life: "I, Saleem Sinai, later variously called Snotnose, Stainface, Baldy, Sniffer, Buddha and even Piece-of-the Moon [...]" (*MC* 9). Whilst, for example, "Snotnose" refers to Saleem's telepathic abilities and the "Midnight Children's Conference" he organises, "Sniffer" stands for his degradation to the subhuman soldier called "man-dog" (*MC* 347) in the Sundarbans episode. Mutability of identity is thus reflected in Saleem's different names and the various roles in life,[23] a multiplication that is wonderfully captured in Mary Pereira's singing, "Anything you want to be, you kin [*sic*] be, / You kin [*sic*] be just what-all you want" (*MC* 383).

The overt protagonist-antagonist dualism can be detected in *The Moor's Last Sigh* as well, although here it is not as powerful and complex as in *Midnight's Children*. Moraes Zogoiby's *alter ego* is his girlfriend Uma who also functions as a more active counterpart opposed to Moraes' generally passive nature. Uma says: "[...] *I will be your mirror, your self's other self, your equal, your empress and your slave*" (*MLS* 248). Their relationship ends when Uma commits suicide; in dying she is passing through various changes, "as if the pages of a book were turning, as if she were giving up, one by one, all her numberless selves" (*MLS* 281). Interestingly, Moraes' father 24—in true 'Jekyll and Hyde manner'—also constructs various selves by letting his identity oscillate between an official business personality and his sly underworld self:

> The truth about Abraham Zogoiby was that he had put on a disguise; had created a mild-mannered secret identity to mask his covert super-nature. He had

> deliberately painted the dullest possible picture of himself [...] over the thrilling but unacceptable reality. The deferential, complaisant surface was what Vasco would have called his 'overneath'; underneath it, he ruled Mogambo-ish underworld [...] (*MLS* 179-80).

The Ground Beneath Her Feet works on a similar level as far as mirror-images and *alter egos* are concerned. Ormus, the leader of the band 'VTO,' is heavily in love with Vina, the singer. In their passionate relationship, one cannot live without the other, but, to make matters worse, they cannot really live with each other: their selves are simultaneously drawn to each other and continuously forced apart. Furthermore, Umeed/Rai can be read as the antagonist to Ormus, for both are fighting over their love to Vina. Then again, Ormus's brothers take up the various shades of self from the respective brothers: "[...] punishment caused Cyrus, too, to conceal himself beneath a falsehood, a self he had borrowed from his sweet-natured twin, which was not truly his"[25] so that their identities have to be seen in relation to each other. Hence this might be interpreted as a metaphor for identity in relation to mutability as well as alterity.

This in fact already leads us to the last point we want to discuss, i.e. the question of *identity* in relation to *alterity*. Identity, of course, cannot be scrutinised in isolation, i.e. only by studying the self: the Other, or rather the self's relation to *Others* has to be taken into consideration as well. Partly, this aspect has been observed in the previous discussion already, but what we are looking into now is the formation of the self in a larger context. This concerns the question of how a migrant who is moving between different nations and cultures is able to form his or her personal identity. This also refers to Bhabha's theory of hybridity and alterity, conceptualising a 'third space' that is used to "deconstruct the boundaries between the self and other."[26] It is this sort of migrant identity that most of Rushdie's novels elaborate, particularly because *travelling* constitutes a most central metaphor in his texts.

In *Midnight's Children*, the leitmotif of the nose bridges the gap between the inside and the outside world (*MC* 10, 307).

Saleem recurrently states: "To understand just one life, you have to swallow the world" (*MC* 109), a remark which is taken up again in *The Moor's Last Sigh*: "We inhale the world and breathe out meaning" (*MLS* 54). In a later passage of *Midnight's Children*, Saleem tries to answer the question:

> Who what am I? My answer: I am the sum total of everything that went before me, of all I have been seen done, of everything done-to-me. I am everyone everything whose being-in-the-world affected was affected by mine. I am anything that happens after I've gone which would not have happened if I had not come. Nor am I particularly exceptional in this matter; each "I," every one of the now-six-hundred-million-plus of us, contains a similar multitude. (*MC* 383).

Here the interaction between personal and collective identity is alluded to already. More or less the same approach to identity/alterity can be found in *The Moor's Last Sigh* when Moraes speaks of "boundaries of your self [which] began to dissolve [...] in crowds or in love" (*MLS* 193). And this aspect of identity-building is taken up yet again in *The Satanic Verses* where Saladin Chamcha and Gibreel Farishta are the two opposing figures. Whereas Saladin tries to adapt to English manners as much as possible (finally becoming "more English than the English"[27]) Gibreel wants to stick to his 'Indianness.' In the course of the novel, Gibreel is seemingly rewarded, because he obtains a "halo" (*SV* 142) and passes his bad breath on to Saladin (*SV* 133), who, in contrast, is being punished for having selected adaptation: Saladin grows horns (*SV* 141) and finally also a hoof. The narrator comments on the migrant status of Gibreel and Saladin:

> Should we even say that these are two fundamentally different types of self? Might we not agree that Gibreel, [...]—has wished to remain, to a large degree, *continuous*-that is, joined to and arising from his past;—[...]-so that his is still a self which, for our present purposes, we may describe as true [...] whereas Saladin Chamcha is a creature of *selected* discontinuities, a *willing* re-invention; his *preferred* revolt against history being what makes him, in our chosen idiom, "false"? [...]-While Gibreel, to follow

> the logic of our established terminology, is to be considered "good" by virtue of *wishing to remain*, for all his vicissitudes, at bottom an untranslated man.
>
> —But, and again but: this sounds, does it not, dangerously like an intentionalist fallacy?—Such distinctions, resting as they must on an idea of the self as being (ideally) homogeneous, non-hybrid, "pure,"—an utterly fantastic notion!—cannot, must not, suffice. (*SV* 427)

The differentiation between good and evil with regard to the migrant's position towards adaptability is not only verbally deconstructed by the narrator. Later, back in India, Gibreel's problem of "sulphurous halitosis" returns with a vengeance on him, and he loses his girl-friend as well as his job before finally committing suicide (*SV* 546). Saladin, on the other hand, is finally reconciled with his father, inherits his wealth and even re-unites with his girl-friend Zeeny Vakil (*SV* 547). Thus, in the end, it is Saladin rather than Gibreel who comes up with a successful concept of a person's *self*-positioning *as migrant* in both a foreign *and* familiar culture.

Goonetilleke argues that the end of *The Satanic Verses* suggests the process of hybridity to have failed.[28] He gives three reasons for this: Saladin's return to his ancestral home, his resuming his original name, and his mother tongue Urdu coming back to him. We contend, however, that this argument is not necessarily valid because Gibreel also comes back to India but fails to 'survive.' Furthermore, Saladin's re-uniting with Zeeny Vakil, who favours "an ethic of historically validated eclecticism, for was not the entire national culture based on the principle of borrowing whatever clothes seemed to fit, Aryan, Mughal, British, take-the-best-and-leave-the-rest?" (*SV* 52) clearly shows that he has decided to live in a culture of hybridity. And, most significantly, Saladin does not go back to his 'one and only former self,' but rather "feels closer to many old rejected selves, many alternative Saladins" (*SV* 523). Thus even individual cultures are in themselves always already hybrid constructs. The migrant travelling between two or more cultures will eventually have to develop a sense of a 'third-space,' or hybrid identity.[29] This is confirmed towards the end of *The Satanic Verses*:

> [...] we are here to change things. I concede at once that we shall ourselves be changed; African, Caribbean, Indian, Pakistani, Bangladeshi, Cypriot, Chinese, we are other than what we would have been if we had not crossed the oceans, if our mothers and fathers had not crossed the skies [...]. We have been made again: but I say that we shall also be the ones to remake this society, to shape it from bottom to top (*SV* 413-14).

In Rushdie's novels, the third space is often alluded to when the respective protagonists fly from one to another country. Thus the aeroplane becomes a powerful symbol for Bhabha's third space of in-betweenness. In *The Satanic Verses*, for example, Saladin and Gibreel fall out of an exploding aircraft towards England and some of their transformations in terms of personality already start there, because not only do the passengers fall out of the plane, it is also, "the debris of the soul, broken memories, sloughed-off selves, severed mother-tongues, violated privacies, untranslatable jokes, extinguished futures, lost loves, the forgotten meaning of hollow, booming words, *land, belonging, home*" (*SV* 4).

When towards the end of *The Moor's Last Sigh*, Moraes Zogoiby has to fly to Granada, he talks about leaving back the "place, language, people and customs I knew [...]; and these, for most of us, are the four anchors of the soul" (*MLS* 383). Accordingly, after his arrival he feels that "I was a nobody from nowhere, like no-one, belonging to nothing," but this is something he has to convince himself of: "That sounded better. That felt true. All my ties had loosened" (*MLS* 388). Later Moraes is no longer sure of anything (*MLS* 414), merely of finding comfort and strength in the Japanese painter he has met. She, the painter, celebrates rootlessness and the autonomy of the self (*MLS* 427). She, however, eventually dies and Moraes has to find another way of claiming his personal identity: after having undergone the change from the (over-)celebrated hybridity of his parental home to the somewhat simplistic concept of a 'mono-identity' à la Raman Fielding, he arrives at the final conclusion: "[the] need for flowing together, for putting an end to frontiers, for the dropping of the boundaries of the self" (*MLS* 433).

Yet another example of an aeroplane serving as a symbol for an inter-cultural 'third space' can be found in *The Ground Beneath Her Feet*. Ormus, the lover and future husband of Vina Apsara, "sheds his old skin [...] like a snake" (*GBHF* 250) when flying from India to Britain. Strikingly, the whole chapter dedicated to the flight is termed 'Membrane,' suggesting that all migrant travellers, by having to penetrate this filter of the membrane, can only save some parts of their identity and thus have to leave back some other parts:

> [...] detached from the indifferent earth, he feels a certain resistance in the air. Something fighting back against the aircraft's forward movement. As if there's a stretchy translucent membrane across the sky, an ectoplasmic barrier, a Wall. [...]. But it's so springy, this invisible restriction, it keeps pushing the airplane back, boeing!, boeing!, until at last the Mayflower breaks through, it's through! Sunlight bounces off the wing into his bleary eye. And as he passes that unseen frontier he sees the tear in the sky, [...]. He intuits that every bone in his body is being irradiated by something pouring through the sky-rip, a mutation is occurring at the level of the cell, of the gene, of the particle. The person who arrives won't be the one who left, or not quite. (*GBHF* 253)

This, finally, is interesting with regard to the migrants' 'cultural translation.' The term translation, as Rushdie himself has pointed out, etymologically derives from the Latin word *translatio* which originally designates a neutral 'bearing across.' Rushdie has said: "having been borne across the world, we [migrants] are translated men. It is normally supposed that something always gets lost in translation; I cling, obstinately, to the notion that something can also be gained."[30] Consequently, Rushdie's novels portray identity not as being precise or monolithic, but rather as various, continuously changing, oscillating between disparate elements.[31] Identity cannot be pinned down easily, it is always—and this has to do with its very nature and is thus wholly independent of whether we talk of a migrant's or a native's identity—process-like rather than fixed. Saladin's statement about his identity in *The Satanic Verses* can therefore be seen as representative for the concept of self that emerges in Rushdie's work: "*I'm not myself today,* he thought. The heart flutters. Life damages the living. None of us are ourselves. None of us are *like this*" (*SV* 65).

Notes

1. Lyotard (1984: *passim*).
2. Kellner (1992: 141).
3. Kellner (1992).
4. cf. Kellner (1992); Jameson (1983).
5. Kellner (1992: 141),
6. Eagleton (1988: 386).
7. Reinfandt (1998: 76).
8. A concise discussion of this kind, with direct reference to Rushdie and numerous suggestions for further reading in the footnotes, can be found in Fletcher's introduction to *Reading Rushdie* (1994: especially 3-10). See also Connor (1989: 231-37).
9. Lange (1998: 369).
10. Hutcheon (1988: 69, our emphasis).
11. cf. Bhabha (1990).
12. Bhabha (1990: 213, our emphasis).
13. Reinfandt (1998: 85, our emphasis). But Rushdie's opinions on hybridity are anything but naive. As Reinfandt argues only shortly afterwards in his article: "there are certainly many passages in *The Moor's Last Sigh* which point to the pitfalls of pluralism of hybridity. Even 'India's deep rooted secularism,' appears to have mutated into an 'inter-community league of cynical self-interest'" (1998: 87).
14. Bhabha (1990: 209, our emphasis).
15. Rushdie 1995 [1981]: 236-37).
16. cf. Subba Rao (1993/4: 92); Shepherd (1990: 35).
17. cf. Rushdie (1991: 22-25).
18. See also Reckwitz (1986: 151); Rajkowska (1987: 17).
19. Rushdie (1995: 278-79).
20. Rushdie (1999: 121-22).
21. Thus Saleem is clearly a 'self-subverting' narrator, an aspect of narrative strategy that supports the (typically postmodern) concept of unstable identity.
22. What is more, he almost randomly designates further people as his parents (cf. Rushdie 1995 [1981]: *passim* but especially 127, 148-49). This seemingly nonsensical multiplication of parentage also points towards

Saleem being in a state of orphanhood and displacement, lacking a symbolic centre. It also comments upon the arbitrariness of identity-building, or, in the words of Durix, "that any identity is purely accidental and often made up" (1989: 181).

23. This is confirmed in *The Ground Beneath Her Feet* when the first person narrator Umeed Merchant comments on his nickname 'Rai': "Pseudonyms, stage names, work-names: for writers, for actors, for spies, these are useful masks, hiding or altering one's true identity" Rushdie (1999: 18). The use of the term 'true identity' reveals that Umeed dreams of what might be called a core identity, which, however, is never fixed throughout the novel.
24. In this novel again, the question of (non-)authentic parentage is being put forward. It is by no means clear whether Abraham Zogoiby really is 'the Moor's' father-it might as well be Pandit Nehru (cf. *MLS* 175). Like Saleem in *Midnight's Children,* Moraes consciously decides on one possibility, i.e. in this case, Moraes chooses to believe that Abraham is his father (cf. *MLS* 177), which may be read as an additional comment upon the fragmentation and the constructedness of identity.
25. Rushdie (1999: 138).
26. Fludernik (1998: 51); cf. also Goetsch (1997).
27. cf. Rushdie (1988: 53).
28. Goonetilleke (1998: 90-91)
29. What the narrator of *The Satanic Verses* also displays is the pressure that the chosen country can apply to the individual immigrant self. The brutal arrest of the immigration officers and the resulting changes of Saladin as a response (Rushdie 1992: 157-64) are a first clue to this, but there is further evidence in the novel. Saladin has to develop masks in school in order to socialise with the other pupils (43), other immigrants in a hospital mutate to animals because "[t]hey have the power of description, and we succumb to the pictures they construct" (168).
30. Rushdie (1991: 17).
31. cf. also Rushdie (1991: 394).

Works Cited

Bhabha, Homi K. "The Third Space (an Interview)." *Identity: Community, Culture, Difference.* Ed. Rutherford. London: Lawrence & Wishart, 1990. 207-21.

Connor, Steven. *Postmodernist Culture: An Introduction to Theories of the Contemporary.* Oxford: Blackwell, 1989.

Durix, Jean-Pierre. "Salman Rushdie's Declaration of Kaleidoscopic Identity." *Declarations of Cultural Independence in the English-Speaking World: A Symposium.* Ed. Luigi Sampietro. Mailand: D'Imperio Editore Novara, 1989. 173-84.

Eagleton, Terry. "Capitalism, Modernism and Postmodernism." *Modern Criticism and Theory: A Reader*. Ed. David Lodge. London: Longman, 1988. 385-98.

Fletcher, M.D. "Introduction: the Politics of Salman Rushdie's Fiction." *Reading Rushdie: Perspectives on the Fiction of Salman Rushdie* (Cross/Cultures Series Vol. 16). Ed. M.D. Fletcher. Amsterdam and Atlanta: Rodopi, 1994. 1-22.

Fludernik, Monika. "The Constitution of Hybridity: Postcolonial Interventions." *Hybridity and Postcolonialism: Twentieth-Century Indian Literature*. Ed. Monika Fludernik. Tübingen: Stauffenburg, 1998. 19-53.

Goetsch, Paul. "Funktionen von Hybridität in der postkolonialen Theorie." *Literatur in Wissenschaft und Unterricht* 30.2 (1997): 135-45.

Goonetilleke, D.C.R.A. *Salman Rushdie*. London: Macmillan, 1998.

Hutcheon, Linda. *A Poetics of Postmodernism: History, Theory, Fiction*. London and New York: Routledge, 1988.

Jameson, Fredric. "Postmodernism and Consumer Society." *The Anti-Aesthetic: Essays on Postmodern Culture*. Ed. Hal Foster. Seattle: Bay Press, 1983. 111-25.

Kellner, Douglas. "Popular Culture and the Construction of Postmodern Identities." *Modernity and Identity*. Ed. Scott Lash and Jonathan Friedman. Oxford: Blackwell, 1992. 141-77.

Lange, Bernd-Peter. "Postcolonial Gothic: Salman Rushdie's *The Moor's Last Sigh*." *Literatur in Wissenschaft und Unterricht* 31.4 (1998): 365-75.

Lyotard, Jean François. *The Postmodern Condition: A Report on Knowledge*. Trans. Geoff Bennington and Brian Massumi. Minneapolis: U Minnesota P, 1984.

Rajkowska, Barbara O. "The Reality of the Alien: An Exploration of Salman Rushdie's Novels." *Revista Canaria de Estudios Ingleses* 13/14 (1987): 9-27.

Reckwitz, Erhard. "Der Roman als Metaroman: Salman Rushdie, *Midnight's Children*; Kazuo Ishiguro, *A Pale View of Hills*; John Fowles, *Mantissa*." *Poetica: Zeitschrift für Sprach-und Literaturwissenschaft* 18.1-2 (1986): 140-64.

Reinfandt, Christoph. "What's the Use of Stories that Aren't Even True: Salman Rushdie as a Test Case for Literature and Literary Studies Today." *Literatur in Wissenschaft und Unterricht* 31.1 (1998): 75-92.

Rushdie, Salman. *Imaginary Homelands. Essays and Criticism 1981-1991*. London: Granta, 1991.

—. *The Satanic Verses*. 1988. Dover (Del.): The Consortium, 1992.

—. *Midnight's Children*. 1981. London: Vintage, 1995.

—. *The Moor's Last Sigh*. London: Cape, 1995.

—. *The Ground Beneath Her Feet.* New York: Henry Holt, 1999.

Shepherd, Ron. "*Midnight's Children* as Fantasy." *The Commonwealth Review* 1.2 (1990): 33-43.

Subba Rao, V.V. "Salman Rushdie's *Midnight's Children*: A Study." *The Indian Journal of English Studies* 32 (1993/4): 87-93.

8

Rushdie's Affiliation with Dickens

MARTINE HENNARD DUTHEIL DE LA ROCHÈRE

> The Ocean of the Streams of Story was in fact the biggest library in the universe. And because the stories were held here in fluid form, they retained the ability to change, to become new versions of themselves, to join up with other stories and so to become yet other stories; so that unlike a library of books, the Ocean of the Streams of Story was much more than a storeroom of yarns.
>
> —Salman Rushdie, *Haroun and the Sea of Stories*

> How stories travel, what mouths they end up in!
>
> —Salman Rushdie, *The Moor's Last Sigh*

Family is one of Salman Rushdie's favourite tropes to investigate the question of individual and collective origins. After the publication of *The Moor's Last Sigh*, the author declared that he saw this novel as

> the completion of what I began in *Midnight's Children*, *Shame* and *The Satanic Verses*—the story of myself, where I came from, a story of origins and memory. But it's also a public project that forms an arc, my response to an age in history that began in 1947. That cycle of novels is now complete. ("The Last Laugh" 21)

Steeped in the complexities of the postcolonial condition, these four novels challenge the traditional values attached to the family not only by exposing the tyranny of families but also by subverting the generative model which underlies the familial system. In *Midnight's Children* and *Shame*, Rushdie thematizes the complex nature of origin and defamiliarizes the hallowed concept of family, notably by holding in suspense the identity of the heroes' biological parents. Born illegally across cultures, Saleem Sinai and Omar Shakil multiply father substitutes while their author satirizes patriarchal authority and family entanglements. In *The Satanic Verses,* he even more daringly transgresses the law of the father by breaking down aesthetic, moral and cultural distinctions (including the one between sacred and profane texts), although Saladin Chamcha's last minute reconciliation with his dying father expresses a desire for rapprochement with the emblem of authority. *The Moor's Last Sigh* dramatises the tyranny of parental rule within the context of a family torn apart by strife, division and violence. Burdened with an extravagant and gifted mother and a big-time crook of a father, Moraes is reduced to insignificance before being abandoned by both. In these novels, the image of the family becomes productive only to the extent that its reproductive structure is called into question. Thus, the vertical, linear, genealogical familial logic gives way to a wide, intricate and changing network of multiple relationships which open up the familial unit to the outside and the other: the old family tree is felled and transformed into the leaves upon which the transformative action of writing can take place.

Rushdie's treatment of the family is part of a wide-ranging critique of naturalised notions that are most intimately bound up with our sense of self and belonging. In "Imaginary Homelands," the novelist insists on the necessity of moving away from essentialist conceptions of race, culture and nation in this era of mass migration. Similarly, he rejects an exclusive allegiance to native traditions to construct his own "family tree." Defining himself as a "literary migrant," Rushdie is happy to list the members of his large and cosmopolitan "literary family," thereby creating a tension between the constraining laws of genealogy and the free affiliative nature of writing. As he puts it in "Imaginary Homelands" (1982):

> We are inescapably international writers at a time when the novel has never been a more international form (a writer like Borges speaks of the influence of Robert Louis Stevenson on his work; Heinrich Böll acknowledges the

> influence of Irish literature; cross-pollination is everywhere); and it is perhaps one of the more pleasant freedoms of the literary migrant to be able to choose his parents. My own-selected half consciously, half not-include Gogol, Cervantes, Kafka, Melville, Machado de Assis; a polyglot family tree against which I measure myself, and to which I would be honoured to belong. (*Imaginary Homelands* 20-21)

Although absent from this list of self-selected parents, Charles Dickens looms large over Rushdie's œuvre. Several interviews nevertheless confirm the influence of the Victorian novelist on his writings. Dickens appears alongside Sterne, Swift, Grass, Joyce, Beckett, Flann O'Brien and Márquez in an early interview with Victoria Glendinning ("A Novelist in the Country of the Mind" 1981, 38). Two years later, Rushdie declared to Chandrabhanu Pattanayak that, rather than Grass and Márquez, the writers he was much more conscious of while writing *Midnight's Children* were Sterne, Dickens and Swift (*Conversations with Salman Rushdie* 17). In particular, he admitted to being influenced by Dickens's technique of playing out fantasy elements against a realistic background:

> He uses a kind of background or setting for his works which is completely naturalistic, down to the tiniest details. And on top of this completely naturalistic background he imposes totally surrealistic images-like the Circumlocution office, which is a civil service department designed to do nothing, or like many of the characters, who are much larger than life. Because they are so precisely rooted in a recognizable real world the fantasy works. What I tried to do-though not quite in the Dickensian way-was to make sure that the background, the bedrock of the book, was right-that Bombay was like Bombay, the cities were like the cities, the different dates were recognizably correct so that the fantasy could be rooted in that kind of reality. (*Conversations with Salman Rushdie* 17-18)

In a 1988 interview with John Clement Ball, Rushdie mentioned *Little Dorrit* and *Bleak House* as sources for his representation of London in *The Satanic Verses*: "And I suppose that is something I've tried to learn from the great man, that fantasy, surrealism, those elements work as intensifications of the real; they work as metaphors of the real world when you can embed them in a believable setting" (*Conversations with Salman Rushdie* 106). In a more recent interview with Heather Neill, Rushdie again insists on Dickens's "huge influence" on his writing, "especially his juxtaposition of a surreal foreground with a minutely naturalistic background" ("Saved by a Sea of Stories," 1998, 7).

In recent years, Rushdie has thus sought to challenge the critical commonplace of the Márquez connection to foreground his affiliation with Dickens, which he seems to consider as a magic realist writer *avant la lettre*. Rather than elaborate on this displacement which deliberately challenges the ascription of simple and single origins to literary movements, I want to suggest that Dickens's fatherly-or indeed fathering-presence is not only perceptible at the general level of style, but also more directly in key passages in Rushdie's novels. This "literary parent" indeed appears at moments where the issue of origin is centrally at stake in *Midnight's children*, *Shame* and *The Satanic Verses*. Specifically, in *Midnight's Children* and in *Shame*, the presence of Dickens haunts the births of Saleem and Omar through allusions to *David Copperfield*. In *The Satanic Verses*, straightforward references to *Our Mutual Friend* are scattered in the climactic scene of the party, so that Dickens is shown to attend another, bleaker kind of birth: the birth of evil in Saladin Chamcha. The enigma of influence which motivates the plot of the first two novels and in turn informs *The Satanic Verses* is thus repeated at the textual level. Furthermore, the main intertexts of *Midnight's Children* turn out to be Dickens's all time favourites, *Tristram Shandy* and the *Arabian Nights*.

The travels of the *Arabian Nights*: from Dickens to Rushdie

> Taking a handkerchief from his pocket, he rubbed briskly: once, twice, thrice.
>
> The lights all went on at once. Zeenat Vakil entered the room.
>
> Salman Rushdie, *The Satanic Verses*

There are several allusions to the *Arabian Nights* in *David Copperfield*. The legacy of David's deceased father to his son consists of "a small collection of books" stocked "in a little room upstairs [...] which nobody else in our house ever troubled" (*David Copperfield* 105). There, David finds relief from his dreary life under the iron rule of Mr and Mrs Murdstone, "reading as if for life" (*David Copperfield,* 106) *Tom Jones, Don Quixote* and *Robinson Crusoe,* along with the *Arabian Nights* and the *Tales of the Genii.* Later on, at the prison-like school of Salem House, David cements his ambiguous relationship with Steerforth by telling him the stories he read as a child, thus taking on, as Steerforth himself remarks, the role of Scheherazade. The references to the *Arabian Nights* occur in two scenes that mark important stages in David's growth as a writer. The first passage emphasises the consolatory and life-giving aspect of reading, since David survives the hardships of his youth by escaping into books. The second represents a transitional period of remembering and retelling before David evolves into a fully-fledged author. Dickens seems to suggest that reading, appropriating and transforming stories ("What ravages I committed on my favourite authors in the course of my interpretation of them, I am not in a condition to say" *David Copperfield* 144) play a crucial role in the creative process. Through David, he is thus paying homage to the seminal works which enabled him to "give birth" to his own original character.

At the beginning of *Midnight's Children,* Saleem declares that in order to tell the story of the thousand and one children of midnight, he "must work fast, faster than Scheherazade, if I am to end up meaning-yes, meaning-something" (*Midnight's Children* 9). When he resumes the story "which [he] left yesterday hanging in mid-air," Saleem again draws parallels between his narrative situation and his illustrious predecessor's. "[J]ust as Scheherazade, depending for her very survival on leaving Prince Shahryar eaten up by curiosity, used to do night after night" (*Midnight's Children* 24), he unravels the thread of his story, on which his own life also hangs. Yet Saleem's flattering comparison with Scheherazade is ironic, as it follows Padma's blunt dismissal of his efforts as so much "writing-shiting" (*Midnight's Children* 24).

In *The Satanic Verses,* Rushdie self-consciously rewrites the scene of David's voracious assimilation of his father's literary heritage when Changez Chamchawala brings the cross-cultural wanderings of the *Arabian Nights* to an end by letting its collected tales rot in his library. Saladin Chamcha's father keeps "a ten-volume set of the Richard Burton translation of the *Arabian Nights*, which was being slowly devoured by mildew and bookworm owing to the deep-seated prejudice against books which led Changez to own thousands of the pernicious things in order to humiliate them by leaving them to rot unread" beside "a magic lamp, a brightly polished copper-and-brass avatar of Aladdin's very own genie-container: a lamp begging to be rubbed" (*The Satanic Verses* 36). By keeping books under lock and key, Changez refuses his son access to what Saladin considers his rightful legacy: a treasure of words and the imaginary worlds they conjure up, represented by Aladdin's magic lamp. Read in the light of Dickens's text, Saladin's trajectory implies that his own father must also die to release a rich, mixed cultural past so that the imaginative and creative faculties of the son are freed to invent a satisfying life for himself at last. Rushdie thus establishes a complex filiation with Dickens by reinscribing his novels along with their original sources, and so bears witness to the constant exchange that took place between the cultures of the East and the West. At the same time, the novelist manifests a profound ambivalence towards the authority figures of both cultures, as he sees them to inhibit *and* nurture the creative process. I want to show how, in *Midnight's Children* and *Shame*, Rushdie's dialogue with *David Copperfield* brings out these tensions.

David Copperfield is born again

> Dickens has created creatures who cling to us and tyrannize over us,
> creatures whom we would not forget if we could,
> creatures whom we could not forget if we would,
> creatures who are more actual than the man who made them.
>
> —G.K. Chesterton

In *Culture and Imperialism*, Edward Said has convincingly argued that mainstream Victorian fiction, including the novels of Charles Dickens, contributed to the imagination of Empire even when these works were only marginally concerned with life in the colonies. While the stories replicate the power relation between the metropolitan centre and its overseas territories, they also sometimes betray unease about the imperial venture. Rushdie, like Said, focuses on the rare but telling moments when the colonial relationship is played out in Dickens's text and alters their significance by repeating and displacing them from a postcolonial perspective.

Midnight's Children playfully emulates Dickens's fictional worlds in being a work of capacious imagination and comic power. Like Dickens, Rushdie enjoys juggling with tones, styles and registers. Similarly, he delights in the invention of larger-than-life characters and in artfully combining social satire, sentimental interests, and reflections on the relation between identity and writing. What Rushdie most significantly adopts from his literary father, however, is the motif of the child of uncertain origin who needs to replace a traumatic past with his own inventions. A changeling raised in a Bombay bourgeois family, Saleem is ejected from the narrower family circle when the enigma of his origin is revealed. In his subsequent life of wandering, he plays the part of the surrogate son to various parental figures. Saleem thus shares the fate of the rejected children that figure in Dickens's major novels: David Copperfield, Oliver Twist, Little Nell, Florence Dombey, poor Jo, and of course Pip, with whom David shares the earliest memory of a visit to a cold tombstone in the nearby churchyard. A "posthumous child," David loses his beloved and frail mother early in the novel and, after suffering the cruelty of his stepfather, is eventually "adopted" by one of his father's aunts, Miss Betsey Trotwood.

The narrator had introduced the character of Betsey Trotwood three pages into the novel, immediately after describing his actual birth: David informs us that she was briefly and unhappily married to a handsome but violent man who left her to try his luck in India "and there, according to a wild legend in our family, he was once seen riding on an elephant, in company with a Baboon; but I think it must have been a Baboo-or a Begum" (*David Copperfield* 51). This passing allusion to imperial Britain in the colonial imagery of elephants, monkeys, servants and exotic mistresses is a vignette which neatly captures the phantasmic quality of European projections on India. Their fabulistic status is revealed, however, by the "wild legend" running in the family as well as through the enigmatic nature of cultural difference; the unfamiliar context defies naming and identification. Description slips over elusive signifiers which muddle the veracity of the account of the life of Betsey's husband in India; hesitating between baboon, baboo and begum, David's imagination is thus let loose in a world of word-play.

India is the place where Dickens "exiles" unpleasant characters. Jack Maldon, the young Mrs Strong's "paramour" (or so David wants us to believe), is expediently sent to India by Mr. Wickfield. While the misrepresentations of India are amusingly discarded in favour of other misrepresentations by David's friends (who promote a reassuringly "tame" version of its "wilderness"), the child's own oriental fantasies are once again based on the suggestive power of the *Arabian Nights*:

> I recollect it was settled by general consent that India was quite a misrepresented country, and had nothing objectionable in it, but a tiger or two, and a little heat in the warm part of the day. For my own part, I looked on Mr. Jack Maldon as a modern Sinbad, and pictured him the bosom friend of all the Rajahs in the East, sitting under canopies, smoking curly golden pipes-a mile long, if they could be straightened out. (*David Copperfield* 300)

The concluding and almost surreal image of the mile long hookah pipe neatly figures the impossibility of putting the reality of India straight.

Much later in the novel, we encounter Betsey Trotwood again when she rescues David from Mr and Mrs Murdstone and enables him to begin a new life "in a new name, and with everything new about [him]" (*David Copperfield* 271-72). In this reconstituted and most unconventional family composed of a gaunt divorcée and her protégé, the eccentric Mr. Dick, David finds at last some happiness and a home where he can "make another beginning," as the heading of chapter fifteen explicitly states, under the new name of Trotwood Copperfield. In this way, David symbolically becomes the son Betsey and her long-gone husband never had, and we may extrapolate that this absent father is one of a line with the British Methwold in *Midnight's Children* and the anonymous "Angrez" in *Shame*, who unwittingly give birth to literary sons.

The first chapter of *David Copperfield* starts with the memorable paragraph where David puts his reader and himself to the test of answering a crucial question:

> Whether I shall turn to be the hero of my own life, or whether that station will be held by anybody else, these pages must show. To begin my life with the beginning of my life, I record that I was born (as I have been informed and believe) on a Friday, at twelve o'clock at night. It was remarked that the clock began to strike, and I began to cry, simultaneously.

In *Midnight's Children*, Saleem first gives a boldly positive answer to this question by taking central responsibility for the history of India before being gradually relegated to its margins. Saleem's parentage turns out to be that of the substituted child of romantic comedy and, like *David Copperfield*, the narrator of *Midnight's Children* begins his narrative-and his life-on the auspicious stroke of midnight before he, like his predecessor, starts "meandering":

> I was born in the city of Bombay [...] once upon a time. No, that won't do, there's no getting away from the date: I was born in Doctor Narlikar's Nursing Home on August 15th, 1947. And the time? The time matters, too. Well then: at night. No, it's important to be more [...] On the stroke of midnight, as a matter of fact. Clock-hands joined palms in respectful greeting as I came. (*Midnight's Children* 9)

Reproducing the typically Dickensian dialogue between the conventions of the fairy-tale and the demands of realist fiction, the inaugural scene provides a key as to how the conflict with origin is to be acted out and originality (and individuality) achieved. If the hybridisation of traditional forms is an essential element of this strategy, the type of intervention performed on the famous opening of Dickens's "favourite child" is equally revealing. By displacing the Dickensian reference in time (August 15th, 1947, India's Independence day) and in space (the city of Bombay), Rushdie repeats Dickens's original text from the perspective of cultural difference. The grafting of otherness on the repeated motif of the birth of a novel echoing the birth of its narrator estranges its origin, thereby enabling originality. Thus, the striking of the clocks which heralds David Copperfield's birth is supplemented in Rushdie's version by the wonderful image of the "clock-hands join[ing] palms in respectful greeting" (*Midnight's Children*, 9). The dead metaphor of the clock-hands is revived through its analogy with the Asian gesture of benevolent salute. Dickens's paternal influence on Saleem's birth is thus welcomed, as it were, from afar. Rushdie thus pays homage to the author of *David Copperfield*, whose presence at the birth of Saleem Sinai is signalled at the beginning of the novel.

David Copperfield also happens to be one of Omar Khayyam Shakil's substitute fathers. A few pages into *Shame*, the peripheral hero of this political allegory alludes to the first sentence of *David Copperfield* as an appropriate commentary on his own calamitous existence. "Whether I shall turn out to be the hero of my own life, or whether that station will be held by anybody else, these pages must show" is thus reappropriated by Omar who, like David, is "destined to be unlucky in life" and "privileged to see ghosts and spirits" (*David Copperfield* 49):

> 'You see before you,' he confided, 'a fellow who is not even the hero of his own life; a man born and raised in the condition of being out of things. Heredity counts, dontyouthinkso?'
>
> 'That is an oppressive notion,' Iskander Harrapa replied. (*Shame* 24)

Omar rounds off his (unacknowledged) citation with a remark on the importance of heredity, in order to explain his condition as a marginal figure in history (and in the story). On a metatextual level, Omar's appeal to the constraining laws of genealogy draws attention to his incapacity to exist as an original character, since he can only conceive of his destiny in terms that are borrowed from another. In the larger context of the history of Pakistan, the narrative also oscillates between a belief in the determinism of "heredity" and a rejection of this "oppressive notion": after the partition, Pakistan is indeed "that country divided into two Wings a thousand miles apart, that fantastic bird of a place, two Wings without a body, sundered by the land-mass of its greatest foe, joined by nothing but God" (*Shame* 178). Rushdie seems to imply that, split from the moment of its creation, Pakistan is doomed to civil war and fratricidal power plays. A hopeless and helpless witness to the relationship between the Westernised Iskander Harrapa and the Islamic General Raza Hyder, in the course of which the adoptive son betrays his spiritual father and puts him to death, Omar can only submit to the violent logic of "unnatural" acts. In Rushdie's version, the political myth of Pakistan is thus recast as the Oedipal or Shakespearean drama, with the difference that, in Rushdie's harsh opinion, "The Zia-Bhutto relationship is tragic-the protégé becomes the executioner-but the figures haven't the stature you can associate with high tragedy. These are people who don't deserve tragedy" ("Salman Rushdie: A Literary Conversation" 248). The history of Pakistan activates Rushdie's own filial anxieties and his ambivalence towards the figure of the father. As a consequence, *Shame*'s fictional world is appropriately riddled with guilt and haunted by the spectres of angry ghosts seeking revenge on those who have humiliated them. The killing of the father, which Rushdie fantasises in the political history of Pakistan, is narrated with a mixture of horror and the suspect complacency of the one who, as Sara Suleri has aptly diagnosed, "tells lurid family tales with the zeal of a distant relative" (*The Rhetoric of English India* 177). If Omar's ventriloquism manifests a desire to evade responsibility, the narrator's grappling with the problematic issue of influence brings out the fear and desire to transgress Freud's original taboo. The related issue of influence and transgression, treated with playful irreverence in *Midnight's Children*, takes on much sinister overtones in *Shame* and culminates in *The Satanic Verses*.

In *Shame*, the context for the quotation from *David Copperfield* not only inscribes circumstantial and cultural difference, as in *Midnight's Children,* but it also ironizes and darkens its significance: while the first mention of David's dilemma occurs in a drinking bout, the second takes place during a questioning when Omar Shakil fails to answer Talvar Ul-Haq's questions and, pathetically ineffectual to the end, confesses to the Chief Martial Law Administrator and Federal Security Force that "Other persons have been the principal actors in my life-story" (*Shame* 283). Incapable of taking responsibility for his deeds as well as for his words, Omar's excuse only precipitates his violent end. The appeal to Dickens is shown to be irrelevant in the immediate context of the questioning ("We are getting nowhere" replies Ul-Haq), and is further dismissed as an inappropriate subtext to the narration of Pakistani history. In this sense, Omar's invocation of *David Copperfield* reverses Saleem's: far from having any life-giving power, it provokes Ul-Haq into shooting him in the heart. This first version of his death is followed by his alternative dispatch in the hands of his retarded wife, which bleakly ends the novel. *Shame* thus symbolically decentres Dickens, along with the character who mimics David: "no longer the hero of Rushdie's novel," Dickens is replaced by the sound and the fury of Jacobean drama, or rather the irreducible difference of historical and political specificity.

Our Mutual Friend revisited

Rushdie deliberately hybridises the Western literary heritage with the Indian oral narrative tradition, from which he borrows the digressive and circumvoluted structure of his novels. The influence of *The Arabian Nights* on Dickens already showed that cross-cultural borrowing was a fundamental source of literary creativity. From the collection of tales (of mainly Indo-Persian but also Arabic and Egyptian origin) and the work of the prolific Victorian writer, Rushdie convokes two characters, Scheherazade and David Copperfield, who play the "literary parents" of Saleem Sinai as he is born in the first pages of *Midnight's Children.* In *The Satanic Verses,* another unlikely couple is present at the birth of evil in Saladin Chamcha: Podsnap and Iago. Saladin's revenge on Gibreel will take the form of anonymous phone calls where he sings doggerel verse implying that Gibreel's girl-friend is unfaithful to him. This gradually drives his friend mad to the point of murdering his beloved and committing suicide.

The Satanic Verses inscribes and displaces the Dickensian and Shakespearean heritage when *Our Mutual Friend* and *Othello* are referred to at a turning-point in the narrative, if only as décor in a postmodern pastiche. The scene of the confrontation at first seems to enact the purely decorative presence of past forms that is commonly associated with postmodern practice and global culture. Yet, in Rushdie's characteristic manner, the literalization of this decorativeness is itself suspect: the invocation of Dickens and Shakespeare at a climactic moment in the narrative reinvests these sources with significance, albeit a different one from the original. Saladin Chamcha and Gibreel Farishta meet again at a party organised by the stammering S. S. Sisodia in the Shepperton film studios where a "huge re-creation of Dickensian London" is staged for "a musical adaptation of the great writer's last completed novel, renamed *Friend!*" (*The Satanic Verses* 421). Sisodia's *Friend!* which clearly alludes to Carol Reed's musical extravaganza *Oliver!* (itself an adaptation of a stage musical by Lionel Bart), points to a long tradition of commercializations of Dickens. This prompts Jay Clayton to suggest, after Rushdie himself, that Dickens "is perhaps the most postmodern nineteenth-century writer" (*Great Expectations* 611).

Dickens commodified serves as a literal background to a tragi-comic replay of *Othello* when Saladin takes revenge on Gibreel for letting him down after the fall:

> What follows is tragedy.—Or, at the least the echo of tragedy, the full-blooded original being unavailable to modern men and women, so it's said.—A burlesque for our degraded, imitative times, in which clowns re-enact what was first done by heroes and by kings. (*The Satanic Verses* 424)

Dickens is recycled as the stage (literal and figurative) on which another icon of British culture, Shakespeare, is to be replayed as burlesque, as the self-conscious and theoretically wise narrator (who knows that literature, just like history, repeats itself only as farce) points out. The *trompe-l'oeil* of Dickens's London and the revamping of *Our Mutual Friend* suggest a fairly complex interplay of allusions, when we recall that Dickens's last completed novel deals precisely with the recycling of dead objects and even of dead people. Ironically, the actor playing the role of Jesse "Gaffer" Hexam, one of the waterside men who makes a living fishing for drowned bodies and robbing them of their valuables in *Our Mutual Friend,* rescues Jumpy Joshi, Saladin and Gibreel's "mutual enemy," knocked cold by Gibreel in the fake Thames during the party. The film producer Sisodia revives, yet transforms by updating, a novel that itself adapts the perennial myth of death and rebirth to nineteenth century London. This theme in turn informs *The Satanic Verses* which begins with "In order to be born again, first you have to die" and goes on to show how the past lives on in new forms in the present.

The relevance of *Our Mutual Friend* to the scene of the party in Rushdie's novel is also evidently linked to the comedy of social life that counterbalances the dark atmosphere of the river and its scavengers. Dickens anatomises the false glitter of the world of Victorian bourgeois society with the Podsnaps and the *nouveaux riches* Veneerings, who "have a house out of the Tales of the Genii, and give dinners out of the Arabian Nights" (*Our Mutual Friend* 249) in the words of Lady Tippins. Rushdie similarly makes fun of their late twentieth century descendants who gravitate to the equally artificial world of the film industry and the media:

> Society grandees, fashion models, film stars, corporation bigwigs, a brace of minor royal Personages, useful politicians and suchlike riff-raff perspire and mingle in these counterfeit streets with numbers of men and women as sweat-glistened as the 'real' guests and as counterfeit as the city. (*The Satanic Verses* 422)

Clayton acutely observes that at the moment of the confrontation between Saladin and Gibreel during the scene of the party, Rushdie "combines familiar postmodern playfulness about the indistinguishability of imitations and originals with more disturbing motifs: nationalism, xenophobia, misogyny, and racism" (*Great Expectations* 1996, 619). Saladin's desire to take revenge on Gibreel will precisely develop from their antagonistic views about national identity and cultural difference. Rushdie's adaptation of *Our Mutual Friend* thus provides an appropriately ironic commentary on the relation between the two main protagonists in the exclamatory and ambiguous *Friend!*. Their former friendship takes a definitive turn for the worse during the party, which prompts a resentful and envious Saladin to play Iago and destroy Gibreel. At the moment when Saladin moves towards Gibreel through the crowd of fashionable people, he "seems to see, *right now*, that same sneer upon Farishta's face, that scorn of an inverted Podsnap, for whom all things English are worthy of derision instead of praise" (*The Satanic Verses* 425-26). Saladin's hatred is partly a reaction to Gibreel's Podsnappian arrogance. More profoundly, it is triggered by the recognition of his own image as Podsnap reflected in the contemptuous sneer of his inverted double, "For are they not conjoined opposites, these two, each man the other's shadow?—One seeking to be transformed into the foreignness he admires, the other preferring, contemptuously, to transform" (*The Satanic Verses* 426).

On another level, the scene repeats the problematic of faithfulness and betrayal in the context of Rushdie's own use and misuse of the literary authorities of the past. In the words of the singing actors, "*What kind of fellow is Our Mutual Friend? What does he intend? Is he the kind of fellow on whom you may depend? Etc. Etc. Etc.*" (*The Satanic Verses* 423). The spokeswoman for Rushdie's answer to his predecessors turns out to be a female guest who, "in an expert parody of the Marine Insurance agent's self-important posture, [...] launches into her own version of the scheduled musical Podsnappery." She thus repeats with an ironic distance the lyrics of the next act of the musical, Mr. Podsnap's solo, which only slightly adapt Dickens's text:

Ours is a Copious Language,
A Language Trying to Strangers;
Ours is the Favoured Nation,
Blest, and Safe from Dangers [...] (*The Satanic Verses* 423)

In the wonderfully comic scene of the original, the fatuous Podsnap condescends to a Frenchman who is at pains to make sense of the conversation. Instead of engaging with his questions, Podsnap keeps correcting his pronunciation:

> 'Our language,' said Mr. Podsnap, with a gracious consciousness of always being right, 'is Difficult. Ours is a Copious language, and Trying to Strangers. I will not Pursue my Question.' (*Our Mutual Friend* 133)

In Rushdie's version, the rhyme pattern of the lyrics, which equate "strangers" with "dangers," exposes further Podsnap's national pride, which translates in a distasteful and distrustful attitude to foreigners. This is particularly striking when Podsnap cuts the Frenchman short as a way of evading a likely challenge of his arrogant assertion that the English Constitution "Was Bestowed Upon Us By Providence." Podsnap's reaction is once again to reassert his authority by taking advantage of the linguistic difficulties of his interlocutor. In this instance, the "otherness" of the Frenchman is explicitly invoked to prevent dialogue:

> 'And ozer countries?—' the foreign gentleman was beginning, when Mr. Podsnap put him right away again. 'We do not say Ozer; we say Other.' (*Our Mutual Friend* 133)

Through Podsnap, Dickens satirizes the self-satisfied English bourgeoisie and mocks the fatuity of a representative member of a society in decline and about to fall. Saladin, Rushdie's grotesque version of the foreigner turned Podsnap, inflects Dickens's critique towards postcolonial issues to address the question of assimilation and mimicry. As the "other" who desperately tries to belong to English society, Saladin is a "second degree" parody himself. By emulating British ways, adopting their tastes and mimicking their accents, he has become "more English than" (*The Satanic Verses* 53). As Steven Connor points out, the Dickens musical reveals to Saladin that cultural identity is not an essence but an "effect-the projection outwards for global consumption by the tourist and culture industries of an Englishness that is in some sense already derived from or dependent upon the images of self from the outside" (*The English Novel in History* 126).

It is revealing that, to cover Gibreel's singing of the hit number of *Mr 420*, "Mera Joota Hai Japani" as they fall towards England at the beginning of *The Satanic Verses* Saladin sings the first stanza of "Rule, Britannia!":

When Britain first, at Heaven's command,
Arose from out the azure main,
This was the charter of the land,
And guardian angels sung this strain—
Rule, Britannia, rule the waves;
Britons never will be slaves.

The lyrics of the original are quoted in a truncated and comically stressed form as "aroooose from out of aaaazure main" and "and guardian aaaaangels sung the strain" (*The Satanic Verses* 6). Unsurprisingly, and with similar parodic intent, Dickens also has Podsnap quote the national anthem as a conclusive authority to end his dialogue with the Frenchman. Saladin's uncritical embrace of Britishness, which Gibreel cruelly exposes as a self-defeating sham at the party, points to the dangers of cultural translation. Being "An Indian translated into an English-medium" (*The Satanic Verses* 58), Saladin in fact identifies with a myth that rejects the difference he represents. Gibreel, a master actor himself, sees through Saladin's act, which outdoes what he believes to be "the real thing." Unwilling to "Decline and Fall Off the British Empire" (to adapt Silas Wegg's misreading of the title, which he mistakes for the author), Saladin responds by eliminating the one who mocks his alienation by causing an even more destructive mental breakdown in Gibreel. *The Satanic Verses*' twice removed parodic version of Podsnappery thus pursues Dickens's critical treatment of "Anglo-centredness" to reflect upon the migrant condition and its dilemmas.

Friend! also crystallises the ambivalent strategy of appropriation at work in the novel. Do Rushdie and Dickens remain mutual friends in *The Satanic Verses*? If a strategy of postcolonial reinscription is evidently at work in Rushdie's adaptation of Dickens, *The Satanic Verses* simultaneously highlights the topicality of the Victorian writer's satire of jingoism and the vanity fair of "Society" in *Our Mutual Friend*. By transposing the novel to the new contexts of an increasingly multicultural world, Rushdie attests to the relevance of Dickens's work while expressing the need to reconsider its significance from a different cultural position. To quote Homi Bhabha; "The process of reinscription and negotiation—the insertion of intervention of something that takes on new meaning" therefore combines a homage to Dickens's insights into human nature and society with "a contestation of the given symbols of authority" (*The Location of Culture* 193) which enables the production of new forms and meanings.

Notes

1. See Martine Hennard Dutheil de la Rochère, *Origin and Originality in Rushdie's Fiction*, esp. Chap. 1.
2. In *Haroun and the Sea of Stories*, however, the father-son relationship is treated in the sentimental mode. Haroun embarks on a quest to rescue his father, the storyteller Rashid Khalifa, and return to him his special gift of storytelling along with his eloped wife. This updated *Arabian Nights* complete with silly princes, corrupt politicians and technological conundrums reads like an allegory of Rushdie's own predicament.
3. On the mixed traditions of his novels, see " 'Commonwealth Literature' Does Not Exist" (1983), "Günter Grass" (1984), and "In Good Faith" (1990) in *Imaginary Homelands*. To these incomplete lists of novelistic influences must of course be added the many sources from high and popular culture that Rushdie delights in hybridising, from Ovid to *The Wizard of Oz*, from the Qur'an to the Bombay talkies. The much noted Grass-Rushdie connection is extensively documented by Patricia Merivale in "Saleem Fathered by Oskar: Intertextual Strategies in *Midnight's Children* and *The Tin Drum*." She discusses similarities in narrative technique, structure, tone and themes, among which "ambiguous paternity [which] forms a large part of [the protagonists'] search for origins" (*Reading Rushdie* 84).
4. Chandrabhanu Pattanayak, "Interview with Salman Rushdie," *The Literary Criterion* 18.3 (1983): 19-22. Reprinted in *Conversations with Salman Rushdie*, ed. Michael Reder (Jackson: UP of Mississippi, 2000) 17-19. See also Ameena Meer, "Salman Rushdie," *BOMB* 27 (Spring 1989): 61-74. Reprinted in *Conversations with Salman Rushdie*, ed. Michael Reder (Jackson: UP of Mississippi, 2000) 110-22, esp. 111.
5. Keith Wilson establishes numerous parallels between *Midnight's Children* and *Tristram Shandy*, another of Rushdie's most commented-upon intertexts, including "ill-starred origins [...] linked to the striking of a clock" (*Reading Rushdie* 65). In the same volume, Nancy E. Batty discusses the shaping influence of the *Arabian Nights* on *Midnight's Children* as a text which "dramatize[s] the problematic relationship of life to art" (*Reading Rushdie* 69).
6. Dickens is not the only novelist to be fascinated by the *Arabian Nights*. Elleke Boehmer traces the widespread influence of the tales in nineteenth century works as diverse as Wordsworth's *The Prelude*,

Charlotte Brontë's *Jane Eyre*, Anthony Trollope's *Tales of All Countries* and De Quincey's *The Confessions of an English Opium Eater*.

7. When he learns that David recalls the stories he read as a child, Steerforth suggests the following arrangement in exchange for his protection and friendship: "'Then I tell you what, young Copperfield,' [...] 'you shall tell 'em to me. I can't get to sleep very early at night, and I generally wake rather early in the morning. We'll go over 'em one after another. We'll make some regular Arabian Nights of it.' I felt extremely flattered by this arrangement, and we commenced carrying it into execution that very evening. What ravages I committed in my interpretation of them, I am not in condition to say, and should be very unwilling to know; but I had a profound faith in them, and I had, to the best of my belief, a simple, earnest manner of narrating what I did narrate; and these qualities went a long way" (*David Copperfield* 144-45).
8. This contrasts with Rushdie's description of his father as "a magical parent of young children" in Ian Hamilton's lively pre-fatwa biography. Rushdie's sister Sameen adds: "We never had a 'story a night.' The story never ended. [...] One story fell into another story. Some of them were rooted in the 'Arabian Nights,' but he would embellish them and some he would tell straight, probably depending on how imaginative or tired he was feeling. That they never ended is what I remember" ("The First Life of Salman Rushdie," 92). Rushdie's loving homage to his story-telling father is of course Rashid Khalifa, Haroun's father in *Haroun and the Sea of Stories*, which he has dedicated to his own son, Zafar.
9. Said notes that "In his new carrier as colonial businessman, Pip is hardly an exceptional figure, since nearly all of Dickens's businessmen, wayward relatives, and frightening outsiders have a fairly normal and secure connection with the empire" (*Culture and Imperialism* xvii). Elleke Boehmer documents this assertion and shows how Australia, like India, "acts to relieve social and sexual embarrassment" in Dickens's novels (*Colonial and Postcolonial Literature* 28). Thus, Mr Micawber believes that "something of an extraordinary nature will turn up on that shore" and fallen Emily is taken to Australia to begin a new life.
10. In the 1869 preface to his novel, Dickens states that "Of all my books, I like this the best. It will be easily believed that I am a fond parent to every child of my fancy, and that no one can ever love that family as dearly as I love them. But, like many fond parents, I have in my heart of hearts a favourite child. And his name is DAVID COPPERFIELD."
11. Omar Khayyam Shakil is named after a poet whose fate is equally trans-cultural, as the narrator takes pains to point out: "Omar Khayyam's position as a poet is curious. He was never very popular in his native Persia; and he exists in the West in a translation that is really a complete reworking of his verses, in many cases very different from the spirit (to say nothing of the content) of the original. I, too, am a translated man" (*Shame* 29).

12. Rushdie has repeatedly stressed the influence of native oral forms on his own novels, which adopt their digressive, repetitive and self-conscious shape. Intent on dislocating origins, Rushdie conflates Western postmodern fiction and the age-old Indian oral tradition in a 1984 interview with David Brooks: "One of the strange things about the oral narrative—which I did look at closely before writing *Midnight's Children*—is that you find there a form which is thousands of years old, and yet which has all the methods of the postmodernist novel [...]. It seems to me that when you look at the old narrative and use it, as I tried to do, as the basis of a novel, you become a postmodernist writer by being a very traditional one." (*Conversations with Salman Rushdie* 59)
13. Steven Connor observes that in *Bleak House* and *Our Mutual Friend*, the city of London functions as a metaphor for the imaginary space of the text. In *The Satanic Verses*, London (or, rather, a re-presentation of Dickens's London) is condensed on the film-set which superposes residential and derelict areas, collapses and conflates class barriers, "telescoping together [...] centres and margins." Alert to the ambivalence of Rushdie's citation, Connor remarks that "There is both mockery and admiration in [his] enjoyment of the vulgar travesty of the novel being brought about in this adaptation" (*The English Novel in History* 124).
14. In his influential essay "Postmodernism and Consumer Society," Fredric Jameson identifies postmodernism as a reaction against the "dead, stifling, canonical [...] reified monuments" (*The Anti-Aesthetic* 112) of the establishment; it notably takes the form of pastiche, a type of "blank parody" which incorporates various texts where traditional distinctions between high culture and mass or popular culture are erased. Although it certainly conflates the "high" and the "low," Rushdie's parody of *Othello* is far from blank. Saladin's reenactment of Iago's destruction of Othello/Gibreel and the beautiful blonde Desdemona/Allie Cone is the ultimate evidence of his alienation to "white" values. Indeed, *Othello* "is an obvious focus for counter-discursive interpretations because it centralises racial issues, presenting miscegenation as not just a metaphorical threat to the white society but as an actualised event" (*Post-Colonial Drama* 24).
15. Gaffer Hexam briefly reappears in the dramatic context of communalist violence in India, when Saladin Chamcha reads about a massacre of Muslims in the newspapers: "In a north Indian town there had been a massacre of Muslims, and their corpses had been dumped in the water, where they awaited the ministrations of some twentieth century Gaffer Hexam" (*The Satanic Verses* 518). In this passage, the Dickensian allusion signals a shift from West to East, and from postmodern levity to real-life tragedy.
16. J. Hillis Miller has stressed the importance of the motif of mirroring in *Our Mutual Friend*, and brilliantly discussed its significance in relation to Dickens's social critique: "The reflection in the mirror is emptied of its solidity and presented as a thin surface of appearance hiding

fathomless depths of nullity" (127). Miller argues that the Veneering dinner parties are already "an elaborate theatrical ceremony resting on nothing, and the people who come to these parties have been so dehumanized by their submission to money that they exist not as human beings, but as their abstract roles, 'Boots,' 'Brewer,' and so on" (*The Victorian Novel* 126).

17. Elleke Boehmer usefully reminds us that such patriotic rhetoric was widespread in the second half of the nineteenth century. She suggests that "In Britain itself, patriotism, called jingoism in its more rabid forms, was perhaps the most powerful medium through which the belief in the Empire was maintained." Theories of racial and cultural superiority combined with the so-called duty to bring civilisation, prosperity and Christianity to the 'savages' conspired to legitimate imperial rule. Indeed, in Boehmer's felicitous phrase, "the Victorians had a genius for fashioning moral ideals which matched their economic needs" (*Colonial and Postcolonial Literature* 35, 36).

Works Cited

Ball, John Clement. "An Interview with Salman Rushdie." *The Toronto South Asian Review* 10.1 (1988): 30-37. Rpt. *Conversations with Salman Rushdie.* Ed. Michael Reder. Jackson: UP Mississippi, 2000. 101-09.

Batty, Nancy E. "The Art of Suspense: Rushdie's 1001 (Mid-)Nights." *Reading Rushdie: Perspectives on the Fiction of Salman Rushdie.* Ed. M.D. Fletcher. Amsterdam: Rodopi, 1994. 69-81.

Bhabha, Homi K. *The Location of Culture.* London and New York: Routledge, 1994.

Boehmer, Elleke. *Colonial and Postcolonial Literature: Migrant Metaphors.* Oxford and New York: Oxford UP, 1995.

Brooks, David. "Salman Rushdie." *Helix* 19/20 (1984): 55-69. Rpt. *Conversations with Salman Rushdie.* Ed. Michael Reder. Jackson: UP Mississippi, 2000. 57-71.

Clayton, Jay. "Is Pip Postmodern? Or, Dickens at the End of the Twentieth Century." *Great Expectations.* Ed. Janice Carlisle. Boston and New York: Bedford Books of St. Martin's Press, 1996. 606-24.

Connor, Steven. *The English Novel in History: 1950-1995.* London and New York: Routledge, 1996.

Dickens, Charles. *David Copperfield.* Harmondsworth: Penguin, 1986.

____. *Our Mutual Friend.* Oxford and New York: Oxford UP, 1991.

Gilbert, Helen and Joanne Tompkins. *Post-Colonial Drama: Theory, Practice, Politics.* London and New York: Routledge, 1996.

Glendinning, Victoria. "A Novelist in the Country of the Mind." *The Sunday Times* 25 Oct. 1981: 38.

Hamilton, Ian. "The First Life of Salman Rushdie." *The New Yorker* 25 Dec. 1995 and 1 Jan. 1996: 90-113.

Hennard Dutheil de la Rochère, Martine. *Origin and Originality in Rushdie's Fiction*. Bern, Berlin: Peter Lang, 1999.

Hillis Miller, J. "Our Mutual Friend." *The Victorian Novel: Modern Essays in Criticism*. Ed. Ian Watt. London, Oxford and New York: Oxford UP, 1971. 123-32.

Jaggi, Maya. "The Last Laugh." *New Statesman and Society* 8 Sep. 1995: 20-21.

Jameson, Fredric. "Postmodernism and Consumer Society." *The Anti-Aesthetic: Essays on Postmodern Culture*. Ed. Hal Foster. Seattle, Washington: Bay Press, 1991. 111-25.

Meer, Ameena. "Salman Rushdie." *BOMB* 27 (Spring 1989): 61-74. Rpt. *Conversations with Salman Rushdie*. Ed. Michael Reder. Jackson: UP Mississippi, 2000. 110-22.

Merivale, Patricia. "Saleem Fathered by Oskar: Intertextual Strategies in *Midnight's Children* and *The Tin Drum*." *Reading Rushdie: Perspectives on the Fiction of Salman Rushdie*. Ed. M.D. Fletcher. Amsterdam: Rodopi, 1994. 83-96.

Neill, Heather. "Saved by a Sea of Stories." *The Sunday Telegraph* 20 Sept. 1998: 7.

Pattanayak, Chandrabhanu. "Interview with Salman Rushdie." *The Literary Criterion* 18.3 (1983): 19-22. Rpt. *Conversations with Salman Rushdie*. Ed. Michael Reder. Jackson: UP of Mississippi, 2000. 17-19.

Rushdie, Salman. *Haroun and the Sea of Stories*. London: Granta and Penguin, 1990.

____. *Imaginary Homelands: Essays and Criticism 1981-1991*. London: Granta and Penguin, 1991.

____. *Midnight's Children*. London: Picador, 1982.

____. *Shame*. London: Picador, 1984.

_____. *The Moor's Last Sigh*. London: Jonathan Cape, 1995.

____. *The Satanic Verses*. London: Viking Penguin, 1988.

Said, Edward. *Culture and Imperialism*. London: Vintage, 1994.

____. *Orientalism: Western Conceptions of the Orient*. Harmondsworth: Penguin, 1991.

"Salman Rushdie: A Literary Conversation." Interview by Kumkum Sangari. *Book Review* 8.5 (April 1984): 247-53.

Suleri, Sara. *The Rhetoric of English India*. Chicago and London: U of Chicago P, 1992.

Wilson, Keith. "*Midnight's Children* and Reader Responsibility." *Reading Rushdie: Perspectives on the Fiction of Salman Rushdie*. Ed. M.D. Fletcher. Amsterdam: Rodopi, 1994. 55-68.

9

'Old Stable Ego of the Character': The Politics of Identity in Rushdie's Fiction

MICHAEL HENSEN

In Salman Rushdie's latest novel *The Ground Beneath Her Feet* (1999) the first-person narrator makes the following statement about the identity of one of the protagonists:

> To her last day, I could always see in her the skittish, disintegrated creature she'd been when she first came to us, looking as if she might run away again at any moment. What a piece of jetsam she was then, what a casualty! Literally selfless, her personality smashed, like a mirror, by the fist of her life. Her name, her mother and family, her sense of place and home and safety and belonging and being loved, her belief in the future, all these things had been pulled out from under her, like a rug. She was floating in a void, denatured, dehistoried, clawing at the shapelessness, trying to make some sort of mark [...]. She was a rag-bag of selves, torn fragments of people she might have become. Some days she sat crumpled in a corner like a string-cut puppet, and when she jerked into life you never knew who would be there, in her skin (Rushdie 1999: 121-22).

From this statement it immediately becomes clear that "the old stable ego of the character" (Lawrence, qtd. in Gorra 1994: 655) and therefore also the traditional approach of the self as being developed out of family or place is to be dismissed when analysing Rushdie's novels. In order to show how Rushdie perceives identity, a closer look at an approach to identity by the social sciences seems to be particularly rewarding as it differentiates between personal and social identity.

1. Personal and Social Identity

Personal identity, according to the psycho-sociologist Erik Erikson, is an individual's "subjective sense of a continuous existence and a coherent memory" (Erikson 1968: 61). According to the sociologist Peter Wagner, who elaborates on Erikson's theory, this definition communicates several messages. Firstly, this means that identity is highly subjective and can only be gained through a self-reflexive process (cf. also Kamm et al 1994: 12), secondly, that this process is used to develop a continuous existence, although there might have been breaks and faults in one's life, and thirdly, that the individual's mind tries to generate a coherent view of itself, i.e. tries to identify past events as part of its own identity (Wagner 1998: 45).

Social identity, by contrast, is the identification of one individual with the other, be it a small group, a religious community, or a nation (Wagner 1998: 45). What is important, however, is the dialectical relationship between these two aspects of the term identity. Social identity, on the one hand, necessitates the existence of several people's personal identities targeting the same objective. On the other hand, personal identity can often only be comprehended in terms of denial or acceptance of collective or cultural values, indicating that there is a gap, or call it *différance* in the Derridaean sense, between society or parts of it and the individual self (Wagner 1998: 46). This difference means that in order to keep one's identity one will have to interpret oneself constantly, and by doing so one is constructing one's own identity. If identity is regarded as a construct (cf. Assmann & Friese 1998: 12-13; Motz 2000; Wagner 1998: 63-65), then the notion of easy coherence in life and continuity of the self is deceptive as there will always be ruptures and discontinuities. This means that in the postmodern or poststructuralist sense identity is to be regarded as an adaptable and thus unstable and fluid entity, and that identity is the product of continuing exchange and endless negotiations (Assmann & Friese 1998: 12).

2. Deconstruction of Identity in the Traditional Sense

2.1 Parents and Family / Family Name

The family (especially the parents) has been traditionally seen as central to a person's identity. In most of Rushdie's novels, however, the protagonists do not really know who their parents are, or if they do, they deliberately choose not to accept this insight.

Saleem Sinai in *Midnight's Children* makes the reader believe that his parents are Ahmed and Amina Sinai, a wealthy Indian couple, and he also describes in great detail their life and experiences. In the middle of the novel it becomes clear, though, that after the delivery the nurse Mary Pereira swapped two babies, so that Saleem is actually not the midnight's child Saleem Sinai, but the baby he was swapped for, i.e. Shiva. This means that Saleem would be the child of the poor busker Wee Willie Winkie and his wife Vanita. But nine months before the delivery Vanita had sexual intercourse with the Englishman William Methwold, so that Saleem turns out to be of Anglo-Indian descent (Rushdie 1982: 118). This is something he constantly denies and he rather chooses to believe that Ahmed and Amina still are his parents (Rushdie 1982: 118). Thus Saleem deliberately makes up, or constructs, his parents and his descent, later also naming other potential parents: the nurse Mary Pereira and Nadir Khan (Rushdie 1982: 127), Mr Schaapsteeker (Rushdie 1982: 148-49) or Picture Singh (Rushdie 1982: 378).

More or less the same holds true for *The Ground Beneath Her Feet* where the protagonist and rockstar Vina Apsara can be seen as having five different parents. She is the American-born child of a Greek-American mother and an Indian father. After the divorce her mother marries again, this time an American by origin, but the second marriage drives the mother mad and being utterly desperate she kills herself and the rest of the family, sparing only her daughter, who is then transferred to other American relatives at the West Coast. But they, having run out of money, contact the girl's Indian relatives who promise to take her as their daughter. As a result of having been treated badly there she flees and finally arrives at the house of the first-person narrator, whose parents Ameer and Vivvy are the last parents to accept her as their child.

This multiplication of parentage in *Midnight's Children*, as well as in *The Ground Beneath Her Feet*, is seemingly nonsensical but works in the way of a reverse pattern: by naming too many parents none seems to be plausible so that both protagonists can be viewed as being in a state of orphanhood and displacement. Accordingly, Juan-Navarro contends that Rushdie's protagonists lack a symbolic centre (Juan-Navarro 1993: 269), which is also underlined by the fact that Saleem is constantly referring to a "hole in the centre of me" (e.g. Rushdie 1982: 192). Nevertheless both protagonists state that they can maintain their identity and they do so by constructing a coherent view of themselves.[1]

This is also true of Moraes Zogoiby, the protagonist of *The Moor's Last Sigh* who is disinherited by his parents and finally kicked out of the parental home:

> I stumbled through them [the gates], giddy, disoriented, lost. I was nobody, nothing. Nothing I had ever known was of use, nor could I any longer say that I knew it. I had been emptied, invalidated; I was, to use a hoary but suddenly fitting epithet, ruined. I had fallen from grace, and the horror of it shattered the universe, like a mirror. I felt as though I, too, had shattered; as if I were falling to earth, not as myself, but as a thousand and one fragmented images of myself, trapped in shards of glass (Rushdie 1995: 278-79).

Despite this shattered vision Moraes has of himself at this moment he later seems to be able to collect himself and claim to have found his true self without needing his parents any more: "I need no longer be what ancestry, breeding and misfortune had decreed, but could enter, at long last, into myself—my true self" (Rushdie 1995: 295). Read on another level, this implies that Moraes' move from his former hybrid identity towards a simplistic and easily determinable one, mirrors the state India is in.[2] At the end of the novel, however, Moraes makes a plea for a broad concept of identity as he conjures up his predecessors from all around the globe: King Arthur, Barbarossa, Finn MacCool and the Worm Ouroboros (cf. Rushdie 1995: 433).

The Ground Beneath Her Feet offers yet another aspect to the point that identity may also be seen as independent of one's family background. Apart from calling five different couples her parents, Vina Apsara, in keeping with the traditions of the music business, makes up her own name: 'Vina' for an Indian musical instrument and also for being morphologically close to 'Divina,' and 'Apsara' who, according to Hindu myth, is a beautiful nymph who is consorting with other mythical beings skilled in music and who is constantly tempting men (cf. Knappert 1991: 52). In the course of the novel it turns out that both parts of her chosen name will prove right for her behaviour: she is not only skilled in all music matters but also in seducing and consuming men. From this it seems possible that by constructing one's name one can also construct one's identity.

2.2 Place and Home

Another element of the traditional view of identity is that a person's character is determined by the environment she or he grows up or lives in. This is questioned in Rushdie's novels because most of the protagonists are migrants who do not see place as a feature by which a person's character is moulded.

In *Grimus* the orphaned protagonist Flapping Eagle is forced to leave his tribe and wander aimlessly around the world, and in *Midnight's Children* Saleem travels the whole Indian subcontinent physically as well as by his telepathic powers. *The Satanic Verses* offers another angle when the Indian protagonists Saladin Chamcha and Gibreel Farishta migrate to England, go back to India in the end, and in between dream themselves into different times and places. Moraes Zogoiby in *The Moor's Last Sigh* travels India as well as Spain, and his father changes his appearance and character according to whether he deals with the world overneath or underneath, i.e. with the underworld (Rushdie 1995: 179-80).

What all these novels also have in common regarding the notion of place is firstly, that one can strike one's roots in any culture, and secondly, that the culture one is brought up in cannot be easily pinned down either. For example, the Cochin-born Moraes is of Jewish-Christian-Muslim descent and Vina Apsara is of Greek-Indian-American origin. This means that the notion of a single, fixed identity cannot easily be ascribed to place and cultural roots because these in themselves already are the product of diversity and intermingling (cf. also Bhabha 1994: 35).

3. Identity and Hybridity

Most of Rushdie's protagonists are migrants, of their own will—migrants who have to construct their personal identity in relation to the often entirely different social identity around them. They have chosen a specific country and culture, and then have the possibility to make themselves at home there and to put down roots. This is something Umeed Merchant, the Indian-born first-person narrator of *The Ground Beneath Her Feet*, senses when he looks at his new house in New York:

> So this is what they feel like, I thought: roots. Not the ones we're born with, can't help having, but the ones we put down in our own chosen soil, the you could say radical selections we make for ourselves (Rushdie 1999: 414).

The question is, however, whether the migrant chooses, or selects to put down roots after all. This may not be the case, taking into account that his or her sense of personal identity might deviate considerably from the (assumed and actual) cultural identities of the appointed destination. What the migrant, usually being a member of a minority, senses is the difference and the tension between him or herself and the Other, and it is up to the migrant how to deal with it. The two extremes possible are either identification with or denial of cultural values.

This theme is developed in *The Satanic Verses*. Whereas the

Indian Gibreel Farishta tries to hold on to a consistent idea of selfhood deciding not to adapt to English society, his fellow countryman Saladin Chamcha chooses to do just that. In the course of the novel Gibreel is rewarded, represented by his obtaining a halo (Rushdie 1992: 142) and passing his bad breath on to Saladin (Rushdie 1992: 133), who is being punished for having selected adaptation: he grows horns (Rushdie 1992: 141) and finally also a hoof. The narrator comments on the migrant status of Gibreel and Saladin:

> Should we even say that these are two fundamentally different *types* of self? Might we not agree that Gibreel, [...]—has wished to remain, to a large degree, *continuous*—that is, joined to and arising from his past;—[...]—so that his is still a self which, for our present purposes, we may describe as true [...] whereas Saladin Chamcha is a creature of *selected* discontinuities, a *willing* re-invention; his *preferred* revolt against history being what makes him, in our chosen idiom, 'false'? [...]—While Gibreel, to follow the logic of our established terminology, is to be considered 'good' by virtue of *wishing to remain*, for all his vicissitudes, at bottom an untranslated man. —But, and again but: this sounds, does it not, dangerously like an intentionalist fallacy?—Such distinctions, resting as they must on an idea of the self as being (ideally) his vicissitudes, at bottom an untranslated man. homogeneous, non-hybrid, 'pure,'—an utterly fantastic notion!—cannot, must not, suffice (Rushdie 1992: 427).

This differentiation between good and evil with regard to the migrant's position towards adaptability is not only verbally deconstructed by the narrator. Later, back in India, Gibreel's problem of sulphurous halitosis returns with a vengeance on him, and he loses his girl-friend and his job before finally committing suicide (Rushdie 1992: 546), whereas Saladin is reconciled with his father, inherits his wealth and reunites with his girl-friend Zeeny Vakil (Rushdie 1992: 547).

Migrants on their quest for identity in their chosen new home can compare their identity with that of the others, and some of the migrants (Saladin, for example) might be able to translate themselves culturally. If they choose to do so, they will have to form their identity in the tension between the already known and the new culture. Thus their identities become hybrid, meaning that their selves will be "composed of different or incongruous elements of heterogeneous sources" (*OED*). The term hybridity has its origins in the 19th-century biological theory, denoting the crossing of two different species (Young 1995: 12). Later, especially in colonial times, the term was used pejoratively for half-breeds, but in the broader sense the term nowadays alludes to the contact between two or more cultures, between the self and the Other (Bhabha 1994: 35; Fludernik 1998b: 11-12). The relationship between these two is dialectical, it is an irreconcilable contradiction and a difference that can never be solved, but one cannot be without the other either. This tension is what Bhabha terms "the third space" (Bhabha in an interview with Rutherford 1990: 211; Bhabha 1994: 37) and he uses this notion to "deconstruct the boundary between the self and other" (Fludernik 1998a: 51). This space between cultures is the one in which migrants move and out of which they will have to develop their personal identity. This idea of migrants' identities is exactly what most of Rushdie's novels elaborate on (cf. also Goetsch 1997: 143). In his essay "Imaginary Homelands"—the term itself being an alternative image for the third space—Rushdie subsequently talks about migrants' identities:

> Our identity is at once plural and partial. Sometimes we feel that we straddle two cultures; at other times that we fall between two stools. But however ambiguous and shifting this ground may be, it is not an infertile territory for the writer to occupy (Rushdie 1991: 15).

What the migrant can gain from his oscillation between the two (or more) cultures is a newness which can only be achieved by bringing together two seemingly incompatible positions. And this is also the answer to one of the narrator's central questions in *The Satanic Verses*: "How does newness come into the world?" (e.g., Rushdie 1992: 8). By breaking up dichotomies, by bringing together two dissimilar views, by joining the self with the Other.

It has to be stated, however, that migrants may also face

serious problems and eventually even the loss of parts of their identity. Problems will inevitably arise if the majority puts pressure on the migrant, and the results of oppression are vividly depicted in Saladin's brutal arrest by several immigration officers (Rushdie 1992: 157-64). And by gaining something new, undoubtedly something old has to be left behind. This, for example, is powerfully outlined by the frequent references to incidents taking place in airplanes, a metaphor for crossing Bhabha's third space, in Rushdie's novels:

In *The Satanic Verses* Saladin and Gibreel fall out of an exploding aircraft towards England, the fall symbolising their fall from grace as well as the fall of Lucifer,[3] and some of their transformations already start during their fall. In *The Moor's Last Sigh* Moraes boards an airplane and notices that his old understanding of his personal identity will probably not work any more:

> You will see that I entered an unfamiliar state of mind. The place, language, people and customs I knew had all been removed from me by the simple act of boarding this flying vehicle; and these, for most of us, are the four anchors of the soul (Rushdie 1995: 383).[4]

And finally in *The Ground Beneath Her Feet* Ormus, the lover and future husband of Vina Apsara, "sheds his old skin [...] like a snake" (Rushdie 1999: 250) when flying from India towards London. Strikingly, the whole chapter dedicated to the flight is termed "Membrane," suggesting that all migrant travellers, by having to penetrate this membrane, can only save some parts of their identity and thus have to leave back some other parts:

> [...] detached from the indifferent earth, he feels a certain resistance in the air. Something fighting back against the aircraft's forward movement. As if there's a stretchy translucent membrane across the sky, an ectoplasmic barrier, a Wall [...]. But it's so springy, this invisible restriction, it keeps pushing the airplane back, boeing!, boeing!, until at last the *Mayflower* breaks through, it's through! Sunlight bounces off the wing into his bleary eye.

> And as he passes that unseen frontier he sees the tear in the sky, [...]. He intuits that every bone in his body is being irradiated by something pouring through the sky-rip, a mutation is occurring at the level of the cell, of the gene, of the particle. The person who arrives won't be the one who left, or not quite (Rushdie 1999: 253).[5]

This also compares with the notion of the migrant's (cultural) translation. The term translation, as Rushdie states, etymologically comes from the Latin word for 'bearing across':

> Having been borne across the world, we [migrants] are translated men. It is normally supposed that something always gets lost in translation; I cling, obstinately, to the notion that something can also be gained (Rushdie 1991: 17).

4. Conclusion

It has become clear that almost all of Rushdie's novels suggest that an individual can never restrain from being influenced by cultural identity. Therefore, it is not surprising that Moraes speaks about "a self without walls" (Rushdie 1995: 288) and finally even draws the parallel between 14th-century multi-ethnic Granada and its Alhambra and the "need for flowing together, for putting an end to frontiers, for the dropping of the boundaries of the self" (Rushdie 1995: 433). Saleem Sinai, too, alludes to the notion of hybrid identity when he says:

> O eternal opposition of inside and outside! Because, a human being, inside himself, is anything but a whole, anything but homogeneous; all kinds of everywhichthing are jumbled up inside him, and he is one person one minute and another person the next (Rushdie 1982: 236-37).

His later approach towards defining his personal identity can succeed only by relating the self to the environment.

> Who what am I? My answer: I am the sum total of everything that went before me, of all I have been seen done, of everything done-to-me. I am everyone everything whose being-in-the-world affected was affected by mine. I am

> anything that happens after I have gone which would not have happened if I had not come. [...] I repeat for the last time: to understand me, you'll have to swallow a world (Rushdie 1982: 383).

Other terms that frequently come up in Rushdie's novels are impurity, intermingling, transformation, mongrelization, mélange, hotchpotch, pastiche and finally palimpsest: What Rushdie has to say about *The Satanic Verses* thus certainly holds true for most of his novels.

> *The Satanic Verses* celebrates hybridity, impurity, intermingling, the transformation that comes of new and unexpected combinations of human beings, cultures, ideas, politics, movies, songs. It rejoices in mongrelization and fears the absolutism of the Pure. Mélange, hotchpotch, a bit of this and a bit of that is how newness enters the world (Rushdie 1991: 394).

All these terms show that in Rushdie's novels identity is not a unitary entity but rather a fragment, not stable but fluid, not single but multiple, not coherent or continuous but hybrid. This does not mean that an individual cannot think himself or herself as coherent. One has to accept, however, certain discontinuities and ruptures in one's biography.

Thus, personal identity has to be seen as a perpetual process of negotiations with oneself and one's environment, which is very much in line with Zygmunt Bauman's statement on postmodern identity-building: "'identity,' though ostensibly a noun, behaves like a verb, albeit a strange one to be sure: it appears only in the future tense" (Bauman 1995: 82). Accordingly, Salman Rushdie goes beyond the theoretical approach outlined in the beginning: today identity arises out of cross-border and cross-continental exchange.

Notes

1. In the case of Saleem Sinai this coherence is mainly achieved by the act of writing: "I must work fast, faster than Scheherazade, if I am to end up meaning—yes, meaning—something" (Rushdie 1982: 9) whereas Vina Apsara achieves this goal by singing. Thus they both construct their identities by means of creating pieces of art, i.e. cultural constructs, and enhance the constructedness of their identity.

2. In this passage India's pluralistic society is severely threatened by semi-fictional Hindu fundamentalists (cf. Rushdie 1995: 290ff).
3. The carrier is named Bostan (Rushdie 1992: 4) after one of the Gardens of Eden (cf. also Aravamudan 1989: 8).
4. In this context Schülting's view of Moraes as being "the most hybrid of characters" in the novel holds true as he "possesses not two, but multiple identities, or, as he says, none at all" (Schülting 1998: 248-49).
5. In the context of this chapter it would also be possible to speak of 'cultural osmosis,' denoting that the contact between cultures is based on negotiation and the process of mutual give and take within the third space.

Works Cited

Aravamudan, Srinivas. 1989. "'Being God's Postman is no Fun, Yaar': Salman Rushdie's *The Satanic Verses*." *Diacritics: A Review of Contemporary Criticism* 19.2: 3-20.

Assmann, Aleida and Heidrun Friese. 1998. "Einleitung." *Identitäten*. Ed. Aleida Assmann and Heidrun Friese. Frankfurt / Main: Suhrkamp. 11-23.

Bauman, Zygmunt. 1995. *Life in Fragments: Essays in Postmodern Morality*. Oxford: Blackwell.

Bhabha, Homi K. 1994. *The Location of Culture*. London: Routledge.

Erikson, Erik H. 1968. "Identity, Psychosocial." *International Encyclopedia of the Social Sciences*, Bk. 7. Ed. David L. Sills. London: Macmillan.

Fludernik, Monika. 1998a. "The Constitution of Hybridity: Postcolonial Interventions." *Hybridity and Postcolonialism: Twentieth-Century Indian Literature*. Ed. Monika Fludernik. Tübingen: Stauffenburg. 19-54.

——. 1998b. "Introduction." *Hybridity and Postcolonialism: Twentieth-Century Indian Literature*. Ed. Monika Fludernik. Tübingen: Stauffenburg. 9-18.

Goetsch, Paul. 1997. "Funktionen von Hybridität in der postkolonialen Theorie." *Literatur in Wissenschaft und Unterricht* 30.2: 135-45.

Gorra, Michael. 1994. "Rudyard Kipling to Salman Rushdie: Imperialism to Postcolonialism." *The Columbia History of the British Novel*. Ed. John Richett. New York: Columbia UP. 631-57.

Juan-Navarro, Santiago. 1993. "The Dialogic Imagination of Salman Rushdie and Carlos Fuentes: National Allegories and the Scene of Writing in *Midnight,s Children* and *Cristobal Nonato*." *Neohelicon: Acta Comparationis Litterarum Universarum* 20.2: 257-11.

Kamm, Jürgen, Norbert Schaffeld and Marion Spies. 1994. *Spuren der Identitätssuche in zeitgenössischen Literaturen*. Trier: WVT.

Knappert, Jan. 1991. *Indian Mythology: An Encyclopedia of Myth and Legend.* London: Aquarian Press.

Motz, Wolfram. 2000. *Die Konstruktion von Identität im schottischen Roman während der Ära des britischen Konservatismus 1979-1997.* Frankfurt / Main: Lang.

Rushdie, Salman. 1996 (1975). *Grimus.* London: Vintage.

——. 1999. *The Ground Beneath Her Feet: A Novel.* New York: Henry Holt.

——. 1991. "Imaginary Homelands." *Imaginary Homelands: Essays and Criticism 1981-1991.* Ed. Salman Rushdie. Harmondsworth: Penguin. 9-21.

——. 1982 (1981). *Midnight,s Children.* London: Macmillan.

——. 1995. *The Moor's Last Sigh.* London: Cape.

——. 1992 (1988). *The Satanic Verses.* Dover (Del.): The Consortium.

Rutherford, Jonathan. 1990. "Interview with Homi Bhabha: The Third Space." *Identity: Community, Culture, Difference.* Ed. Jonathan Rutherford. London: Lawrence and Wishart. 207-21.

Schülting, Sabine. 1998. "Peeling off History in Salman Rushdie's *The Moor's Last Sigh.*" *Hybridity and Postcolonialism: Twentieth-Century Indian Literature.* Ed. Monika Fludernik. Tübingen: Stauffenburg. 239-60.

Wagner, Peter. 1998. "Fest-Stellungen. Beobachtungen zur sozialwissenschaftlichen Diskussion über Identität." *Identitäten.* Ed. Aleida Assmann and Heidrun Friese. Frankfurt / Main: Suhrkamp. 44-72.

Young, Robert J.C. 1995. *Colonial Desire: Hybridity in Theory, Culture and Race.* London: Routledge.

Bibliography of the Rushdie Criticism

JOEL KUORTTI

1. PRE-1995 CRITICAL WORKS

Supplement to Joel Kuortti, *The Salman Rushdie Bibliography* (1997)

1981

Mukherjee, Meenakshi. "Irreverent, Exuberant and Metaphoric: *Midnight's Children*." *Indian Book Chronicle* 6.23 (Dec. 1981): 381-82.

Nadeau, Raymond. "The Essence of India Captured Remarkably: *Midnight's Children* by Salman Rushdie." *Washington Post* June 28 (1981).

1982

Blaber, Ron. "Darkness and Hope: *Midnight's Children*." *Reviews Journal* (CRNLE) 2 (1982): 33-35.

1983

Jay Cantor, Jay. "Pathos and Beauty in a Modern Fable: *Shame* by Salman Rushdie." *Washington Post* Nov. 20 (1983).

Jaidka, Manju. "The World of Fantasy: *Shame*." *Indian Book Chronicle* 8.22, Nov. 16 (1983) 371-73.

Mukherjee Blaise, Bharati. "Mimicry and Reinvention." *The Commonwealth in Canada*. Ed. Uma Parameswaran. Calcutta: Writers Workshop, 1983. 147-57.

1984

"Rushdie, A Minor Nirad Chaudhuri: *Shame*." *The Literary Half-Yearly* 25.1 (Jan. 1984): 120-23.

1985

Dhawan, R.K. "The Artist as Historian: Some New Writers." *Three Contemporary Novelists*. Ed. R. K. Dhawan. New Delhi: Classical Publishing Company, 1985. 1-32.

Commonwealth Fiction. In 3 vols. Ed. R.K. Dhawan. New Delhi: Classical Publishing House, 1988. 238-68.

Goodwin, Ken. "The Image of the National Child in the Work of Atwood, Rushdie, Soyinka, and White." *Literature and Commitment: A Commonwealth Perspective*. 3rd Commonwealth in Canada Conference, 1985. Ed. Govind Narain Sharma. Toronto: TSAR, 1988. 15-25.

Mathur, O.P. "*Midnight's Children* and the Indian Identity." *Indian Journal of English Studies* 25 (1985): 42.

1986

Jussawalla, Feroza. "Fact versus Fiction: Attenborough's *Gandhi* and Salman Rushdie's *Midnight's Children*." *ACLALS Bulletin* 7.4 (1986): 70-78.

Kaul, K.R. "A Sealed Chutney Bottle: *Midnight's Children*." *Indian Book Chronicle* 11.11&12 (Nov.-Dec. 1986): 248.

1987

Chandra, Suresh. "The Metaphor of *Shame*: Rushdie's Fact-Fiction." Chandra. *Culture and Criticism: New World Literature*, Series 2. Delhi: B.R. Publishing Corporation, 1987. 61-70. *The Commonwealth Review* 12 (1990): 77-84. *The Novels of Salman Rushdie*. Ed. G.R. Taneja and Rajinder Kuman Dhawan. New Delhi: Indian Society for Commonwealth Studies, 1992. 77-84.

Jaidev. "Salman Rushdie: The Indian Postmodernist." *Punjab Journal of English Studies* 2 (1987): 29-38.

Marwah, Anuradha. "Riding A Jaguar: *The Jaguar Smile: A Nicaraguan Journey*." *The Book Review* 11.2 (Mar.-Apr. 1987): 41-45.

Murti, K.V. Suryanarayan. "Secular Fantasy: Salman Rushdie's Fiction." Murti. *Kohinoor in the Crown: Critical Studies in the Indo-English Literature*. New Delhi: Sterling, 1987. 171-79.

Pandit, M.L. "Fantasy in Salman Rushdie's *Midnight's Children*." *The Indian Novel in English*. Ed. Ravi Nandan Sinha and R.K. Sinha. Ranchi: Ankit Publishers, 1987. 87-92.

Pandit. *New Commonwealth Writing: A Critical Response*. New Delhi: Prestige, 1996. 45-49.

1988

Carter, Angela. "Angels in Dirty Places: *The Satanic Verses.*" *The Guardian* Sep. 23 (1988): 30; in *The Rushdie File*. Eds. Lisa Appignanesi and Sara Maitland. London: 4th Estate, 1989. 10-2 and Syracuse: Syracuse UP, 1990; as "Salman Rushdie: *The Satanic Verses.*" Carter. *Shaking a Leg: Journalism and Writings*. Ed. Jenny Uglow. London: Chatto and Windus, 1997. 586-88.
http://books.guardian.co.uk/reviews/generalfiction/0,6121,99006,00.html

1989

Ahmedi, Arshad. *Rushdie, Haunted by His Unholy Ghosts.* (1989) London. Avon Books. 1997.

Ali, Siddiq. "*Midnight's Children* as Historiography." *Osmania Journal of English Studies* 25 (1989): 130-09.

Engineer, Asghar Ali. "The Storm Over *Satanic Verses.*" *Indian Book Chronicle* 14.4 (Apr. 1989): 94-95.

Hussain, Nasser. "Hyphenated Identity: Nationalistic Discourse, History, and the Anxiety of Criticism in Salman Rushdie's *Shame.*" *Qui Parle: Literature, Philosophy, Visual Arts, History* 3.2 (1989): 1-18.

Kamaluddin, Sabiha. "*Midnight's Children*: History as a Truncated Narrative." *Osmania Journal of English Studies* 25 (1989): 124-29. *Critical Responses: Commonwealth Literature*. New Delhi: Sterling, 1993. 169-73.

Kaul, R.K. "A Journey Through Nicaragua: *The Jaguar Smile: A Nicaraguan Journey.*" *Indian Book Chronicle* 14.1 (Jan. 1989): 12-14.

Lowndes, Colin. "The Unforgivable: *The Satanic Verses.*" *The Toronto South Asian Review* 7.2 (Win 1989): 74-76.

Mojtabai, A.G. "Magical Mystery Pilgrimage: *The Satanic Verses.*" *The New York Times Book Review* 94.5 (29 Jan. 1989): 3 & 37. Repr. abr. in *Contemporary Literary Criticism* 55. Detroit: Gale Research Inc., 1989. 225-26. As "Looking History in the Eye" in *New York Times. The New York Times Book Review* 146 (6 Oct. 1996): 99.

Parameswaran, Uma. "*The Satanic Verses.*" *New Literatures Review* 17 (Sum 1989): 97-98.

Raman, Ratna. "Passage to More than India: Shifting Perspectives in *Kim, A Passage to India* and *Midnight's Children*." *Recent Commonwealth Literature*, I. Ed. R.K. Dhawan, P.V. Dhamija and A.K. Shrivastava. New Delhi: Prestige, 1989. 181-93.

Samuel, Julian. "Salman Rushdie in the Age of Reason." Ramjas College, University of Delhi, Jan. 1989. *US/THEM: Translation, Transcription and Identity in Post-Colonial Literary Cultures*. Ed. Gordon Collier. Cross/Cultures: Readings in the Post/Colonial Literatures in English, 6. Amsterdam and Atlanta, GA: Rodopi, 1992. 201-07.
http://www.indiastar.com/jsamuel.html

Shukla, Malini. "Modes of Narration in Salman Rushdie's *Shame*." *Indian Scholar* 11.1 (Jan. 1989): 65-72.

Singh, Satindra. "Rushdie's Guilt." *Indian Book Chronicle* 14.4 (Apr. 1989): 93-94.

Verma, Charu. "Padma's Tragedy: A Feminist Deconstruction of *Midnight's Children*." *Panjab University Research Bulletin (Arts)* 20.2 (1989): 59-65.

webcurrent.com. "*The Satanic Verses*, a Review." Monday Literary Club (1989).
http://www.webcurrent.com/rushdie.html#top

1990

Alexander, Meena ."Bursting the Margins: Explosive Play in *The Satanic Verses*." *The Toronto South Asian Review* 8.3 (Spr 1990): 28-33.

Chaussee, Griffith A. "A Textual Unicorn: Identity and Islamic Reference in Salman Rushdie's *Shame*." *The Toronto South Asian Review* 8.3 (Spr 1990): 17-27.

Cornwell, Neil. *The Literary Fantastic: from Gothic to Postmodernism*. New York and London: Harvester Wheatsheaf, 1990.

King, Bruce. "*The Rushdie File*." *World Literature Today* 64.3 (Sum 1990): 529-30.

Lurdos, Michele. "Passage to Pakistan." *Ailleurs imagines*. Paris: Didier Erudition, 1990. 133-36.

Lurie, Alison. "Another Dangerous Story from Salman Rushdie: *Haroun and the Sea of Stories." The New York Times Book Review* 95.44 Nov. 11 (1990): 1 & 59. http://www.nytimes.com/books/98/07/12/specials/lurie-rushdie.html

Kerr, David. "Migration and the Human Spirit in Salman Rushdie's *The Satanic Verses." The Commonwealth Review* 2.1-2 1990-91): 168-80. *Australian and Indian Literature.* Ed. David Kerr and R. K. Dhawan. New Delhi: Indian Society for Commonwealth Studies, 1991: 168-80.

Merivale, Patricia. "Saleem Fathered by Oskar: *Midnight's Children,* Magic Realism, and *The Tin Drum." ARIEL* 21.3 (July 1990): 5-21. *Reading Rushdie: Perspectives on the Fiction of Salman Rushdie.* Ed. M.D. Fletcher. *Cross/Cultures: Readings in the Post/Colonial Literatures in English,* 16. Amsterdam and Atlanta, GA: Rodopi, 1994. 83-96. *Magical Realism: Theory, History, Community.* Ed. Lois Parkinson Zamora and Wendy B. Faris. Durham: Duke UP, 1995. 329-45.

Myers, David. "From Satiric Farce to Tragic Epiphany: Salman Rushdie's *The Satanic Verses." The Commonwealth Review* 21.2 (1990-1): 144-67. *Australian and Indian Literature.* Ed. David Kerr and R. K. Dhawan. New Delhi: Indian Society for Commonwealth Studies, 1991: 144-67.

Pathak, R.S. "Salman Rushdie's Treatment of Alienation." *Indian Fiction in English: Problems and Promises.* Ed. R.S. Pathak. New Delhi: Northern Book Centre, 1990. 155-69.

Pipes, Daniel. *The Rushdie Affair: The Ayatollah, the Novelist and the West.* Carol, USA: Birch Lane Press, 1990. Indian edition with a Foreword by Koenaard Elst. New Delhi: Voice of India, 1998.

Raina, M.L. "Is Realism a Dead Duck? Observations on the Return of Epic." *Voice from India: Critical Essays on Literature: A Festschrift for Prof. R.K. Kaul.* Ed. Jasbir Jain and Francine E. Krishna. Jaipur: Printwell Publishers, 1990. 154-69.

Reddy, P. Bayapa. "A Political Novel on India: Salman Rushdie's *Midnight's Children.*" Reddy. *Studies in Indian Writing in English.* New Delhi: Prestige, 1990. 70-78.

Reddy, P. Bayapa. "*Shame*: A Point of View." *The Commonwealth Review* 1.2 (1990): 94-101. Reddy. *Studies in Indian Writing in English.* New Delhi: Prestige, 1990: 79-87. *The Novels of Salman Rushdie.* Ed. G.R. Taneja and Rajinder Kuman Dhawan. New Delhi: Indian Society for Commonwealth Studies, 1992. 94-101.

Sardar, Ziauddin and Merryl Wyn Davies. *Distorted Imagination: Lessons from the Rushdie Affair.* London: Grey Seal, 1990; Kuala Lumpur: Berita, 1990. http://msanews.mynet.net/books/lessons/

Schaefer, Claudia. "Media/Mediation: Central America According to the New Journalists." *Nature, Society, and Thought* 3.2 (1990): 135-43.

Women Against Fundamentalism. The Rushdie Affair. http://www.gn.apc.org/waf/j1p12.htm

1991

Dhar, T.N. "A Fable of Our Times: *Haroun and the Sea of Stories.*" *Indian Book Chronicle* 16.4 (Apr. 1991): 5.

Doreswamy, Vani. "Visible Peripheries, Invisible Centres: Imperialism as a Sexual Allegory in *Midnight's Children* and *Shame.*" Rajkot, Feb. 1991. *Contemporary Indian Fiction in English.* Ed. Avadesh K. Singh. Papers of a conference, Rajkot, Feb. 1991. New Delhi: Creative Books, 1994. 45-62. *Commonwealth Quarterly* 19.47 (Dec.-Mar. 1994): 45-62.

Harris, Roy and Christopher New. "English versus Islam: The Asian Voice of Salman Rushdie." *Asian Voices in English.* Ed. Mimi Chan and Roy Harris. Hong Kong: Hong Kong UP, 1991. 87-100.

Hissom, James. "Rushdie's Labyrinth: Polytheism and Narrative Displacement in *The Satanic Verses.*" *The Bulletin of the West Virginia Association of College English Teachers* 13.1 (1991): 1-9.

Ismail, Qadri. "A Bit of This and a Bit of That: Rushdie's Newness." *Social Text* 9.4 (29) (1991): 117-24.

Kapadia, Novy. "Political Allegory: A Comparison of Rushdie's *Haroun and the Sea of Stories* and Joseph Conrad's *Nostromo*." *Indian English Literature: Since Independence*. Ed. K. Ayyappa Paniker. New Delhi: The Indian Association for English Studies, 1991. 55-68. *The Novels of Salman Rushdie*. Ed. G.R. Taneja and Rajinder Kuman Dhawan. New Delhi: Indian Society for Commonwealth Studies, 1992. 217-29.

Mathur, O.P. "A Metaphor of Reality: A Study of the Protagonist of *Midnight's Children*." *Indian English Literature: Since Independence*. Ed. K. Ayyappa Paniker. New Delhi: The Indian Association for English Studies, 1991. 69-78.

Mufti, Aamir. "Reading the Rushdie Affair: An Essay on Islam and Politics." *Social Text* 9.4 (29) (1991): 95-116.

1992

Coppola, Darlene P. and Carlo Coppola. "Rushdie's *The Satanic Verses*: Some Freudian Aspects." *South Asian Review* 16.13 (1992): 84-91.

Duffy, Andrew Enda. "Engendering Monsters." *South Asian Review* 16.13 (1992): 98-109.

Esposito, John L. "'Islamic Fundamentalism' and the West." Esposito. *The Islamic Threat: Myth or Reality?* New York and Oxford: Oxford UP, 1992. Ch. 6, 168-212 & 223-25.

Esposito, John L. "The Significance of the Rushdie Affair." From ch.6 "'Islamic Fundamentalism' and the West" Esposito. *The Islamic Threat*. 1992. 190-93. http://msanews.mynet.net/books/threat/6.6.html

Ferrell, Robert. "Sympathy for the Devil: Salman Rushdie's *The Satanic Verses*." *South Asian Review* 16.13 (1992): 29-37.

Green, Martin. "Gandhi and *The Satanic Verses*." *South Asian Review* 16.13 (1992): 38-47.

Habib, M.A.R. and Tracy K. Habib. "Reader Response: Theory and Orientalism: Is *The Satanic Verses* Teachable?" *South Asian Review* 16.13 (1992): 15-28.

Kanaganayakam, Chelva. "Rushdie in Focus: Salman Rushdie." *World Literature Written in English* 32.1 (Spr 1992): 117-19.

Kern, Suzan. "'His Word Against Mine': An Exploration of Bakhtinian Polarity in Salman Rushdie's *The Satanic Verses.*" *South Asian Review* 16.13 (1992): 78-83.

Lindblad, Ishrat. "Salman Rushdie's *The Satanic Verses*: Monoism Contra Pluralism." *From Commonwealth to Post-Colonial.* Ed. Anna Rutherford. Sydney: Dangaroo Press, 1992. 83-90.

Marrouchi, Mustapha. "Living in the Aftermath of the Death of Ouroboros, Kraken, Leviathan." *South Asian Review* 16.13 (1992): 48-62.

Mookerjea, Sourayan. "Irradiations of History: The Author, Cosmopolitanism and *The Satanic Verses.*" *World Literature Written in English* 32.2-33.1 (1992-3): 107-21.

Pathak, R.S. "Identity Crisis in the Novels of Salman Rushdie." *Quest for Identity in Indian English Writing,* Part I: Fiction. Ed. R.S. Pathak. New Delhi: Bahri Publications, 1992. 112-34.

Al-Raheb, Hani. "Salman Rushdie's *The Satanic Verses*: Fantasy for Religious Satire." *Literary Criterion* 27.4 (1992): 31-41.

Ross, Robert L. "Reading Afterwords Afterwards: *Haroun and the Sea of Stories.*" *South Asian Review* 16.13 (1992): 93-97.

Seshadri Crooks, Kalpana. "Freedom of Speech and the Post-Colonial 'Double Take': Rushdie, Islam and the Enlightenment." *South Asian Review* 16.13 (1992): 1-14.

Suter, David W. "Of the Devil's Party: The Marriage of Heaven and Hell in *Satanic Verses.*" *South Asian Review* 16.13 (1992): 63-77.

Wilson, Keith. "*Imaginary Homelands: Essays and Criticism 1981-1991.*" *ARIEL* 23.2 (Apr. 1992): 137-39.

1993

Afzal-Khan, Fawzia. "Myth De-Bunked: Genre and Ideology in Rushdie's *Midnight's Children* and *Shame.*" *South Asian Review* 17.14 (1993): 76-84.

Aghassi, Hamid H. Mirza. *Fallacies of Satanic Verses: Rushdiesm on Trial.* San Marino, CA: Tarmasal, 1993.

Crane, Ralph J. "Like a Distant Drum Beating Loudly: The Exiled Pen of Salman Rushdie: *Haroun and the Sea of Stories.*" *Reviews Journal* (CRNLE) 2 (1993): 11-18.

Cundy, Catherine. "Rushdie's Women." *Wasafiri* 18 (1993): 13-17.

Ellerby, Janet Mason. "Narrative Imperialism in *The Satanic Verses.*" *Multicultural Literatures through Feminist/ Poststructuralist Lenses.* Ed. Barbara Frey Waxman. Knoxville: U of Tennessee P, 1993. 173-89.

Norman Mailer. "Dear Salman." *The Sunday Times,* Books Feb. 14 (1993): 8. *The Rushdie Letters: Freedom to Speak, Freedom to Write.* Ed. Steve MacDonogh. Lincoln: U of Nebraska P, 1993. Dingle: Brandon Book Publishers Ltd, 1993. 73. *Letters of a Nation: a Collection of Extradordinary American Letters.* Ed. Andrew Carroll. New York: Broadway Book, 1997. "Norman Mailer To Salman Rushdie." http://www.rjgeib.com/thoughts/burning/mailer-rushdie.html

Mehta, Digish. "Fiction of the Interface: Kipling and Rushdie." *Contemporary Indian Fiction in English.* Ed. Avadhesh K. Singh. New Delhi: Creative, 1993. 28-32.

Pothier, Jacques. "Southern Modes of Commitment: Faulkner and Rushdie." *Faulkner, His Contemporaries, and His Posterity.* Ed. Waldemar Zacharasiewicz. Tubingen: Francke, 1993. 360-71.

Purushotham, K. "Rushdie's Images of *Bharateeya Nari* in *Midnight's Children.*" *Kakatiya Journal of English Studies* 13 (1993): 90-103. *Indian Fiction in English.* Eds. Mallikarjuna Rao and Rajeshwar Mittapalli. New Delhi: Atlantic, 1999. 240-51.

Yussef, Saeed. "The Time Wasted for Salman Rushdie." *The Toronto South Asian Review* 11.2 (Win 1993): 49-55.

1994

Bennett, David. "Postmodernism, Postcolonialism and 'the Rushdie Affair.'" *Meridian* 13.2 (1994): 138-58.

Cropley Gonzalez, Madelena. "The Birth of Revolt through Historiographic Metafiction in Salman Rushdie's *Midnight's Children* and *The Satanic Verses*." *Historicite et metafiction dans le roman contemporain des Iles Britanniques*. Ed. Max Duperray. Aix-en-Provence: U de Provence, 1994. 197-206.

Gonzalez, Maria Luz. "Subversion of History and the Creation of Alternative Realities in Salman Rushdie." *Revista Canaria de Estudios Ingleses* 28 (1994): 41-51.

Gowda, H.H. Anniah. "Salman Rushdie and His Fictional Craft." Ed. S. Ramamurthy. *New Nations, New Voices: Essays on Commonwealth Literature*. Papers presented to Dr. K.S. Ramamurti. Tiruchi: 1994. 56-64.

Hand, Felicity. "Challenging the Centre: The Response of British Asian Writers." *Revista Canaria de Estudios Ingleses* 28 (1994): 81-93.

Hayes, Michael. "Autobiography in the Pacific: Changing Functions of Self, Writing and Nation." *New Literatures Review* 27 (Sum 1994): 29-44.

Juan Hatchard, Luis de. "Saleem's Historical Discourse in *Midnight's Children*." *Miscelanea: A Journal of English and American Studies* 15 (1994): 331-45.

Kumar, N. Sunil. "The Whale and the Wail of Commitment." *Malayalam Literary Survey* 18.2 & 3 (Apr.-Sep. 1994): 143-50.

Lewis, Robin Jared. "Salman Rushdie: *Midnight's Children*." *Masterworks of Asian Literature in Comparative Perspective: A Guide for Teaching*. Ed. Barbara Stoler Miller. Armonk, NY: Sharpe, 1994. 178-88.

An-Na'im, Abdullahi. "What Do We Mean by Universal?" *Index on Censorship* 23.4-5 (1994): 120-28.

Natarajan, Nalini. "Woman, Nation, and Narration in *Midnight's Children*." *Scattered Hegemonies: Postmodernity and Transnational Feminist Practices*. Eds. Inderpal Grewal and Caren Kaplan. Minneapolis: U of Minnesota P, 1994. 76-89.

Rao, K.R. "'Handcuffed to History': Rushdie's Narratology." *Journal of Indian Writing in English* 22.2 (July 1994): 37-40.

Rayan, Krishna. "Suggestion or Statement? Three Contemporary Cases." *New Quest* 106 (July-Aug. 1994): 203-08 & 234.

Reddy, K. Venkata. "The Novel of Novels: Salman Rushdie's *Midnight's Children*." *Critical Studies in Commonwealth Literature*. New Delhi: Prestige, 1994. 158-62.

Segal, Hanna. "Salman Rushdie and the Sea of Stories: A Not-So-Simple Fable about Creativity." *The International Journal of Psycho-Analysis* 75.3 (June 1994): 611-88. *Psychoanalysis, Literature and War: Papers 1972-1995*. New Library of Psychoanalysis. Ed. J. Steiner. New York and London: Routledge, 1997.

Sharma, I.K. "Three Expatriate Writers: *Homeless by Choice*." *Indian Book Chronicle* 19.9 (Sep. 1994): 12.

Syal, Pushpinder. "The Composite Structure of Salman Rushdie's *Midnight's Children*." *Structure and Style in Commonwealth Literature*. New Delhi: Vikas, 1994. 129-54.

Virani, Hanif. "Freedom and Responsibility: The Case of *The Satanic Verses*." *Toronto Review of Contemporary Writing Abroad* 12.3 (Fall 1994): 67-73.

Wallia, C.J.S. "*East, West: Stories* by Salman Rushdie." *India, Star Review of Books* (1994).
http://www.indiastar.com/eastwest.htm

Wallia, C.J.S. "*East, West: Stories* by Salman Rushdie." IndoLink (1994).
http://www.indolink.com/Book/book34.html

1995

Ahmad, Aijaz. "The Politics of Literary Postcoloniality." *Race and Class* 36.3 (Jan. 1995): 1-20.

Aji, Aron R. "'All Names Mean Something': Salman Rushdie's *Haroun* and the Legacy of Islam." *Contemporary Literature* 36.1 (1995): 103-29.

Aravamudan, Srinivas. "Fables of Censorship: Salman Rushdie, Satire and Symbolic Violence." *Western Humanities Review* 49.4 (1995): 323-29.

Ascroft, Bill, Gareth Griffiths and Helen Tiffin, eds. *The Postcolonial Studies Reader*. London and New York: Routledge, 1995.

Al-Azm, Sadik. "The Rabelais and Joyce of Our Times!" *Freedom of Expression: the Acid Test.* Ed. Niels Fried-Nielsen Stockholm: Nordic Council, 1995. 116-20.

Balasubramanian, Radha. "The Similarities between Mikhail Bulgakov's *The Master and Margarita* and Salman Rushdie's *The Satanic Verses.*" *International Fiction Review* 22.1-2 (1995): 37-46.

Bedford, Carmel. "Who Will Break the Deadlock?" *Freedom of Expression: the Acid Test.* Ed. Niels Fried-Nielsen Stockholm: Nordic Council, 1995. 30-35.

Bemrose, John. "Tower of Babble: *The Moor's Last Sigh.*" 9 Oct. 1995): 85.

Carey-Abrioux, Cynthia. "In the Name of the Nation: Salman Rushdie's *Shame.*" *Commonwealth Essays and Studies* 18.1 (1995): 48-55.

Cook, Rufus. "'Fusions, Translations, Conjoinings': Cultural Transformation in Salman Rushdie's Work." *World Literature Written in English* 34.2 (1995): 27-37.

Coover, Robert. "There's No Place Like Oz: *East, West.*" *The New York Times Book Review* 100.3 Jan. 15 (1995): 1 & 16-17.
http://www.nytimes.com/books/99/04/18/specials/rushdie-eastwest.html

Culver, Stuart. "A Conversation about *Haroun and the Sea of Stories*: There's No Place Like Home: Salman Rushdie and the Myth of Oz." *Western Humanities Review* 49.4 (1995): 317-22.

Desai, Anjana. "The Veils of Salman Rushdie." *Margins of Erasure: Purdah in the Subcontinental Novel in English.* Ed. Jasbir Jain and Amina Amin. New Delhi: Sterling, 1995. 145-55.

"*East, West.*" *Indian Literature* 38.2 (Mar.-Apr. 1995): 188.

Eder, Richard. "Born of Flight: *East, West.*" *The Los Angeles Times,* Book Review Jan. 29 (1995): 3.

Egeland, Jan. "Norway's Involvement in the Rushdie Affair." *Freedom of Expression: the Acid Test.* Ed. Niels Fried-Nielsen. Stockholm: Nordic Council, 1995. 36-42.

Ekman, Kerstin. "What Can We Learn from the Rushdie Affair?" *Freedom of Expression: the Acid Test.* Ed. Niels Fried-Nielsen. Stockholm: Nordic Council, 1995. 89-94.

Fried-Nielsen, Niels, ed. *Freedom of Expression: the Acid Test.* Stockholm: Nordic Council, 1995.

Fried-Nielsen, Niels. "The Nordic Countries as an Outpost of Freedom of Expression." *Freedom of Expression: the Acid Test.* Ed. Niels Fried-Nielsen. Stockholm: Nordic Council, 1995. 12-20.

Gasiorek, Andrzej. *Post-War British Fiction: Realism and After* London: Edward Arnold, 1995.

Gobel, Walter and Damian Grant. "Salman Rushdie's Silver Medal." *Laurence Sterne in Modernism and Postmodernism.* Ed. David Pierce and Peter de Voogd. Amsterdam: Rodopi, 1995. 87-98.

Grant, Damian. "East, West: Home's Best? Salman Rushdie's Cultural Questioning." *Ateliers* 2 (1995): 33-39.

Gudmundsson, Einar Már. "The Tyranny of Words." *Freedom of Expression: the Acid Test.* Ed. Niels Fried-Nielsen. Stockholm: Nordic Council, 1995. 95-101.

Gurnah, Abdulrazak. "Displacement and Transformation in *The Enigma of Arrival* and *The Satanic Verses.*" *Other Britain, Other British: Contemporary Multicultural Fiction.* Ed. A. Robert Lee. London and East Haven: Pluto Press, 1995. 5-20.

Haarde, Geir H. "The Challenge of Freedom of Expression." *Freedom of Expression: the Acid Test.* Ed. Niels Fried-Nielsen. Stockholm: Nordic Council, 1995. 7-8.

Halliday, Fred. "`Islam Is in Danger': Authority, Rushdie, and the Struggle for the Migrant Soul. *The Next Threat: Western Perceptions of Islam.* Ed. Jochen Hippler and Andrew Lueg. Trans. Laila Friese. Ser. Transnational Institute Series. London and Boulder, Co.: Pluto Press and Transnational Institute, 1995. Orig. *Feinbild Islam.* Chapter 4.

Home, Stewart. *Neoism, Plagiarism and Praxis.* Edinburgh and San Francisco: AK Press, 1995.

Iyer, Sanjay. "East, West No Home is Best: *East, West.*" *Indian Review of Books* 4.3, 16 Jan.-15 Feb. (1995): 2-3.

Iyer, Sanjay. "A Palimpsest of Life: *The Moor's Last Sigh.*" *Indian Review of Books* 5.1, 16 Sep.-15 Nov. (1995): 68-69.

Jensen, Axel. "God Does Not Read Novels." *Freedom of Expression: the Acid Test.* Ed. Niels Fried-Nielsen. Stockholm: Nordic Council, 1995. 43-51.

Juárez Hervás, Luisa. "An Irreverent Chronicle: History and Fiction in Salman Rushdie's *Midnight's Children.*" *Telling Histories: Narrativizing History, Historicizing Literature.* Ed. Susan Onega. Amsterdam and Atlanta: Rodopi, 1995. 73-84.

Kastholm, Claes. "The Crime of Silence." *Freedom of Expression: the Acid Test.* Ed. Niels Fried-Nielsen. Stockholm: Nordic Council, 1995. 121-25.

Khan, Yunus. *Answer to Salman Rushdie's 'Satanic Verses'.* Lahore: Combine Graphics, 1995.

King, Bruce. "*East, West.*" *World Literature Today* 69.3 (Sum 1995): 650-51.

Kleveland, Åse. "Freedom of Expression-the Most Demanding of All Freedoms." *Freedom of Expression: the Acid Test.* Ed. Niels Fried-Nielsen. Stockholm: Nordic Council, 1995. 60-71.

Krishnan, R.S. "Telling of the Tale: Text, Context, and Narrative Act in Rushdie's *Haroun and the Sea of Stories.*" *International Fiction Review* 22.1-2 (1995): 67-73.

Krishnaswamy, Revathi. "Mythologies of Migrancy: Postcolonialism, Postmodernism and the Politics of (Dis)Location." *ARIEL: A Review of International English Literature* 26.1 (1995): 125-46.

Kundera, Milan. "A Writer's Rights. " An extract of Milan Kundera, *Testaments Betrayed* (London: Faber & Faber, 1995). *Biblio: A Review of Books* 1.5 (Oct. 1995): 6.

Kureishi, Hanif. *The Black Album.* London: Faber & Faber, 1995.

Lal, P. "Salman the Magnificent: *The Moor's Last Sigh.*" *Indian Book Chronicle* 20.10 & 11 (Oct.-Nov. 1995): 5-8.

Majid, Anouar. "Can the Postcolonial Critic Speak? Orientalism and the Rushdie Affair." *Cultural Critique* 32 (1995-6): 5-42.

Mann, Harveen Sachdeva. "'Being Borne Across': Translation

and Salman Rushdie's *The Satanic Verses.*" *Criticism: A Quarterly for Literature and the Arts* 37.2 (1995): 281-308.

Massé Sophie. "Transfictional Identities in Salman Rushdie's *Grimus.*" *Etudes Britanniques Contemporaines,* 8. Montpellier: PU Montpellier, 1995. 89-95. http://perso.worldonline.fr/ebc/ebc87.html

Mathur, O.P. "A Metaphor of Reality: a Study of the Protagonists of Rushdie's *Midnight's Children.*" *Image of India in the Indian Novel in English 1960-1985.* Ed. Sudhakar Pandey and R. Raj Rao. Hyderabad: Orient Longman, 1993. 113-22; *Symbolism in Indian Fiction in English.* Ed. Ramesh K. Srivastava. Jalandhar: ABS Publications, 1997. 170-78; Mathur. *Indian Political Novel and Other Essays.* Allahabad: Kitab Mahal, 1995. 67-78.

Mathur, O.P. "Sense and Sensibility in Salman Rushdie's *Shame.*" Mathur. *Indian Political Novel and Other Essays.* Allahabad: Kitab Mahal, 1995. 79-90.

Milley, Craig. "*East, West* by Salman Rushdie." *Maroon-News* 1995. http://kendrick.colgate.edu/maroon/ArchivesS95/Text2.17.95/milley.html

Mishra, Vijay. "Postcolonial Differend: Diasporic Narratives of Salman Rushdie." *ARIEL: A Review of International English Literature* 26.3 (1995): 7-45.

Narasimhaiah, C.D. "Spurious Reputations: Vikram Seth, Salman Rushdie and Shashi Tharoor." *Essays in Commonwealth Literature: Heirloom of Multiple Heritage.*" Delhi: Pencraft, 1995. 118-26.

Nygaard, William. "Of the Necessity of Publishing Salman Rushdie." Niels Fried-Nielsen, ed. *Freedom of Expression: the Acid Test.* Stockholm: Nordic Council, 1995. 75-80.

Panjabi, Kavita. "From Community to Nation: Contradiction or Transition? A Comparison of *Midnight's Children, Neighbours* and *The Temple Pavillion.* " *ICLA '91 Tokyo: The Force of Vision, II: Visions in History; Visions of the Other.* Ed. Gerald Gillespie, Margaret Higonnet and Sumie Jones. Tokyo: International Comparative Literature Association, 1995. 234-41.

Parameswaran, Uma. "Purdah in Salman Rushdie, Attia Hosain and Rama Mehta." *Margins of Erasure: Purdah in the Subcontinental Novel in English.* Ed. Jasbir Jain and Amina Amin. New Delhi: Sterling, 1995. 33-48.

Pillai, Nita. "Fabulous Realism: *The Moor's Last Sigh.*" *The Book Review* 19.12 (Dec. 1995): 28-29.

Plotz, Judith. "*Haroun* and the Politics of Children's Literature." *Children's Literature Association Quarterly* 20.3 (1995): 100-04.

Al-Raheb, Hani. "Religious Satire in Rushdie's *Satanic Verses.*" *Journal of the Fantastic in the Arts* 6.4 (24) (1995): 330-39.

Raj, Alok. "Moor, Moor! *The Moor's Last Sigh.*" *The India Magazine* 15.11 (Oct. 1995): 60-65.

Ramachanndra, Ragini and Jayashree Sanjay. "A Report on the Proceedings of a Two-Day Seminar on 'Four Indian Novelists' held at Dhvanyaloka, Mysore (Nov. 7-8, 1993)." *The Literary Criterion* 30.3 (1995): 71-77.

Rangachari, Latha and Evangelini Manickam. "The Story Teller Silenced: A Study of Rushdie's *Haroun and the Sea of Stories.*" *Literary Criterion* 30.4 (1995): 15-24.

Rockwood, Bruce L. "Speech as a Universal Right: International Law and the Case of Salman Rushdie." *Conscience, Consensus and Crossroads in Law.* Eighth Round Table on Law and Semiotics. Ed. Roberta Kevelson. New York: Peter Lang, 1995. 271-90.

Ruth, Arne. "Endgame." Niels Fried-Nielsen, ed. *Freedom of Expression: the Acid Test.* Stockholm: Nordic Council, 1995. 21-29.

Sagar, Aparajita. "Cultural Imperialism and the Indo-English Novel: Genre and Ideology in R. K. Narayan, Anita Desai, Kamala Markandaya and Salman Rushdie." World Literature Today 69.1 (Win 1995): 233.

Schori, Pierre. "Rushdie, or the Intifada of the Imagination." *Freedom of Expression: the Acid Test.* Ed. Niels Fried-Nielsen. Stockholm: Nordic Council, 1995. 72-74.

Sen, Suchismita. "Memory, Language, and Society in Salman Rushdie's *Haroun and the Sea of Stories.*" *Contemporary Literature* 36.4 (1995): 654-75.

Seshadri, Veena. "And Warily the Twain Shall Meet: *East, West.*" *Indian Review of Books* 4.3, 16 Jan.-15 Feb. (1995): 3-4.

Singh, Harminder. "*The Moor's Last Sigh.*" *The Book Review* 19.9 (Sep. 1995): 38.

de Souza, Eunice. "A Sombre Sigh: *The Moor's Last Sigh.*" *Biblio: A Review of Books* 1.4 (Aug.-Sep. 1995): 4-5.

Stroemme, Sigmund. "The Nygaard Affair-a Political Challenge to the Nordic Countries." *Freedom of Expression: the Acid Test.* Ed. Niels Fried-Nielsen. Stockholm: Nordic Council, 1995. 52-59.

Swain, S.P. "Theme of Fragmentation: Rushdie's *Midnight's Children.*" *Literary Half-Yearly* 36.2 (1995): 29-40.

ten Kortenaar, Neil. "*Midnight's Children* and the Allegory of History." *Ariel: A Review of International English Literature* 26.2 (1995): 41-62.

Thompson, Jon. "Superman and Salman Rushdie: *Midnight's Children* and the Disillusionment of History." *Journal of Commonwealth and Postcolonial Studies* 3.1 (1995): 1-23.

Tikkanen, Märta. "Finland-Far from Atolls and Ayatollahs." *Freedom of Expression: the Acid Test.* Ed. Niels Fried-Nielsen. Stockholm: Nordic Council, 1995. 102-6.

Walker, Steven F. "Magical Archetypes: Midlife Miracles in *The Satanic Verses.*" *Magical Realism: Theory, History, Community.* Ed. Lois Parkinson Zamora and Wendy B. Faris. Durham: Duke UP, 1995. 347-69.

Wilson, Robert R. "Supporting Salman Rushdie, II." *Mattoid* 49 (1995): 16-30.

Wivel, Henrik. "Rushdie's Magic Mirror." *Freedom of Expression: the Acid Test.* Ed. Niels Fried-Nielsen. Stockholm: Nordic Council, 1995. 107-15.

2. CRITICISM 1996-2001

1996

Aikant, Satish C. "Salman Rushdie's *Midnight's Children*: The Middle Ground of Diaspora." *Interrogating Post-Colonialism: Theory, Text and Context.* Ed. Harish Trivedi and Meenakshi Mukherjee. Rashtrapati Nivas: Indian Institute of Advanced Study, 1996. 213-20.

Aji, Aron and Katrina Runge. "Haroun's Mystic Journey: Salman Rushdie's *Haroun and the Sea of Stories.*" *No Small World: Visions and Revisions of World Literature.* Ed. Michael Thomas Carroll. Urbana: National Council of Teachers of English, 1996. 131-45.

Allen, Brooke. "Sound and Fury: *The Moor's Last Sigh.*" *New Criterion* 14.7 Mar. 1996): 59-62.

Bhaduri, Seema. "In Quest of Form: a Study of Structural Motifs in Salman Rushdie's *Midnight's Children.*" *Indian Writing Today: Essays in Honour of Professor L.S.R. Krishna Sastry.* Ed. C.R. Visweswara Rao. New Delhi: Indian Association for English Studies, 1996. 95-104.

Branzeu, Pia. "Imaginary Cities." *B.A.S.: British and American Studies Revista de Studii Britanice si Americane* 1.1 (1996): 56-62.

Challakere, Padmaja. "Migrancy as Paranoid Schizophrenia in Salman Rushdie's *East, West.*" *South Asian Review* 20.17 (1996): 66-74.

Connor, Steven. *The English Novel in History, 1950 to the Present.* London and New York: Routledge, 1996.

Costa, Horacio. "The Fundamental Re-Writing: Religious Texts and Contemporary Narrative: Gore Vidal's *Live from Golgotha*; Salman Rushdie's *The Satanic Verses*; Jose Saramago's *O Evangelho Segundo Jesus Cristo.*" *Dedalus: Revista Portuguesa de Literatura Comparada* 6 (1996): 245-53; *Poligrafias: Revista de Literatura Comparada* 1 (1996) 189-98.

Cundy, Catherine. *Salman Rushdie.* Manchester: Manchester UP, 1996.

Davies, J.M.Q. "Aspects of the Grotesque in Rushdie's *The Satanic Verses.*" *AUMLA: Journal of the Australasian Universities Language and Literature Association* 85 (1996): 29-37.

Docker, John. "*The Satanic Verses* as a Post-Modern Novel." *Crossing Cultures: Essays on Literature and Culture of the Asia Pacific.* Ed. Bruce Bennett, Jeff Doyle, Satendra Nandan and Loes Baker. London: Skoob, 1996. 149-53.

Donnerstag, Jurgen. "Hybrid Forms of Multiculturalism in the Fiction of Salman Rushdie." *Nationalism vs.*

Internationalism: (Inter)National Dimensions of Literatures in English. Ed. Wolfgang Zach and Ken L. Goodwin. Tubingen: Stauffenburg, 1996. 455-60.

Forsyth, Neil and Martine Hennard. "'Mr Mustapha Aziz and Fly': Defamiliarization of 'family' in Salman Rushdie's *Midnight's Children*." *Families*. Ed. Werner Senn. Spell: Swiss Papers in English Language and Literature, 9. Tübingen: Gunter Norr, 1996. 197-206.

Frank, Katherine. "Mr. Rushdie and Mrs. Gandhi." *Biography: An Interdisciplinary Quarterly* 19.3 (1996): 245-58.

Gimpelevich, Zina. "Skaldin, Bulgakov and Rushdie: Who Art Thou, Then? Similarities in *The Wanderings and Adventures of Nikodim the Elder, The Master and Margarita* and *The Satanic Verses*." *Canadian-American Slavic Studies* 30.1 (1996): 69-80.

Goonetilleke, D.C.R.A. "*Haroun and the Sea of Stories* and Rushdie's Partial/Plural Identity." *World Literature Written in English* 35.2 (1996): 13-27. In *Crossing Cultures: Essays on Literature and Culture of the Asia Pacific*. Ed. Bruce Bennett, Jeff Doyle, Satendra Nandan and Loes Baker. London: Skoob, 1996. 155-71.

Gray, Paul. "Writing to Save His Life: *The Moor's Last Sigh*." *Time* 147.9 Feb. 26 (1996): 49.

Habib, Imtiaz. "Interrogating Cultures: Hybrid Subjectivity as Third Space in R. K. Narayan's *The Guide*, V.S. Naipaul's *A House for Mr. Biswas*, and Salman Rushdie's *Midnight's Children*." *Studies in the Humanities* 23.1 (1996): 28-52.

Hazarika, Sanjoy." Telling Tales, Salmanesquely: *Haroun and the Sea of Stories*." *The Book Review* 20.11 (Nov. 1996): 9.

Hitchens, Christopher. "A Subverting Sensualist." *Nation* 262.1 (1 Jan. 1996): 8.

Jussawalla, Feroza. "Rushdie's Dastan-E-Dilruba: *The Satanic Verses* as Rushdie's Love Letter to Islam." *diacritics* 26.1 (1996): 50-73.

Kamra, Sukeshi. "Replacing the Colonial Gaze: Gender as Strategy in Salman Rushdie's Fiction." *Between the Lines: South Asians and Post-Coloniality*. Ed. Deepika Bahri and Mary Vasudeva. Philadelphia: Temple UP, 1996. 237-49.

Kane, Jean M. "The Migrant Intellectual and the Body of History: Salman Rushdie's *Midnight's Children.*" *Contemporary Literature* 37.1 (1996): 94-118.

Kaul, R.K. "A Family Saga, Of Merchants, Painters and Gangsters: *The Moor's Last Sigh.*" *Indian Book Chronicle* 21.1 & 2 (Jan.-Feb. 1996): 8-9.

Kim, Soonsik. *Colonial and Post-colonial Discourse in the Novels of Yom Sang-sop, Chinua Achebe, and Salman Rushdie.* New York: Peter Lang, 1996.

King, Bruce. "*The Moor's Last Sigh.*" *World Literature Today* 70.3 (Sum 1996): 694-95.

Kirpal, Viney. "Postmodern Strategies in the Indian English Novel." *Littcrit* 22.2 (Dec. 1996): 21-34.

Kundera, Milan. "The Day Panurge No Longer Makes People Laugh." An extract of Milan Kundera, *Testaments Betrayed* (London: Faber & Faber, 1995). *Critical Quarterly* 38.2 (Sum 1996): 33-50.

Langeland, Agnes Scott. "Rushdie's Language." *English Today* 12.1 (45) (1996): 16-22.

Lenz, Millicent. "The Magic of Story vs. the Panjandrums of Tyranny: Salman Rushdie's *Haroun and the Sea of Stories.*" *Paradoxa: Studies in World Literary Genres* 2.3-4 (1996): 369-78.

Lernout, Geert. "'What Shall We Do with the Shrunken Tailor?': Salman Rushdie's Intertextuality." *A Talent(ed) Digger: Creations, Cameos, and Essays in Honour of Anna Rutherford.* Ed. Hena Maes-Jelinek, Gordon Collier and Geoffrey V. Davis. Amsterdam and Atlanta: Rodopi, 1996. 319-23.

Maitland, Sara. "The Author Is Too Much with Us: *The Moor's Last Sigh.*" *Commonweal* 123.3 (9 Feb. 1996): 22-23.

Majid, Farida. "Law, Literature and Islam: The Misbegotten Cultural, Historical and Semiotic Parameters." *Law and Literature Perspectives.* Ed. Bruce L. Rockwood and Roberta Kevelson. New York: Peter Lang, 1996.

McLeod, John. "Authority and Tension: Postmodernism and Writing History." *Modernity-Postmodernity: From the*

Personal to the Global. Ed. Barrie Axford and Gary Browning; Oxford Brookes University: Oxford, 1996.

Moka Dias, Brunda. ""The Stuff That Dreams Are Made Of': Interpreting Dreams in Salman Rushdie's *The Satanic Verses.*" *Journal of the Fantastic in the Arts* 7.4 (28) (1996): 60-73.

Mukherjee, Meenakshi. "*Haroun and the Sea of Stories*: Fantasy or Fable?" *The Postmodern Indian English Novel.* Ed. Viney Kirpal. Bombay: Allied, 1996. 29-40.

Narayan, Shyamala A. "*Reading Rushdie: Perspectives on the Fiction of Salman Rushdie.*" *The Journal of Indian Writing in English* 24.2 (July 1996): 43-44.

Netton, Ian Richard. *Text and Trauma: an East-West Primer.* Richmond: Curzon Press, 1996.

Neumann, Anne Waldron. "Fundamental Verities and Provisional Truths: *The Moor's Last Sigh.*" *Quadrant* 40.3 Mar. 1996): 75-77.

Noor, Ronny. "Misrepresentation of History in Salman Rushdie's *Midnight's Children.*" *Notes on Contemporary Literature* 26.2 (1996): 7-8.

Pandit, M.L. "Salman Rushdie's *The Moor's Last Sigh*: Yet Another Controversial Novel." *New Commonwealth Writing: A Critical Response.* New Delhi: Prestige, 1996. 64-69.

Pandit, M.L. "Subversion of Faith as Fiction: Salman Rushdie's *The Satanic Verses* and Shashi Tharoor's *The Great Indian Novel.*" *New Commonwealth Writing: A Critical Response.* New Delhi: Prestige, 1996. 57-63.

Pandit, M.L. "The Writer as Historical Witness: Salman Rushdie's *Midnight's Children.*" *New Commonwealth Writing: A Critical Response.* New Delhi: Prestige, 1996. 50-56.

Parameswaran, Uma. "'Impressive Women, but the Chains Are No Fictions': Women in Rushdie's *Shame.*" *Women's Writing. Text and Context.* Ed. Jasbir Jain. Jaipur and New Delhi: Rawat Publications, 1996. 141-57.

Parameswaran, Uma. "We-They Paradigm in Rushdie's *The Satanic Verses.*" Parameswaran. *Saclit: An Introduction to South-Asian-Canadian Literature.* Madras: Eastwest Books, 1996. 219-35.

Parnell, Tim. "Salman Rushdie: from Colonial to Postmodern Poetics." *Writing India: 1757-1990: the Literature of British India*. Ed. Bart Moore-Gilbert. Manchester: Manchester UP, 1996. 236-60.

Petersson, Margareta. *Unending Metamorphoses: Myth, Satire and Religion in Salman Rushdie's Novels*. Lund and Bromley: Lund UP and Chartwell Bratt, 1996.

Plotz, Judith. "Rushdie's Pickle and the New Indian Historical Novel: Sealy, Singh, Tharoor, and National Metaphor." *World Literature Written in English* 35.2 (1996): 28-48.

Raghavendra, M.K. "The Minor Sensibility in Search of Major Subjects." *Indian Review of Books* 6.1, 16 Sep.-15 Nov (1996): 36-39.

Rubin, Merle. "Extravagant, Madcap Vision of an Indian Clan: *The Moor's Last Sigh*." *Christian Science Monitor* 88.50 (7 Feb. 1996): 13.

Rush, Norman. "Doomed in Bombay: *The Moor's Last Sigh*." *The New York Times Book Review* 145 (14 Jan. 1996): 7. http://www.nytimes.com/

Sadri, Ahmad. "Another Look at Rushdie." *The Iranian* (July 1996).
http://www.iranian.com/July96/Opinion/Rushdie/Rushdie.html

Sandahl, Stella. "All or Nothing: *The Moor's Last Sigh*." *The Toronto Review of Contemporary Writing Abroad* 14.2 (Win 1996): 77-82.

Schulze-Engler, Frank. "Riding the Crisis: *The Satanic Verses* and the Silences of Literary Theory." *Fusion of Cultures?* Ed. Peter O. Stummer and Christopher Balme. Amsterdam: Rodopi, 1996. 193-203.

Shapiro, Laura and Daniel Pedersen. "The Prisoner in the Tower: *The Moor's Last Sigh*." *Newsweek* 127.2 8 Jan. 1996): 70.

Sharma, Shailja. "Aestheticized Angst: Rushdie and the Idea of Home." *South Asian Review* 20.17 (1996): 75-79.

Sood, Sujay. "The Politics of Escapism: Rushdie's *The Moor Last Sigh*." *Commonwealth Essays and Studies* 19.1 (1996): 96-101.

D'Souza, Frances. "A World without Censorship?" *English Today* 12.4 (48) (1996): 39-42.

Trivedi, Harish. "Hate the Book.and the Booker." *Indian Review of Books* 6.1, 16 Sep.-15 Nov. (1996): 23-24.

Wallia, C.J.S. "The Rushdie Phenomenon: a Second Look: *The Moor's Last Sigh by Salman Rushdie." IndiaStar Review of Books* (1996). http://www.indiastar.com/rsighs.htm

Werbner, Pnina. "Allegories of Sacred Imperfection: Magic, Hermeneutics, and Passion in *The Satanic Verses.*" *Current Anthropology* 37 (supplement) (1996): 55-86. York: Peter Lang, 1996. 209-54.

Wood, James. "Salaam Bombay! *The Moor's Last Sigh.*" *New Republic* 214.12 18 Mar. 1996): 38-41.

1997

Amnesty International. *Iran. Eight Years of Death Threats; Salman Rushdie.* May 1 (1997). MDE 13/17/97. XY/N-1 http://www.web.amnesty.org/ai.nsf/index/MDE130171997

Bhaya Nair, Rukmini. "What Did Rushdie Mean and Why?" *The Hindu* Aug. 17 (1997): 33.

Bhaya Nair, Rukmini. "Why Does Rushdie Offend?" *Seminar* 437 " INDIA 1995" Jan. (1996): 103-09.

Brennan, Timothy. "Salman Rushdie (1947-)." *British Writers*: Supplement IV. Ed. George Stade and Carol Howard. New York: Scribner's, 1997. 433-57.

Cantor, Paul A. "Tales of the Alhambra: Rushdie's Use of Spanish History in *The Moor's Last Sigh.*" *Studies in the Novel* 29.3 (1997): 323-42.

Chew, Shirley. "Voices After midnight: *The Vintage Book of Indian Writing: 1947-1997.*" *The Times Literary Supplement* 4923, Aug. 8 (1997): 26.

Conner, Marc C. "*Midnight's Children* and the Apocalypse of Form." *Critique: Studies in Contemporary Fiction* 38.4 (1997): 289-99.

Connolly, Clara and Pragna Patel. "Women Who Walk on Water: Working across 'Race' in Women against Fundamentalism." *The Politics of Culture in the Shadow of Capital.* Ed. Lisa Lowe and David Lloyd. Durham: Duke UP, 1997. 375-95.

Cook, Rufus. "Cultural Displacement and Narrative Duplicity." *Centennial Review* 41.2 (1997): 205-16.

Coundouriotis, Eleni. "Materialism, the Uncanny, and History in Toni Morrison and Salman Rushdie." *Lit: Literature Interpretation Theory* 8.2 (1997): 207-25.

D'haen, Theo. "Salman Rushdie's *The Moor's Last Sigh*; or, The Emotional Depths of Postmodernism." *Emotion in Postmodernism.* Ed. Gerhard Hoffmann and Alfred Hornung. Heidelberg: Carl Winter Universitatsverlag, 1997. 225-35.

Diwakar, Jasmine. "*The Moor's Last Sigh.*" *Journal of Literature and Aesthetics* 5.1 (Jan.-June 1997): 92.

Doctor, Geeta. "Tales From the Babalog: *The Vintage Book of Indian Writing: 1947-1997.*" *Indian Review of Books* 6.11, 16 Aug.-15 Sep. (1997): 6-9.

Dutheil, Martine Hennard. "The Epigraph to *The Satanic Verses*: Defoe's Devil and Rushdie's Migrant." *Southern Review: Literary and Interdisciplinary Essays* 30.1 (1997): 51-69.

Dutheil, Martine Hennard. "Postcolonial Strategies: Rushdie's Tropicalized Tropes." *GRAAT: Publication des Groupes de Recherches Anglo Americaines de l'Universite Francois Rabelais de Tours* 16 (1997): 129-41.

Finn, Leonard G. "Failings of Form in Salman Rushdie's *Shame.*" *Journal x: A Journal in Culture and Criticism* 2.1 (1997): 35-65.

Fugmann, Nicole. "Situating Postmodern Aesthetics: Salman Rushdie's Spatial Historiography." *REAL: The Yearbook of Research in English and American Literature* 13 (1997): 333-45.

Gorra, Michael. *After Empire: Scott, Naipaul, Rushdie*. Chicago and London: U of Chicago P, 1997.

Gowda, H.H. Anniah. "Salman Rushdie." *The Literary Half-Yearly* 38.1 (Jan. 1997): 79-86.

Harper, Graeme. "As if by Magic: World Creation in Postcolonial Children's Literature." *ARIEL* 28.1 (Jan. 1997): 39-52.

Huggan, Graham. "Prizing "Otherness": A Short History of the Booker." *Studies in the Novel* 29.3 (Fall 1997): 412-33.

King, Bruce. " *After Empire: Scott, Naipaul, Rushdie.*" *World Literature Today* 71. 3 (Sum 1997): 660-61.

King, Bruce. "*Salman Rushdie.*" *World Literature Today* 71. 3 (Sum 1997): 648.

Kumar, Sudhir. "Secularizing the Literary Space: Problems and Possibilities." *New Quest* 123 (May-June 1997): 147-56.

Kuortti, Joel. *The Salman Rushdie Bibliography: A Bibliography of Salman Rushdie's Work and Rushdie Criticism.* Frankfurt Peter Lang, 1997.

Kuortti, Joel. "Dreams, Intercultural Identification and *The Satanic Verses.*" *Contemporary South Asia.* July 1997): 191-200.

Kuortti, Joel. *Place of the Sacred: the Rhetoric of the 'Satanic Verses' Affair.* Frankfurt: Peter Lang, 1997.

Leonard, Philip. "Degenerescent Lections: Legal Fictions in Rushdie, Derrida, and Bhabha." *New Formations: A Journal of Culture Theory Politics* 32 (1997): 109-19.

Loomba, Ania. "Kathakali Othello." *The India Magazine* 17.2 (Jan. 1997): 26-33.

Madhavan, N.S. "Language Barriers: *Vintage Book of Indian Writing 1947-1997.*" *Biblio: A Review of Books* 3.7-8 (July-Aug. 1997): 22-3.

Maes-Jelinek, Hena. "Postmodernism and Its Others: Cross Cultural Counterpoints in British Fiction." *Anglistik: Mitteilungen des Verbandes deutscher Anglisten* 8.1 (1997): 61-73.

Maslon, Slawomir. "Matter of Paradise." *The Wild and the Tame: Essays in Cultural Practice.* Ed. Wojciech Kalaga and Tadeusz Rachwal. Katowice: Uniwersytet Slaski, 1997. 101-06.

Massé, Sophie. "Language versus Languages in *The Satanic Verses.*" *Commonwealth Essays and Studies* 20.1 (1997): 72-76.

May, Brian. "Back to the Future: History in /and the Postcolonial Novel." *Studies in the Novel* 29.3 (Fall 1997): 267-73.

Maya, D. "Narrative Strategies in Raja Rao's *Kanthapura* and Salman Rushdie's *Midnight's Children.*" *College English Review* 1.4 (July-Aug. 1997): 30-34.

Merivale, Patricia. "The Telling of Lies and 'The Sea of Stories': 'Haroun,' 'Pinocchio' and the Postcolonial Artist Parable." *ARIEL: A Review of International English Literature* 28.1 (1997): 193-208.

Mujeebuddin, Syed. "Centres and Margins: *Shame*'s 'Other' Nation" *Kakatiya Journal of English Studies* 12 (Dec. 1997): 39-52.

Priskil, Peter. *Salman Rushdie: Portrait of a Poet.* Freiburg: Ahrimand-Verlag, 1997.

Purushottam, K. "Six-hundred-and-thirty-five-day-long Midnight: Rushdie's Representation of Indira Gandhi's Emergency." *Revaluations* 3.1 (1997): 25-38.

Rajan, Rajeswari Sunder. "The Third World Academic in Other Places; or, the Postcolonial Intellectual Revisited." *Critical Inquiry* 23.3 (Spr 1997): 596-616.

Rege, Josna E. "Victim into Protagonist? *Midnight's Children* and the Post-Rushdie National Narratives of the Eighties." *Studies in the Novel* 29.3 (1997): 342-75.

Satchidanandan, K. "*Moor's Last Sigh.*" *Indian Literature* 40.4 (July-Aug. 1997): 5-8.

Sen, Nabaneeta Dev. "An Open Letter to Salman Rushdie." *The India Magazine* 17.9 (Aug. 1997): 71-74.

Sharpe, Jenny. "The Limits of What Is Possible: Reimagining Sharam in Salman Rushdie's *Shame.*" *Jouvert: A Journal of Postcolonial Studies* 1.1 (1997): 18 para.

Shekhar, S. "*The Moor's Last Sigh*: Quest for the True Self." *Indian Fiction of the Nineties.* Ed. R.S. Pathak. New Delhi: Creative, 1997. 185-92.

Singh, Manjeet. "*The Vintage Book of Indian Writing, 1947-1997* edited by Salman Rushdie and Elisabeth West." *IndiaStar Review of Books* (1997). http://www.indiastar.com/manjeet.html

ten Kortenaar, Neil. "Postcolonial Ekphrasis: Salman Rushdie Gives the Finger Back to the Empire." *Contemporary Literature* 38.2 (1997): 232-59.

Uprety, Sanjeev Kumor. "Disability and Postcoloniality in Salman Rushdie's *Midnight's Children* and Third World Novels." *The Disability Studies Reader.* Ed. Lennard J. Davis. New York: Routledge, 1997. 366-81.

Wallhead, Celia M. "Schema Disruption in the Re-writing of History: Salman Rushdie's *East, West.*" *Cuadernos de filología Inglesa* 6.2 (1997): 65-80.

Wallhead, Celia M. "The Subversive Sub-Text of Spices in Salman Rushdie's *The Moor's Last Sigh.*" *Revista Canaria de Estudios Ingleses* 35 (1997): 61-76.

1998

Asnani, Shyam M. "Identity Crisis of Indian Immigrants: Comparison of Three Novels." *Writers of Indian Diaspora: Theory and Practice.* Ed. Jasbir Jain. Jaipur and New Delhi: Rawat, 1998. 73-81.

Ball, John Clement. "'A City Visible but Unseen': The (Un)Realities of London in South Asian Fiction." *Journal of Comparative Literature and Aesthetics* 21.1-2 (1998): 67-82.

Ball, John Clement. "Pessoptimism: Satire and the Menippean Grotesque in Rushdie's *Midnight's Children.*" *English Studies in Canada* 24.1 (1998): 61-81.

Beck, Rudolf. "Close Encounters of the Third Kind: Salman Rushdie's Short Story Cycle *East, West.*" *Anglia: Zeitschrift fur Englische Philologie* 116.3 (1998): 355-80.

Boehmer, Elleke. "Post-Colonial Literary Studies: A Neo-Orientalism?" *Oriental Prospects: Western Literature and the Lure of the East.* Ed. C.C. Barfoot and Theo D'haen. Amsterdam: Rodopi, 1998. 239-45.

Bush, Ronald. "Rereading the Exodus: *Frankenstein, Ulysses, The Satanic Verses,* and Other Postcolonial Texts." *Transcultural Joyce.* Ed. Karen R. Lawrence. Cambridge: Cambridge UP, 1998. 129-47.

Bush, Ronald. "Monstrosity and Representation in the Postcolonial Diaspora: *The Satanic Verses, Ulysses,* and *Frankenstein.*" *Borders, Exiles, Diasporas.* Ed. Elazar Barkan and Shelton Marie Denise. Stanford, CA: Stanford UP, 1998. 234-56.

Cody, Michael. "Rushdie's *The Satanic Verses.*" *Explicator* 56.4 (Su 1998): 218-20.

Cropley Gonzalez, Madelena. "The Cliche as Subversion in *The Satanic Verses.*" *Le Cliche.* Ed. Gilles Mathis. Toulouse: PU du Mirail, 1998. 279-300.

Dayal, Samir. "The Liminalities of Nation and Gender: Salman Rushdie's *Shame." Journal of the Midwest Modern Language Association* 31.2 (1998): 39-62.

Dutheil, Martine Hennard. "Rushdie's Affiliation with Dickens." *Dickens Studies Annual: Essays on Victorian Fiction* 27 (1998): 209-26.

Ellerby, Janet Mason. "Fiction under Siege: Rushdie's Quest for Narrative Emancipation in *Haroun and the Sea of Stories." Lion and the Unicorn: A Critical Journal of Children's Literature* 22.2 (1998): 211-20.

Elst, Koenraad. "The Rushdie Rules." *Middle East Quarterly* 5.2 (June 1998) 31-43. http://www.meforum.org/meq/june98/rushdie.shtml

Erickson, John. "The View from Underneath: Salman Rushdie's *Satanic Verses." Islam and Postcolonial Narrative.* Cambridge: Cambridge UP, 1998. 129-60, 184-88.

Finney, Brian. "Demonizing Discourse in Salman Rushdie's *The Satanic Verses." ARIEL: A Review of International English Literature* 29.3 (1998): 67-93.

Goonetilleke, D.C.R.A. *Salman Rushdie.* New York: St. Martin's, 1998.

Greiner, Donald J. "Salman Rushdie, William Kohler, and the Writer as Hostage in The Tunnel." *Into The Tunnel: Readings of Gass's Novel.* Ed. Steven G. Kellman and Irving Malin. Newark: U of Delaware P, 1998. 84-89.

Harris, Susan Cannon. "Invasive Procedures: Imperial Medicine and Population Control in *Ulysses* and *The Satanic Verses.*" *James Joyce Quarterly* 35.2-3 (1998): 373-99.

Henighan, Stephen. "Coming to Benengeli: The Genesis of Salman Rushdie's Rewriting of Juan Rulfo in *The Moor's Last Sigh." The Journal of Commonwealth Literature* 33.2 (1998): 55-74.

Ho, Cynthia. "Salman Rushdie (19 June 1947-)." *Dictionary of Literary Biography,* 194: British Novelists since 1960, 2nd ser. Ed. Merritt Moseley. Detroit, Washington and London: Gale Research, 1998. 249-61.

Huggan, Graham. "Consuming India." *ARIEL: A Review of International English Literature* 29.1 (1998): 245-58.

Iftekharukddin, Farat. "Postmodernism and Quantum Realities in Salman Rushdie's *Midnight's Children*: Regional Insights and National Outcomes." *Literature of Region and Nation*. Proceedings of the 6th International Literature of Region and Nation Conference, 2-7 Aug. 1996. Ed. Winnifred M. Bogaards. Saint John: Social Sciences and Humanities Research Council of Canada, with University of New Brunswick in Saint John, 1998. 413-22.

Knerr, C.P. "Analysis of 'The Free Radio'." Oct. (1998). http://www.rit.edu/~cpk8576/dyn/publications/short_story/ss_analysis.shtml

Kuortti, Joel. *Fictions to Live In: Narration as an Argument for Fiction in Salman Rushdie's Novels*. Frankfurt: Peter Lang, 1998.

Loomba, Ania. "'Local Manufacture Made in India Othello Fellows': Issues of Race, Hybridity and Location in Post-Colonial Shakespeares." *Post-Colonial Shakespeares*. Ed. Ania Loomba and Martin Orkin. London: Routledge, 1998. 143-63.

McNab, Chris. "Derrida, Rushdie and the Ethics of Mortality." *The Ethics in Literature*. Ed. Andrew Hadfield, Dominic Rainsford and Tim Woods. Houndmills: Macmillan, 1998. 136-51.

Moss, Laura. "'Forget Those Damnfool Realists!': Salman Rushdie's Self Parody as the Magic Realist's 'Last Sigh'." *Ariel: A Review of International English Literature* 29.4 (1998): 121-39.

Mukherjee, Meenakshi. "Politics and Children's Literature: A Reading of *Haroun and the Sea of Stories*." *ARIEL: A Review of International English Literature* 29.1 (1998): 163-77.

Narayan, Shyamala A. Review of *Vintage Book of Indian Writing 1947-1997*. *ARIEL* Jan. 1998): 263-67.

Pipes, Daniel. "Salman Rushdie's Delusions, and Ours." *Commentary* 106.6 (1998): 51-53.

Rajakrishnan, V. "The Land of the Dead in Salman Rushdie's *The Moor's Last Sigh*, and Some Reflections Based on

Indian Response to the Theme of Exile." *Indian Literature* 42.3 (185) (1998): 143-54.

Schulting, Sabine. "Peeling off History in Salman Rushdie's *The Moor's Last Sigh.*" *Hybridity and Postcolonialism: Twentieth Century Indian Literature*. Ed. Monika Fludernik. Tubingen: Stauffenburg, 1998. 239-60.

Singh, Ram Ayodhya. *Salman Rushdie's* Midnight's Children (*A Critical Study*). Bareilly: Prakash Book Depot, 1998.

1999

El-Affendi, Abdelwahab. *An Age of Darkness: Media Failure in the Muslim World.* London 1999. Ch.7, "Censorship by the People" at http://msanews.mynet.net/books/media/chap7.html

Allen, Brooke. "Mister Multiplicity." *New Leader*

Arana, Marie. "Shake, Rattle and Roll: *The Ground Beneath Her Feet,* by Salman" 82.6 (17 May 1999): 16-17. "Rushdie." *Washington Post,* Book World Apr. 25 (1999): 11.

Bassi, Shaul. "Salman Rushdie's Special Effects." *Coterminous Worlds: Magical Realism and Contemporary Post-Colonial Literature in English.* Ed. Elsa Linguanti, Francesco Casotti and Carmen Concilio. Amsterdam: Rodopi, 1999. 47-60.

Bhaya Nair, Rukmini. "Rushdie and His Hero, Condemned to Linger at the Gateway of India: *The Ground Beneath Her Feet.*" *India Today* May 3 (1999). http://www.india-today.com/itoday/03051999/books3.html

Birkerts, Sven. "Sex, Drugs, and That Other Thing: *The Ground Beneath Her Feet* by Salman Rushdie." *Esquire* (May 1999): 61.

Biswell, Andrew. "On Salman Rushdie." *Stand Magazine* 1.2 (new series) (June 1999). http://www.people.vcu.edu/~dlatane/1.html

Booker, M. Keith, ed. *Critical Essays on Salman Rushdie.* New York: G.K. Hall, 1999.

"Boys' Toys: *The Ground Beneath Her Feet* and *An Equal Music.*" *Economist,* Review 351 (15 May 1999): 12-13.

Bradney, Anthony. "Reading Blasphemy: The Necessity of Literary Analysis in Legal Scholarship." *Law and Literature*. Ed. Michael Freeman and Andrew D.E. Lewis. Oxford: Oxford UP, 1999. 533-54.

Brians, Paul. "Annotating *The Satanic Verses*: An Example of Internet Research and Publication." *Computers and the Humanities* 33.3 (1999): 247-64.

Brinzeu, Pia. "A Palimpsest City: Bombay in Salman Rushdie's *The Moor's Last Sigh*." *B.A.S.: British and American Studies Revista de Studii Britanice si Americane* 4.2 (1999): 9-14.

Carey, Joanna. "Liquid Inspiration: *Illustrated Edition of Haroun and the Sea of Stories*." *Guardian* Oct. 26 (1999). http://www.guardian.co.uk/Archive/Article/0,4273, 3917980,00.html

Carson, Tom. "Tales From the Flip Side: *The Ground Beneath Her Feet* by Salman Rushdie." *Wall Street Journal* (Eastern ed.). (16 Apr. 1999): W10.

Coeyman, Marjorie. "Rushdie Looks at Life's Emotional Earthquakes. *Christian Science Monitor* 91.97 15 Apr. 1999): 16.

Davies, Mark. "Aspects of the Grotesque in Rushdie's *The Satanic Verses*." *Seriously Weird: Papers on the Grotesque*. Ed. Alice Mills. New York: Peter Lang, 1999. 51-61.

Dell'Aversano, Carmen. "Worlds, Things, Words: Rushdie's Style from *Grimus* to *Midnight's Children*." *Coterminous Worlds: Magical Realism and Contemporary Post-Colonial Literature in English*. Ed. Elsa Linguanti, Francesco Casotti and Carmen Concilio. Amsterdam: Rodopi, 1999. 61-69.

Dhar, T.N. "Problematizing/Criticizing History with Rushdie." *History-Fiction Interface: M.R. Anand, Nayantara Sahgal, Salman Rushdie, Shashi Tharoor and O.V. Vijayan*. New Delhi: Prestige, 1999. 159-206.

Dutheil de la Rochère, Martine Hennard. *Origin and Originality in Rushdie's Fiction*. Frankfurt,: Peter Lang, 1999.

Ganesh, Latha. "Rushdie and Roy." *Explorations: Arundhati Roy's 'The God of Small Things'*." Ed. Indira Bhatt and

Indira Nityanandam. Creative New Literatures, 27. New Delhi: Creative, 1999. 103-12.

Gardner, James. "Rock and Rushdie: *The Ground Beneath Her Feet*." *National Review* 51.9 (17 May 1999): 61-62.

Glaister, Dan. "After the *Satanic Verses*, the Romantic Lyrics." *Guardian Unlimited* Jan. 22 (1999). http://www.guardian.co.uk/Archive/Article/0,4273, 3811222,00.html

Gorra, Michael. "It's only rock and roll but I like it: *The Ground Beneath Her Feet*." *TLS* (Apr. 1999): 25.

Grant, Damian. *Salman Rushdie*. Plymouth: Northcote House, with British Council, 1999.

Gray, Paul. "Ganja Growing in the Tin: *The Ground Beneath Her Feet* by Salman Rushdie." *Time* 26 Apr. 1999): 99.

Islam, Syed Manzurul. "Writing the Postcolonial Event: Salman Rushdie's August 15th, 1947." *Textual Practice* 13.1 (1999): 119-35.

Kakutani, Michiko. "Turning Rock-and-Roll Into Quakes: *The Ground Beneath Her Feet*." *The New York Times Book Review* 148 (13 Apr. 1999): E7. http://www.nytimes.com/

Khoyratty, Farhad. "Brave New Words for Brave New Worlds? Illocutionary Force in *Paul et Virginie* and *The Satanic Verses*." *Powerful Bodies: Performance in French Cultural Studies*. Ed. Victoria Best and Peter Collier. Bern: Peter Lang, 1999. 187-98.

Kuortti, Joel. "'Nomsense': Salman Rushdie's *The Satanic Verses*." *Textual Practice* 13.1 (1999): 137-46.

Kuortti, Joel. "*Shame*: A Necklace of Stories." *Postcolonialism and Cultural Resistance*. Ed. Jopi Nyman and John A. Stotesbury. Joensuu: Faculty of Humanities, University of Joensuu, 1999. 117-22.

Kuortti, Joel. "`What Kind Am I?' Identity, Genre, and *The Satanic Verses* Controversy." *Translating Cultures*. Ed. Isabel Carrera Suárez, Aurora García Fernández and M.S. Suárez Lafuente. Oviedo: KRK Ediciones and Hebden Bridge: Dangaroo Press, 1999. 195-202.

Lange, Bernd-Peter. "Dislocations: Migrancy in Nabokov and

Rushdie." *Anglia: Zeitschrift fur Englische Philologie* 117.3 (1999): 395-411

La'Porte, Victoria. *An Attempt to Understand the Muslim Reaction to 'The Satanic Verses'*. Symposium series, 53. Lewiston and Lampeter: Edwin Mellen Press, 1999.

Lee, Hermione. "*The Ground Beneath Her Feet,* by Salman Rushdie." *Guardian Unlimited* Mar. 28 (1999). http://www.guardian.co.uk/Archive/Article/0,4273,3845313,00.html

Leonard, John. "Rushdie as Orpheus, on Guitar: *The Ground Beneath Her Feet* by Salman Rushdie." *Nation* 268.17 (10 May 1999): 25-32.

Lethem, Jonathan. "Rock of Ages: *The Ground Beneath Her Feet* by Salman Rushdie." *Village Voice* 44.16 (27 Apr. 1999): 45.

Limaye, Kancham. "Going Global: *The Ground Beneath Her Feet* by Salman Rushdie." *Reason* 31.6 (Nov. 1999): 62-65.

McGrath, Charles. "Rushdie Unplugged: *The Ground Beneath Her Feet.*" *New York Times Book Review* 148 (18 Apr. 1999): 8.
http://www.nytimes.com/books/99/04/18/reviews/990418.18mcgrat.html

McLaughlin, Robert L. "Book Reviews: *The Ground Beneath Her Feet.*" *Review of Contemporary Fiction* 19.3 (Fal. 1999): 173.

Milne, Lorna. "Olfaction, Authority, and the Interpretation of History in Salman Rushdie's *Midnight Children,* Patrick Suskind's *Das Parfum,* and Michel Tournier's *Le Roi des Aulnes.*" *Symposium: A Quarterly Journal in Modern Literatures* 53.1 (1999): 23-36.

Mishra, Pankaj. "The Emperor's New Clothes: *The Ground Beneath Her Feet* by Salman Rushdie." *New Statesman* 128 (9 Apr. 1999): 42-45.

Morel, Michel. "*Haroun and the Sea of Stories*: The Oblique Fight of the Tale-Teller." *Theory and Literary Creation/ Theorie et creation litteraire.* Ed. Jean-Pierre Durix. Dijon: Editions Universitaires de Dijon, 1999. 99-110.

Mossman, Mark. "Salman Rushdie's *Midnight's Children*:

National Narrative as a Liminal Voice." *Midwest Quarterly* 41.1 Aut 1999): 66-78.

Mukherjee, Meenakshi, ed. *Rushdie's 'Midnight's Children': a Book of Readings*. Delhi: Pencraft International, 1999.

Neumann, Fritz Wilhelm. "*The Moor's Last Sigh*: Rushdie's Intercultural Family Saga." *Intercultural Encounters: Studies in English Literatures*. Essays Presented to Rudiger Ahrens on the Occasion of His Sixtieth Birthday. Eds. Heinz Antor and Kevin L. Cope. Heidelberg: Carl Winter Universitatsverlag, 1999. 467-78.

Parks, Tim. "Gods and Monsters: *The Ground Beneath Her Feet*." *The New York Review of Books* May 6 (1999): 12-16.

Pathak, R.S. "History and the Individual in Salman Rushdie's Novels." *Modern Indian Novel in English*. Pathak. New Delhi: Creative, 1999. 114-33.

Pathak, R.S. "Rushdie on the Novel and Novelists." *Modern Indian Novel in English*. New Delhi: Creative, 1999. 134-46.

Power, Carla. " Rock 'n' Roll Rushdie." *Newsweek* 133.16 (19 Apr. 1999): 72. Excerpted http://www.youtwo.net/news_archives.adp?newsid=5943

Price, David W. "Critiquing the Past: Salman Rushdie's *Midnight's Children*." *History Made, History Imagined: Contemporary Literature, Poiesis, and the Past*. Urbana: U of Illinois P, 1999. 121-51.

Purushotham, K. "Rushdie's Images of *Bharateeya Nari* in *Midnight's Children*." *Indian Fiction in English*. Ed. Mallikarjuna Rao and Rajeshwar Mittapalli. New Delhi: Atlantic, 1999. 240-51.

Sawhney, Simona. "Satanic Choices: Poetry and Prophecy in Rushdie's Novel." *Twentieth Century Literature: A Scholarly and Critical Journal* 45.3 (1999): 253-77.

Swan, Toril. "A Feast of Senses: Rhetorical Devices in the Prose of Salman Rushdie with Special Reference to Metaphors and Adverbs." *Nordlit: Arbeidstidsskrift i litteratur* 6 (1999): 119-32.

Wallia, C.J.S. " *The Ground Beneath Her Feet* by Salman Rushdie." *IndiaStar Review of Books* (1999). http://www.indiastar.com/wallia20.html

Weisbard, Eric. "Wide World Webs: Review of *The Gypsy Road* (vengaboys), *The Party Album* (Alula), *The Ground Beneath Her Feet* (Rushdie)" *Village Voice* (25 May 1999): 119-20.

Wilson-Smith, Anthony. "The Revival of Salman Rushdie." *Maclean's* 112.21 (24 May 1999): 54-55.

Wood, James. "Child of the Gods: Salman Rushdie's *The Ground Beneath Her Feet.*" *Guardian Unlimited* Apr 3 (1999). http://www.guardian.co.uk/Archive/Article/0,4273, 3848011,00.html

Wood, James. "An Exile's Sigh for Home: *The Ground Beneath Her Feet* by Salman Rushdie." *Guardian Unlimited* Apr. 14 (1999). *Guardian Weekly* Apr. 18 (1999): 28. http://www.guardian.co.uk/Archive/Article/0,4273, 3854239,00.html

Wood, James. "Lost in the Punhouse: *The Ground Beneath Her Feet* by Salman Rushdie." *The New Republic* 220.17-8 (26 Apr. 1999): 94-99. http://www.thenewrepublic.com/archive/0499/042699/wood042699.html

Wood, Michael. "The Orpheus of MTV: *The Ground Beneath Her Feet.*" *The New York Times Book Review* 148 (18 Apr. 1999): 7. http://www.nytimes.com/

Wormald, Mark. " The Uses of Impurity: Fiction and Fundamentalism in Salman Rushdie and Jeanette Winterson." *An Introduction to Contemporary Fiction: International Writing in English since 1970.* Ed. Rod Mengham. Cambridge: Polity, 1999. 182-202.

2000

Baker, Stephen. "'You Must Remember This': Salman Rushdie's *The Moor's Last Sigh.*" *The Journal of Commonwealth Literature* 35.1 (2000): 43-54.

Balaswamy, P. "A Post-modern, Provocative, Metropolitan

Mother India: Aurora Zogoiby of Rushdie's *The Moor's Last Sigh.*" *The Atlantic Literary Review* 1.2 (Oct.-Dec. 2000): 86-96.

Ball, John Clement. "Acid in the Nation's Bloodstream: Satire, Violence, and the Indian Body Politic in Salman Rushdie's *The Moor's Last Sigh.*" *International Fiction Review* 27.1-2 (2000): 37-47.

Cook, Rufus. "The Art of Uncertainty: Cultural Displacement and the Devaluation of the World." *Critique: Studies in Contemporary Fiction* 41.3 (2000): 227-35.

Dingwaney Needham, Anuradha. "Re-Playing the Indian Subcontinent: Salman Rushdie's Method(s) of Critique." In Dingwaney-Needham.*Using the Master's Tools: Resistance and the Literature of the African and South-Asian Diasporas.* New York: St. Martin's Press, 2000. Ch. 2.

Fenwick, Mac. "A Vision of Unity: Braithwaite, Ngugi, Rushdie and the Quest for Authenticity." *Postcolonizing the Commonwealth: Studies in Literature and Culture.* Ed. Rowland Smith. Waterloo, ON: Wilfrid Laurier UP, 2000. 181-88.

Green, David A. "Authoritarians and Chamchas: Social Milieux and Politics in Grass's *Die Blechtrommel* and Rushdie's *Midnight's Children.*" *The Novel in Anglo-German Context: Cultural Cross-Currents and Affinities.* Conference Papers, University of Leeds, 15-17 Sep. 1997. Ed. Susanne Stark. Amsterdam: Rodopi, 2000. 357-68.

Heffernan, Teresa. "Apocalyptic Narratives: the Nation in Salman Rushdie's *Midnight's Children.*" *Twentieth-Century Literature* 46.4 (2000): 470-91.

Hofele, Andreas. "Wasteland Sprouting: Salman Rushdie's *The Satanic Verses* and the Cityscapes of Modernism." *Theme Parks, Rainforests and Sprouting Wastelands: European Essays on Theory and Performance in Contemporary British Fiction.* Ed. Richard Todd and Flora Luisa. Amsterdam, Netherlands: Rodopi, 2000. 41-54.

Horrocks, David. "The Undisciplined Past: Novel Approaches to History in Grass and Rushdie." *The Novel in Anglo-*

German Context: Cultural Cross-Currents and Affinities. Conference Papers, University of Leeds, 15-17 Sep. 1997. Ed. Susanne Stark. Amsterdam: Rodopi, 2000. 347-55.

Israel, Nico. *Outlandish: Writing between Exile and Diaspora.* Stanford: Stanford UP, 2000.

King, Bruce. "*The Ground Beneath Her Feet.*" Review. *World Literature* (Win 2000): 161.

Linguanti, Elsa. "Origin, Origins, Originality: Salman Rushdie's *East, West,* David Malouf's *Antipodes,* and Wilson Harris' *The Womb of Space.*" *The Atlantic Literary Review* 1.2 (Oct.-Dec. 2000): 72-85.

Maunsell, Jerome Boyd. "Paperback of the Month: *The Ground Beneath Her Feet.*" *The Times* Feb. 5 (2000). http://www.times-archive.co.uk/news/pages/tim/2000/02/05/timbooboo01019.html

Merritt, Stephanie. "Rock'n'roll Legends: Salman Rushdie's *The Ground Beneath Her Feet.*" *Guardian Unlimited* Jan. 30 (2000). http://www.guardian.co.uk/Archive/Article/0,4273,3956573,00.html

Prasannarajan, S. "Rushdie and the Ground Reality." *India Today* Oct. 15 (2000). http://www.india-today.com/webexclusive/columns/prasana/20001015.html

Prodhani, Jyotirmoy. "Chasing a Home and the Expatriate Experience: a Study of the Expatriate Narratives with Special Reference to Rushdie's *Midnight's Children. Contemporary Indian Literature: Positions and Expositions.* Ed. Santosh Gupta. Jaipur and New Delhi: Rawat, 2000. 129-36.

Reder, Michael R., ed. *Conversations with Salman Rushdie.* Jackson: U of Mississippi P, 2000.

Sanga, Jaina. *Salman Rushdie's Postcolonial Metaphors: Migration, Translation, Hybridity, Blasphemy, and Globalisation.* Westport: Greenwood Press, 2000.

Sarvan, Charles. "The Term 'Racism' and Discourse." *Journal of Commonwealth Literature* 35.2 (2000): 130-07.

Spearey, Susan. "Dislocations of Culture: Unhousing and the Unhomely in Salman Rushdie's *Shame.*"

Postcolonizing the Commonwealth: Studies in Literature and Culture. Ed. Rowland Smith. Waterloo, ON: Wilfrid Laurier UP, 2000. 167-80.

Su, Jung. "Articulating Silence: The Expropriation of the Periphery in *Shame.*" *EurAmerica: A Journal of European and American Studies* 30.2 (2000): 71-109.

Tonkin, Boyd. "*Fury,* by Salman Rushdie." *Independent* Aug. 24 (2001). http://www.independent.co.uk/story.jsp?story=90458

Trussler, Michael. "Literary Artifacts: Ekphrasis in the Short Fiction of Donald Barthleme, Salman Rushdie, and John Edgar Wideman." *Contemporary Literature* 41.2 (2000): 252-90.

Wagner, Erica. "Rushdie Lost in the Valley of The Dolls: *Fury,* by Salman Rushdie." *The Times.* Aug. 15 (2001). http://www.thetimes.co.uk/article/0,,217-2001282180, 00.html

Walden, George. "Rushdie's valley of the dolls: *Fury,* by Salman Rushdie." *London Evening Standard* Aug. 20 (2001). http://www.thisislondon.co.uk/dynamic/lifestyle/books/top_review.html?in_review_id=445852andin_review_text_id=395434

Weiss, Timothy. "At the End of East/West: Myth in Rushdie's *The Moor's Last Sigh.*" *Jouvert: A Journal of Postcolonial Studies* 4.2 (2000): 47 para.

2001

Allen, Brooke. "*Fury.*" Review. *Atlantic Monthly* 288.2 Sep. 2001): 138-39.

Baena, Rosaliá. "Telling a Bath-Time Story: *Haroun and the Sea of Stories* as a Modern Literary Fairy Tale." *The Journal of Commonwealth Literature* 36.2 (2001): 65-76.

Bassi, Shaul. "The (Un)making of Saladin Chamcha: Rushdie's Subversion of the Bildungsroman." *Studies in Indian Writing in English.* Vol. 2 Ed. Rajeshwar Mittapalli and Pier Paolo Piciucco. New Delhi: Atlantic, 2001. 108-21.

Carey-Abrioux, Cynthia. "'Coming Unstuck': Salman Rushdie's Short Story 'The Courter." *Telling Stories: Postcolonial Short Fiction in English.* Ed. Jacqueline Bardolph. Ser.

Readings in the Post/Colonial Literatures in English, 47. Amsterdam and Atlanta: Rodopi, 2001. 315-22.

Chauhan, Pradyumna S., ed. *Salman Rushdie Interviews: a Sourcebook of His Ideas.* Westport: Greenwood Press, 2001.

Cowley, Jason. "The Sense of an Ending: Review of *Underworld* (DeLillo), *Fury* (Rushdie), *The Secret Agent* (Conrad)." *New Statesman* 17 Dec. 2001): 108-09.

Eder, Richard."The Beast in Me: *Fury,* by Salman Rushdie." *New York Times Book Review* 9 Sep. 2001): 8.

Fletcher, M.D. "Painting, Palimpsest, and Politics in *The Moor's Last Sigh.*" *Social Alternatives* Oct. 2001): 51-54.

Gates, David. "Raging Bull: *Fury* by Salman Rushdie." 17 Sep. 2001): 68.

Hoffert, Barbara. "*Fury.*" Review. *Library Journal* 126.13 1 Aug. 2001): 166.

Holdsworth, Nick. "Opening the Book on Dissent." *Times Higher Education Supplement* 20 Apr. 2001): 17.

Holmes, Frederick M. "The Postcolonial Subject Divided between East and West: Kureishi's *Black Album* as an Intertext of Rushdie's *The Satanic Verses.*" *Papers on Language and Literature* 37.3 (2001): 296-313.

Hooper, Brad. "Upfront: Advance Reviews: *Fury* by Salman Rushdie." *Booklist* 1-15 June 2001): 1798.

"In Brief: Salman Rushdie-the new Humphrey Bogart?" *Guardian Unlimited* Feb. 9 (2001) http://www.guardian.co.uk/Archive/Article/0,4273, 4133811,00.html

Kakutani, Michiko. "*Fury*: Salman Rushdie's Millennial Manhattan." *The New York Times Book Review* Aug. 31 (2001). http://www.nytimes.com/2001/08/31/books/31BOOK. html

Khair, Tabish. *Babu Fictions: Alienation in Contemporary Indian English Novels.* Oxford: Oxford UP, 2001.

Kumar, Amitava. "The Bend in Their Rivers: Review of *Fury* (Rushdie) and *Half a Life* (Naipaul)." *Nation* 26 Nov. 2001): 32-37.

Lamb, Gregory M. "Salman Rushdie Meets Reality TV." *Christian Science Monitor* (15 June 2001): 13.

Leonard, John. "Puppet Show: *Fury* by Salman Rushdie." *The New York Review of Books* Oct. 4 (2001) 35-37.

Macris, Anthony. "Rage Slave: *Fury* by Salman Rushdie." *Newsweek* 119 (11 Sep. 2001): 70-71.

Mahoney, Blair. "Rushdie and his World: The Carnivalesque, Masquerade, and Grotesque Realism in his Fiction." *The Atlantic Literary Review* 2.1 (Jan.-Mar. 2001): 84-104.

May, Brian. "Memorials to Modernity: Postcolonial Pilgrimage in Naipaul and Rushdie." *ELH* 68 (2001): 241-65.

Pirbhai, Mariam. "The Paradox of Globalization as an 'Untotalizable Totality' in Salman Rushdie's *The Ground Beneath Her Feet.*" *International Fiction Review* 28.1-2 (2001): 54-77.

Prasannarajan, S. "Fun And Fury In New York: *Fury.*" *India Today* Aug. 27 (2001). http://www.india-today.com/itoday/20010827/books.shtml

Ramsey-Kurz, Helga. "Does Saleem Really Miss the Spittoon?: Script and Scriptlessness in *Midnight's Children.*" *The Journal of Commonwealth Literature* 36.1 (2001): 127-45.

Reiland, Ralph R. "War, Theocrats, and All That." *Humanist*Jan.-Feb. 2002): 44-45.

Rollason, Christopher. "Rushdie's Un-Indian Music: *The Ground Beneath Her Feet.*" *Studies in Indian Writing in English.* Vol. 2. Ed. Rajeshwer Mittapalli and Pier Paolo Piciucco. New Delhi: Atlantic, 2001. 122-57.

Rubin, Merle. "A State of Wrath: *Fury* by Salman Rushdie." *Christian Science Monitor* 93.198 (6 Sep. 2001): 14.

"Signifying Nothing: *Fury* by Salman Rushdie." *Economist* 360 25 Aug. 2001): 66.

Sutherland, John. "The Sound and the Fury: *Fury* by Salman Rushdie." *The Guardian* Aug. 25 (2001). http://www.guardian.co.uk/Archive/Article/0,4273,4244846,00.html

Tandon, Bharat. "Confusion in the Doll's House: *Fury* by Salman Rushdie." *TLS* 7 Sep. 2001): 4-5.

Thorne, Matt. "*Fury* by Salman Rushdie." *The Independent on Sunday* Aug. 25 (2001).

Wood, James. "The Nobu Novel: *Fury* by Salman Rushdie." *New Republic* 24 Sep. 2001): 32-36.

Zaleski, Jeff. "*Fury* by Salman Rushdie." *Publishers Weekly* 248.29 16 July 2001): 166.

CONTRIBUTORS

Balaswamy, P. : Department of English, Pondicherry University, Pondicherry 605 014 India.

Ball, John C. : Department of English, University of New Brunswick, P.O. Box 4400, Fredericton, NB E3B 5A3 Canada.

Dutheil de la Rochère, Martine Hennard : Section d'anglais, BFSH II, 1015 Lausanne, Switzerland.

Hensen, Michael : English Literature and Culture, University of Passau, Innstr. 25 94032 Passau, Germany.

Kuortti, Joel : Department of English, FIN-33014 University of Tampere, Finland.

Linguanti, Elsa : Via Dei MIlle 26, 56100 PISA, Italy.

Petry, Mike : Pontstr. 66, 52062 Aachen, Germany.

Rollason, Christopher : 17 avenue Foch, 4ème, F-57000 Metz, France.

Wallhead, Celia M. : Dept of English Philology, University of Granada, Campus de Cartuja, 18070 Granada, Spain.